Married to the Work

How to Be a Leader after God's Own Heart

W.D. Frazee
with Mark Finley

TEACH Services, Inc.
PUBLISHING
www.TEACHServices.com • (800) 367-1844

World rights reserved. This book or any portion thereof may not be copied or reproduced in any form or manner whatever, except as provided by law, without the written permission of the publisher, except by a reviewer who may quote brief passages in a review.

The author assumes full responsibility for the accuracy of all facts and quotations as cited in this book. The opinions expressed in this book are the author's personal views and interpretations and do not necessarily reflect those of the publisher.

This book is provided with the understanding that the publisher is not engaged in giving spiritual, legal, medical, or other professional advice. If authoritative advice is needed, the reader should seek the counsel of a competent professional.

Copyright © 2024 Medical Missionary Pioneers Inc.
Copyright © 2024 TEACH Services, Inc.
ISBN-13: 978-1-4796-1677-0 (Paperback)
ISBN-13: 978-1-4796-1678-7 (ePub)
Library of Congress Control Number: 2024906068

All Scripture references, unless otherwise indicated, are taken from the King James Version of the Bible. Public domain.

Cover Design by Arnold Famini

Published by

Table of Contents

Who Was W.D. Frazee and What Is Special About This Book?..........v

Chapter 1 An Organization of Love....................7

Chapter 2 Individuality and Cooperation...........................19

Chapter 3 Balance.................................31

Chapter 4 The Great Demonstration..............................43

Chapter 5 Order and Authority.................................59

Chapter 6 Authority from Heaven.............................73

Chapter 7 Theocracy................................85

Chapter 8 Leadership with Love.................................95

Chapter 9 God Takes the Reins 109

Chapter 10 Promotion from Above...........................123

Chapter 11 Succession and Apprenticeship 135

Chapter 12 The Golden Rule...............................147

Chapter 13 Christian Discipline............................159

Chapter 14 Counsel and Committee Work, Part 1 173

Chapter 15 Counsel and Committee Work, Part 2 191

Chapter 16 How to Start a Leadership............................205

Chapter 17 The Most Expensive Wool 217

Chapter 18 Content Without Promotion [Mark Finley] 229

Chapter 19 The Three Arks That Didn't Float 241

Chapter 20 Fellow Workers with Him............................253

Chapter 21 Steps to Miracles 265

Chapter 22 Less Attempted, More Achieved 273

Chapter 23 The Secret Formula of Success.........................285

Chapter 24 Married to the Work 295

Who Was W.D. Frazee and What Is Special About This Book?

W.D. Frazee (1906–1996) was educated in medical science at Loma Linda and in health evangelism by the legendary J.H.N. Tindall. In 1942, Elder Frazee and a faithful team of pioneers established Wildwood Lifestyle Center and Health Institute (formerly known as Wildwood Sanitarium and Medical Missionary Institute) where physicians, nurses, pastors, and laymen received practical training in medical evangelism. From its humble beginnings, Wildwood has echoed the vision of the founders, nurtured in a prayerful study of the Scriptures and Spirit of Prophecy counsels. Today, it continues to educate medical missionary evangelistic workers from all over the world at its country outpost near Chattanooga, Tennessee. In 1985, during his retirement years, Elder Frazee established "Pioneers Memorial," which is now "W.D. Frazee Sermons."

WD Frazee

Thousands of audio files on various topics are distributed each year, and tens of thousands have gone around the world. We store, copy, and distribute the sermons of W.D. Frazee, E.A. Sutherland, Dr. Charles Thomas, and other pioneers of medical missionary work. Our goal is to remind this generation of the success and struggles of our self-supporting pioneers so that we may build on their experiences to finish the work in this generation. You can view Elder Frazee's sermon titles available in audio and transcribed format on our website, WDFsermons.org. We also have eBooks and many other special features on the site, including many free instant downloads. Visit 1ref.us/wf1 or use this QR code:

Among the many topics on which Elder Frazee preached, leadership was one on which he placed careful importance. He had lived through significant Adventist history in which the transition of major leaders brought serious challenges. Having witnessed these challenges firsthand, he made it a point to train new leaders and not try to do all the work himself. This book on leadership is a compilation of some of his most expedient messages on leadership. Chapter 18 is a sermon that Elder Frazee preached jointly with Elder Mark Finley while he was serving at Wildwood. Most of the chapters are from classes that he taught on the topic. Many prominent leaders in our church today have received encouragement, counsel, and admonition through these timeless messages. It is our prayer at W. D. Frazee Sermons, whether you are currently involved in leadership or feel that God will call you to that office, that your soul may find the practical instruction in this book useful in making you a leader after God's own heart.

CHAPTER 1

An Organization of Love

There is a text I love, hidden away in the Song of Solomon, which is descriptive of the church in its final warfare here on earth: "Who is she that looketh forth as the morning, fair as the moon, clear as the sun, and terrible as an army with banners?" (Song of Sol. 6:10).

In *Testimonies for the Church, volume five,* speaking of the church after the shaking and sifting have done their work, the prophet says: "Then will the church of Christ appear 'fair as the moon, clear as the sun, and terrible as an army with banners'" (p. 82).

You will find in *Early Writing* another picture of this same group—the remnant after they have received the Latter Rain and are giving the Loud Cry:

"They moved in exact order like a company of soldiers" (*Early Writings*, p. 271). Both of these Spirit of Prophecy statements with the Bible verse compare the church to an army. Do you know the difference between an army and a mob? Both have a lot of people, but an army is organized. The devil can use a mob. He can also use an army. But God compares His church in its final warfare not to a mob but to an army.

I want to study with you in this chapter God's plans of organization. Another way to put that is "how to get things done."

Every institution needs to learn this. There are a lot of things to be done around an institution. The question is, how do you get them done?

Every home needs to learn this lesson. Are there things to be done around a home? Every day. Parents, how do you get things done? How do you get the children to cooperate? This book is not primarily a book on child guidance, but the principles we're going to study have to do with guiding children, as well as adults, about how to work together.

In school, is it necessary to get things done? How do you get students to study? How do you get them to learn? How do you get them to behave? Or does it make any difference? And does it make any difference what methods we use?

If a patient can't sleep, there are certain pills that you can give them, and they will go to sleep. Some people think that a better way is to give them a fomentation, a neutral bath, or a massage. Of course, it doesn't make any difference, just so they go to sleep. Or does it?

In this book, we are going to study how God gets things done. And remember, all of this is with the goal of understanding how we enter into God's program for the final battle of the church. We are going to be in that battle. May it please God, and I hope we'll all be on God's side. But God can never let the last battle be joined until the members of His army know their places and His methods. What a shame it would be to see the world's methods brought into the church of Christ, either in the Christian institution, the Christian home, the Christian school, or the Christian church itself.

Matthew 6 covers the sermon on the mount and the Lord's Prayer, in particular. He gave this prayer more than once. On one occasion, when the disciples found Him praying alone, when He stopped, they said, "Lord, teach us to pray as John also taught his disciples," and He gave them this prayer.

In the midst of this prayer, you'll find this request that we are going to read here: "Thy kingdom come. Thy will be done in earth, as it is in heaven" (Matt. 6:10). Do you want God's kingdom to come? A kingdom is a government with a king in charge. Does God have a government? Yes, and this teaches us to pray that God's government come. Come where? On earth. That is the rest of the verse: "Thy will be done in earth, as it is in heaven."

Does God get things done in heaven? When He speaks, the angels move, but they are not afraid. In the Lord's Prayer, we are taught to pray that His kingdom will come where? Here on earth. Let me ask you something. If you and I are praying that prayer meaningfully, will we try to carry out the principles of heaven in whatever we lead out?

Suppose we're in a school, and we want to get some things done. We want students to study, and we want them to behave while they're studying. If we're praying the Lord's Prayer understandingly, we are praying that God's kingdom (government) will come into our schoolroom and that

His will, will be done there as it is in heaven. Wouldn't you like to be in a schoolroom like that? Can we have one right here now? By God's grace, we want nothing less than that.

Let's be very practical about this. How can you get every one of your workers to show up on time? That would please the master. Suppose I were rich, and I could pay everyone to be on time here every time.

Instead of doing it that way, suppose we would go back a few years in our thinking and suppose the teacher would say, "Now, everyone that is late is going to get a whipping." Do you think that might help some people to be here on time? Or suppose that the leader had the power (which he doesn't) to say, "Now, if anyone is late, then he can't have any breakfast tomorrow morning." Do you think that might help? It might help someone.

You may be thinking, "Brother Frazee, where are you going with this?" I'm trying to get you to think. You may say that I am trying to get you to be on time. No. I hope you will all be on time. But I want to tell you something; I would rather have you be late with the right motive than on time with the wrong motive.

If a group of people is trying to do something together, whether it's harvesting a crop, or putting up a building, or doing any other job, it takes cooperation. There is more than one way to get people to be on time. Or is there something more important?

There have been some dictatorships that have gotten some colossal things done. But the method they used was to put a bayonet to people's backs. Don't you think, if you had a sword right behind you, and you could just feel the point of it, and you knew that if you didn't do what you were told it was going to stick you, don't you think it would help the muscles to move in harmony with what was demanded?

Here in America, we don't usually have bayonets motivating people to do things. Instead of having bayonets behind people urging them forward, we have something in front of people—a paycheck. There are all sorts of incentives used. In these great factories, the job is to get a man to produce. If he can produce more, pay him more. I suppose we would prefer that to the bayonet. But in each case, the response can be wholly selfish. Do you see that?

A wicked infidel will move if a bayonet is at his back or if you can offer him enough money. Of course, after you have given it to him for a while, he may go on strike unless you raise the wage, but it still produces millions of automobiles every year.

Now, if in our homes and our institutions and our work program, we are using either one of those incentives, how much better are we than the publican? If the way we get things done is through fear or bribery, we still are not helping to answer the prayer: "Thy kingdom come. Thy will be done in earth, as it is in heaven" (Matt. 6:10). "Well," you say, "Brother Frazee, be practical. After all, we have to get buildings up, get food on the table, and wash the dishes. If people do it through love, that is wonderful, but if they won't, we still have to get the work done." Or do we?

When I came to Wildwood many years ago, one of the men who helped in laying the foundations used to say to us, "What this place does to us is more important than what we do to the place. The great thing is not getting the work done; it's getting us done." To be "done" means that we are ready to go to heaven and fit into the plan of government up there. Are you ready?

In Psalms 103 is a picture of God's government in action. Let's see how it works: "The Lord hath prepared his throne in the heavens; and his kingdom ruleth over all. Bless the Lord, ye his angels, that excel in strength, that do his commandments, harkening unto the voice of his word" (Ps. 103:19, 20).

And who is pictured here as responding when God speaks? The angels. Now notice what it says: "[They] do his commandments, harkening unto the voice of his word" (Ps. 103:20).

Here is a picture of the government of God. The angels listen. Did you ever watch a child that could hear fine if he were called to supper but had difficulty hearing if he were called to work? It is the same child with the same ears. The picture of the angels here is that they are bending over anxiously to get the least whisper of God's will.

Don't you think that foremen and supervisors would like to have helpers like that? Would not church officers like to have members like that? Instead of having to milk or pump to get cooperation in missionary work and funds, people are trying to find out what needs to be done so they can have a part in it with time or money? Wouldn't parents like to have children like that? That is the way heaven is, according to what we read in the Lord's Prayer.

The reason that you are given the job as a leader is so that you can learn how to get things done using heaven's method. You are either a present leader or a potential leader learning how to get things done using heaven's method. Heaven's methods of leadership are as different from the world as heaven is different from earth.

Believe me, dear friend, we will never learn from the world how to carry on heaven's plan of government. We won't learn it from the big business in America. We won't learn it from all the classes that human beings have invented on how to win friends and influence people. To know how heaven carries on its plan of government, we will have to study the books that heaven has given us, and there we'll find it.

> "Christ designs that heaven's order, heaven's plan of government, heaven's divine harmony, shall be represented in His church on earth" (*The Desire of Ages*, p. 680). In *Testimonies, volume eight*, is another statement that goes with the previous one: "God desires that heaven's plan shall be carried out, and heaven's divine order and harmony prevail, in every family, in every church, in every institution" (*Testimonies for the Church, vol. 8*, p. 140).

That takes in everything. Anything we are a part of in work, in study, in religious worship, in the home, everything is to carry out heaven's plan of government.

In the book *Sons and Daughters of God*, page 255, you will find a similar statement. But in that statement, it includes this thought: "Everything that is to be managed." So you see, if we're managing nurses, these are the principles. If we're managing farmers, these are the principles. If we're managing students, these are the principles—the principles of heaven.

What are the principles of heaven? Here is the first one. I would like to have you memorize this quote: "Order is heaven's first law and the Lord desires His people to give in their homes a representation of the order and harmony that pervade the heavenly courts" (*Counsels on Health*, p. 101).

"You mean when people come into my house, they are to see a place as orderly as heaven?"

That is God's ideal. And if I haven't gotten there yet, I ought to be on the road. If I haven't arrived at the top, I should be on the trail. It's wonderful that we have a Savior who is standing at the mercy seat holding up His wounded hands, praying for us, and making up our deficiencies in a lot of things, isn't it? But let's remember that, "When it is in the heart to obey God when efforts are put forth to this end, Jesus accepts this disposition and effort as man's best effort, and He makes up for the deficiency with His own divine merit" (*Selected Messages*, Book 1, p. 382).

> The righteousness of Jesus is not to cover our laziness; it's to cover our inabilities.

The righteousness of Jesus is not to cover our laziness; it's to cover our inabilities. Those of us who have lacked training in order do not become suddenly transformed. It's by beholding that we become changed. But if my goal is the mountain top, I can thank God that, all the way up, He counts me as having attained. But I show my faith in that, not by lying down on the trail and saying, "Well, God counts me as up there, so I'll just lie here." No. I show my faith and my desire by doing what keeps moving.

So, I am to pray to God to help me to learn heaven's first law. This is kindergarten—basic to everything.

What do you think order is? Everything has a place, and everything is in its place. The only way a thing can be in its place is to have a place. Get rid of those things that have no place. Is there a place for cigarettes? No.

Now with that, let's say that order is a time for everything and everything on time. A time and place for everything and everything in place and on time. That includes people. Does God have in the universe a place for everything? Does He have some extra stars that He doesn't know where to put? No. Does He have a place for you and me?

"Not more surely is the place prepared for us in the heavenly mansions than is a special place designated on earth where we are to work for God" (*Christ's Object Lessons*, p. 327). Do you mean there is a special place where God wants me? In the military, soldiers have a definite place. They have a particular branch of the military to which they are assigned, like the medical corp. In the medical corps, soldiers have a particular number. There is a specific place where the soldiers report for duty from time to time. That is the way an army is run, and that is the way things are in heaven. And this says that as surely as God has a place for us in heaven, He has a special place on earth where we are to work for Him.

Now, I want to give you what, to me, is one of the most wonderful statements on this, found anywhere in the writings of the Spirit of Prophecy:

> It is the very essence of all right faith to do the right thing at the right time… If His people are watching the indications of His providence… their efforts, rightly directed, will produce a hundredfold greater results than can be accomplished with the same means and facilities in another channel where God is not so manifestly working. (*Testimonies for the Church*, vol. 6, p. 24)

Think of it; if I'm in the right place, I can get a hundred times more done.

God uses the illustration of the human body with its various organs to represent the church. How many livers do you have? Just one. Is that enough? Apparently, because you have two kidneys. Suppose my liver would look around and say, "I wish I could be a kidney instead of a liver."

Suppose it could choose to try to fill that place. Would that be helpful? No. I already have two kidneys. But I need that one liver, and I need it in its place.

Or suppose the liver should begin to look up and say, "I wish I could get promoted. I have been here now for a long time. I wish I could move up and be a lung. Eventually, I hope to get up in the skull and take the place of the brain." Would that be a good idea?

There are people who are very dissatisfied with what they are doing now, and they're only counting the days until they can get a change of work. Oh, I am so glad to know that, in heaven's plan of government, there is a particular place for me. And that, for me, is the most wonderful thing in the world. If every worker in an institution knows that, and every student in a school knows that, and every member of a home knows that, you see what a wonderful thrill it can be.

I am filling an important place. It may be a little thing. It may be just a tiny little wheel in a watch, but if I would reach in there and take out one of those wheels, it would not work anymore. Did one man stop the success of the whole army of Israel at Ai? Yes.

Oh, there is a special place in God's plan of government for me. And order is a place for everything and everyone in their place. And this is heaven's first law.

> Law and love are connected, and they are in God's plan of government.

Now, there is something before order. "Oh," you say, "but, Brother Frazee, you just read that order is heaven's first law." Yes, but there is something before the first. Order is heaven's first law, but there is something before law. It's love. Love is the source of law.

I want you to see this relationship between law and love in the following verse: "From his right hand went a fiery law for them. Yea, he loved the people" (Deut. 33:2, 3).

Law and love are connected, and they are in God's plan of government. They aren't always connected in the world. Did you ever hear a sergeant in the army that gave a law that didn't have much love in it? But in heaven's plan of government, behind every law is love. "The law of God, in the home life and in the government of nations, flows from a heart of infinite love" (*Child Guidance*, p. 259).

Every time God gives a law, it comes from love. Is that where the Sabbath came from? Is that where the commandment to honor your parents and not to steal came from? Yes. Do you believe that? Whenever God tells an angel to do something, it comes from a loving heart. Do you suppose that is one reason the angels love to be near the throne? They know that God wouldn't tell them to do a thing unless His motive was love.

Don't you like to be around folks who love you? That is why the beings up in heaven love to be there. God loves them so much. And He never tells them to do anything unless it's through love.

Now, let's see what that means. Let's use Gabriel as an example in an illustration. Before God tells Gabriel to do anything, God can think of any one of a thousand things that He might tell Gabriel to do, but He picks out the one that will make Gabriel the happiest and please him the most. Is that right, or is that going too far?

If you love someone, and you're going to take them a bouquet, wouldn't you pick out the kind of flower that they like most? If you love someone and you're going to make them a birthday dinner, would you think of all the foods they don't like and say, "Well, they're good for them; I'm going to cook them anyway"? "Oh," you say, "Brother Frazee, I am afraid you are getting very impractical." No. We're studying how things are done in heaven. Let me read this again: "The law of God, in the home life and in the government of nations, flows from a heart of infinite love" (*ibid.*).

So, it's love that prompts everything that God tells people to do. It's so in heaven, and it's so on earth for the people who will listen.

Now, this becomes a challenge to you and me as work supervisors, parents, teachers, and church officers. If we're following the principles of heaven and the plan of heaven, before we ask anyone to do anything, we'll first stop and think, "Now, what would be the most loving thing to ask them to do? What would be the thing that would help them the most and please them the most?"

"Oh," someone says, "well, I could never get my child to wash dishes." One of the sweetest testimonials on behalf of a mother that I've ever heard came from a teenage girl. She and I were talking about this matter of useful work being a lesson book that heaven uses to teach us and what joy and satisfaction there is in work. She said, "You know, I don't remember that I ever heard my mother tell me that. But," she said, "I learned it by watching her and working with her." That girl loves to work. Why? Her mother loves to work, and I'm sure that her mother never said to her, "You've got to go in there and wash the dishes. After all, you helped to dirty them. And you better wash them. I've got some other things to do."

Of course, I know all children aren't angels. But oh, the challenge to us as parents, teachers, and supervisors is to wrestle with God on our knees and find heaven's way to learn these principles and teach them.

Sometimes when people have either been kept awake through drugs or put to sleep through drugs, if you take all that away and put them on a normal program, they can become sick. What is the answer? Well, the answer is not to go back to drugs.

The person that just feels down when he or she goes off drugs and doesn't have any energy to do anything until they get that cup of coffee or that bottle of Coke, maybe what they need is a little rest. Maybe what they need are some good fruit juices to flush out the system of the poisons and to build up some real energy in the body with the natural sugars. But the point is, it's worth the depression to get rid of the false power.

And so it is, my dear friend, in the institution, home, school, or church. If our way of getting things done has been through earthly methods, and we try to follow these principles of heavenly leadership, we may at first come up with some results that make some feel sick. We may say, "This just doesn't work." But friend, we must have faith.

Jesus selected twelve men, and He drew them with Him. For three years, He tried to teach these principles. Not long before the end of those three years, two of His best students came to Him and asked for first place in the kingdom. Is that what He'd been teaching them? Where had they learned that? They learned that in this world. They even got their mother to go along with them. She was ambitious for her boys. Is that okay, or is there something higher, deeper, or broader than human ambition?

My point is that after three years, Jesus still had students who hadn't learned this lesson that you and I are trying to study here. But did Jesus get discouraged? Did He change His methods? Did He say, "Well, after all, I guess this won't work; we're going to have to start giving out prizes to those who do a little more than others. Then maybe we can get something done"? Did He offer to make an honor roll? Wouldn't the disciples have been interested in that? Peter and John and James and Matthew would have worked hard to get on that honor roll. Don't you think so? That was just the kind of thing they were used to and interested in. But Jesus said, "…it shall not be so among you" (Matt. 20:26).

He told them that that is the way gentiles get things done, but that isn't God's way. "Whosoever will be chief among you, let him be your servant: Even as the Son of man came not to be ministered unto, but to minister, and to give his life" (Matt. 20:27, 28).

Every time Jesus asked someone to do something, it was through love. What kind of response did Jesus desire and expect? "If ye love me, keep my commandments" (John 14:15).

Notice that love not only prompts Jesus to give the law; love is what prompts the disciple to obey. So, love from above prompts the law, and love in the human heart prompts obedience. Is that success? Yes. Now it takes both. But which comes first? Only by love is love awakened.

So, if you're a parent and you are having trouble with your children in getting them to respond through love, it may be they need to see more love in you. This doesn't mean some soft, sentimental mush that allows all kinds of sin and transgression.

Some people's idea of love is letting people lie in bed in the morning and then giving them candy to eat any time, all day long. That is the way to be really sweet to people. If any vision of that kind is in your mind when we use the word love, then you don't understand what love is. The best way to find out what love is, is to study the life of Jesus because He came down here to demonstrate love. But now, in John 14:15, Christ expects not only that His commands shall come from love but that obedience shall come from us.

But suppose you don't love Him. Well, keep them, anyway. It would be nice if you did it through love, but if you don't have love enough for Him, maybe you'll get a prize if you do it, so do it for the prize. Or maybe you will get a whipping if you don't, so do it to keep from the whipping.

You can't really keep them without love. Not only that, but as some of you have mentioned, all that matters with Him is love. It isn't getting the work done; it's getting us done that His heart is set on. The work is a laboratory in which we are learning these principles. The problems of life are the disciplines through which we learn to understand these methods.

So, I ask you two questions. First, when you give directions, do you do it through love? Second, when you follow directions, do you do it through love? If you can answer "yes" to both those questions, then the prayer is being fulfilled: "Thy kingdom come. Thy will be done on earth, as it is in heaven" (Matt. 6:10). If anything different from that is your experience, if anything less than that is in your life, there is something to pray and work for and something to believe in.

May we kneel together in prayer?

Heavenly Father, we've seen a high standard in this study. Like a great mountain peak, it beckons us, and it challenges us. But who could be satisfied to remain in the valley when this glorious experience is set before us? And we thank Thee, dear Jesus, that You came down from the heights of heaven and lived these glorious principles in this selfish, grasping, and cruel little world. They broke Thy dear heart, Savior. But oh, we thank Thee that the demonstration was made. And now our hearts rejoice that once again, here in human flesh, on earthly soil, the demonstration is to be made in its fullness. The principles of Thy kingdom are to be revealed. God grant that we, kneeling here now, shall be a part of the demonstration. And whatever we may have learned in our past experience that doesn't agree with this, we pray that Thou wilt blot it out of our hearts and minds. We pray that Thou wilt help us, that Thy kingdom shall come into our institution, hearts, and homes, for Jesus' sake, amen.

CHAPTER 2
Individuality and Cooperation

Let us turn to Daniel 12:3 for our opening verse. Notice that this verse is in the setting of the coming time of trouble. Let me ask, when do stars come out? When the night falls. But they are there before night falls. They are not made when darkness comes. They simply appear then.

"And they that be wise shall shine as the brightness of the firmament; and they that turn many to righteousness as the stars for ever and ever" (Dan. 12:3).

Does God have some stars? Yes. And they are going to do what? Shine. Everyone who is normal has a desire to accomplish something, and the purpose of Christian leadership is not to put it to sleep or discourage it. Not at all. It is far from that. The purpose of the gospel is to enable us to reach the highest heights and accomplish the most, both in this world and in the world to come. Can you think of any greater destiny than this?

God's stars shine forever and ever. There are Hollywood stars and television stars, but the names of those men and women come and go. They are in the headlines today, and tomorrow hardly anyone remembers them. But God's stars a million years from now will be shining brighter than ever.

Whom does this say are God's stars? They that turn many to righteousness. We often think of souls that we win represented as stars in our crown, and this is correct. But in this particular verse, it isn't the souls that we win that are spoken of as stars. It is the ones who do the soul-winning.

Oh, I hope you will be one of God's stars. I hope you will be shining for God when the night falls—when the time of trouble breaks. And the deeper the darkness, the more brilliant the stars. But remember, the stars are not made when the night falls; they are there beforehand.

Have you thought of what it means to be one of God's stars? You need to take a second look and see if you want to be one of God's stars or not. "There is one glory of the sun and another glory of the moon, and another glory of the stars: for one star differeth from another star in glory" (1 Cor. 15:41).

There are no two stars alike. Are you still sure you want to be one of God's stars? The price of it is to be different. In this world, that is a price. Of course, in heaven, everyone likes this; it's God's way. "Forever, O Lord, Thy word is settled in heaven" (Ps. 119:89). They don't have any problem with it up there. In this world, it is a cross for some people to find themselves different from others. That is the power of fashion. Someone gets elected as president, and his wife has a particular hairdo, and at once, ten million people across the country want to look like the president's wife. There is something new coming along all the time. People want to look like someone else.

There is tremendous pressure to conform. It isn't just in dress; it's in everything. People are interested in what some television celebrity eats or smokes or what clothes he or she wears. This affects the sale of many products. If you have one eye even half-open, you will notice that the world today is being regimented. But God's program is just the opposite of that.

> Your individuality is what makes you valuable. Did you ever see anyone like you? Sometimes when I ask that question, someone will say, "It's a good thing." It is a good thing. Your value would be decreased by at least 50 percent if there were a duplicate. If there were three people like you, it would decrease even further. But you are of infinite value because you are different from everyone else.

Someone says, "I thought you gave a quote in a previous chapter that they moved in exact order like a company of soldiers." Yes, but they are not regimented. They don't move in exact order because they have become a part of a machine. One star differs from another star in glory. Have you ever noticed the different colors of the stars? If it is clear tonight, and you are in the northern hemisphere, look for Antares and Mars. Do you know what color they are? Antares and Mars are red. If you look for Arcturus, you will notice that it's red, too. Vega is blue-white.

If people haven't noticed that, they just look up and say, "There are stars." Like people who look out and say, "There is a bird out there."

You ask, "What kind of bird?"

They say, "I don't know."

Is there more than one kind of bird? Do they look different? Do they sing differently? I mentioned three red stars, but each one of them is different in intensity from the other two. So, what we are reading here is still true. Whether it is a yellow star, a white star, a blue star, or a red star, every star is different from every other star in the universe.

Did you ever look at a snow crystal under a magnifying glass? This is interesting. When the snow comes this winter, catch some of them as they fall. And under a magnifying glass, look at the formations of those crystals. If you have them on something dark, you can see the patterns better. And as you look at that little snow crystal under a magnifying glass, you see that it has six sides. Look at another one. How many sides does it have? Occasionally, there is a three-sided one, but you probably won't see that; that is very rare.

If you were making trillions of snow crystals, each one with six sides, how many different patterns do you think you could make? Don't you think you would run out of ideas pretty soon? But God never does. It is extremely rare to find snow crystals with nearly the same patterns. Lace makers in Switzerland get new patterns for their laces by examining the snowflakes as they fall. God is trying to tell us that everything He makes is made by a separate pattern.

If that is true of a star, and it's true of a snow crystal, what about you? Your individuality is what makes you valuable. Did you ever see anyone like you? Sometimes when I ask that question, someone will say, "It's a good thing." It is a good thing. Your value would be decreased by at least 50 percent if there were a duplicate. If there were three people like you, it would decrease even further. But you are of infinite value because you are different from everyone else.

If people could get hold of that, would they be interested in the fashions of this world? No. They would be saying, "Lord, what did you make me to be? If you made me a blond, I want to be a blond. If you made me a brunette, I want to be a brunette. If you made me with blue eyes, I want to be blue-eyed." The converted heart says, "Lord, I want to be the individual that you made me."

So here is our problem—how are we going to get a group of people to work together if each one is different from all the others? Everywhere we turn, it takes cooperation. How do you take people who are individuals and have them fit together and work together? That is the problem. When God made individuals and gave them the job of working together, He posed one of the greatest problems of eternity. But He is not going to end up having lost either one. He is not going to lose the advantages of working together; neither is He going to lose the advantages of individuality.

What lesson do bees teach us? Organization, cooperation. Every bee has its place. They are well organized—the queen has her work, the drones have theirs, and the workers have theirs. Among the workers, some of them are doing one thing and some another, but they are all cooperating and working together. Do you know how they do it?

It is a regimented organization. The hive is everything; the individual is nothing. When winter comes, they leave the drones out to starve or freeze. They don't need them anymore; winter is coming on. You say, "That is cruel." Yes. There are a lot of things in the natural world around us that are cruel. My point is that the bees give us a wonderful example of what a group of individuals working together can do. But it's at the sacrifice of the individual.

You likely have seen an individual butterfly fluttering around. It is not common to see them in large swarms. They don't live in hives nor have queens. I guess every butterfly is her own queen. I would like that—I would like to be my own boss, and nobody tells me what to do. There are advantages to the butterfly life. The butterfly can go to this flower and fly over to this one, spend the night wherever it chooses. She is accountable to no one. Which do you think contributes more to this world's well-being, the bees or the butterflies?

My point is that, in Christian leadership, we are to learn how to combine the advantages of the bee's program with the advantages of the butterfly's program. The butterfly is an individualist; the bees are regimented. God seeks through His church to demonstrate that He can get the advantages of group action without sacrificing the important advantages of individuality. As a work supervisor, you need to know that. As a church officer, you need to know that. In the home, the school, the church, and everything with which you are connected, there must be a studied effort and aim to get people to work together without sacrificing their individuality.

If you get things done at the sacrifice of individuality, do you know what you are preparing people for? You are preparing them for the mark of the beast: "These have one mind and shall give their power and strength unto the beast" (Rev. 17:13). They have one mind in this confederacy. But who is leading them? The beast. And as the result, they are making war with the Lamb.

What good would it do if you were so efficient in your work management that you got everyone to work together just like stormtroopers, and in the end, the people you taught to work that way end up fighting Jesus? Even if you turned out a business that was superior, or you got some harvest ingathering goals in the process, or your students got high grades in their final examinations, if in the process of accomplishing these things, we produce people who lose their individuality, what have we accomplished? It is worse than nothing.

When you get this viewpoint, then you will see why it was that Jesus kept His methods with the twelve disciples, even though they didn't appear to be advantageous many times. It is better to fail a quiz or even a six-week test and pass the final examination than it is to get good marks day by day and flunk out at the end. The final examination that is ahead of us is the time of trouble.

Go back in your imagination to the time of Nebuchadnezzar in Daniel 3. Nebuchadnezzar told the people to worship the golden image. He even told them when to do it—as soon as you hear the music, down you go. And what did all those people do? They knelt. That is, all but three. They were different—they were God's stars. Oh, what brilliant stars they were! But they didn't become stars that day. They had learned that back in their Judean homes. They were taught the principles of being different there. Do you know why they were different in Babylon? They had learned to be different in Jerusalem. And even in Jerusalem, dear ones, you will have plenty of opportunities to learn that lesson. Of course, just being different isn't enough. We want to be different by being like Jesus.

I want to ask a question. If our pattern is Jesus, how can each one of us be like Jesus, and still, each one of us be different from all the rest? Because He is infinite. He has so many facets to His character that I can look at Him and copy all that I see. But you look at Him from a little different angle, and you see things in His character that don't impress me so much, and we can end up, all of us, being like Jesus, and yet all of us different, one from another. Isn't that wonderful? And when God gets us all together, it is wonderful to get acquainted with different people.

Wouldn't you like to sit down and have a visit with Enoch? How about having Shadrach tell us about the time he spent in the fiery furnace? How about having Joseph tell us about his experiences in the dungeon? How about having James and Ellen White tell us about how they got the work started in New England and New York? My point is that every one of those people is going to be different. That is why it will be a privilege, pleasure, and rare experience to get acquainted with each one of them.

Elder Luther Warren (1864–1940) used to say, "My best Friend has made arrangements for me to become personally acquainted with everyone that has ever lived in this world that is worth knowing." It is going to take quite a bit of time to really get acquainted with each one of them.

Oh friend, wouldn't it be too bad to spoil it? It would be too bad to twist or pervert a single characteristic. So, we want to study how to get people to work together without sacrificing their individuality.

One of the first places to learn this is in the home. The following statement is talking to a young man and woman who were just married:

> While you are to blend as one, neither of you is to lose his or her individuality in the other. God is the owner of your individuality. Of Him you are to ask: What is right? What is wrong? How may I best fulfill the purpose of my creation? 'Ye are not your own; for ye are bought with a price.' (*Testimonies for the Church*, vol. 7, p. 45)

The blending of husband and wife is the closest union that this world knows. And yet, even here, individuality is to be preserved. Can that be done and still blend? Oh, yes. That is the assignment. And so with every other experience in life.

In the church, are we to blend? Yes. Notice how perfect the blend is to be: "That they all may be one as Thou, Father, art in Me, and I in Thee, that they also may be one in Us: that the world may believe that Thou hast sent Me" (John 17:21).

How close is to be the unity of the members in the church? They are to be one—just as united as Jesus and His Father. The Father and the Son are both individuals, but they blend together so nicely. Neither one has ever had a disagreement or had to give in to the other. All that one wants is what the other wants.

Do you think you could have it that way in an institution? Jesus prayed for it. He is not praying for the impossible. His prayer is going to be answered.

This is a wonderful page. I invite you to study the first three paragraphs. Listen carefully as I read some of these sentences:

> God desires to bring men into direct relation with Himself. In all His dealings with human beings He recognizes the principle of personal responsibility. He seeks to encourage a sense of personal dependence and to impress the need of personal guidance. His gifts are committed to men as individuals.... (*Testimonies for the Church, vol. 7*, p. 176)

So, it isn't enough for me to ask the priest or preacher what I'm supposed to do.

> ...In all this, God is seeking to bring the human into association with the divine, that through this connection man may become transformed into the divine likeness.... (ibid.)

As an individual, I've got to look individually to God to develop the pattern that God has for my life.

> ...Then the principle of love and goodness will be a part of his nature. Satan, seeking to thwart this purpose, constantly works to encourage dependence upon man, to make men the slaves of men. (ibid.)

Satan is behind slave labor. Though slavery can build grand monuments, it can also build concentration camps. It can do great things, make great dams and all sorts of public works projects. But in doing it, Satan is not only after getting a job done, he is getting the people done. And when they are done in his oven, they are burned to a crisp. They all look alike. Listen carefully to this next sentence:

> In all our dealing with one another, God desires us carefully to guard the principle of personal responsibility to and dependence upon Him.... (ibid.)

If I am a teacher, I am to be careful not to make my students stereotypes of myself. I don't want you to think just the way I think. If I'm a work supervisor, I don't want you to do your work exactly as I do. But suppose I do it "just right?"

Some educators visited old communist Russia once. They went to a large institution where there were hundreds of children. The visitors were shown around, and they noticed the efficiency of it all. But they also noticed that all the tools and furniture were arranged for right-handed children.

One of the visitors asked one of the supervisors, "What do you do for left-handed children?"

They answered, "We don't have any."

What happened to a child who was born left-handed? He was made over into a right-handed child—he was regimented. This actual occurrence is a fit illustration of the communist system. The state is everything; the individual is of small importance.

We don't have to go to atheistic communism to find that pattern. We have a great example of it in religion. In fact, every false religion that is of any size relies on this principle. Under the name of Christianity, we have the Roman Catholic system, which exactly follows this principle. This is what Luther rebelled against; this is what Zwingli, Calvin, and Knox cried out against—the regimentation of the individual.

Interestingly enough, God has warned the Seventh-day Adventist Church of this principle: "Satan's skill is exercised in devising plans and methods without number to accomplish his purposes. He works to restrict religious liberty and to bring into the religious world a species of slavery" (*Testimonies for the Church*, vol. 7, pp. 180, 181). What does "species" mean? A kind, a variety of slavery. And the devil is trying to bring this into the religious world.

> Organizations, institutions, unless kept by the power of God, will work under Satan's dictation to bring men under the control of men,

and fraud and guile will bear the semblance of zeal for truth and for the advancement of the kingdom of God. (*ibid.*)

Wouldn't it be nice if everyone in the church would follow the reforms? It would, provided it is an individual response. But if it is the response to mass pressure, then God isn't interested in it.

As far as the effect upon the character, what difference does it make whether we follow the fashions of the world because of the mass pressure, or we yield to the pressure of a group that is teaching reforms? Is that a good question? It is a very important question. "There is a motto: 'When in Rome, do as the Romans do.' But that is Romanism. They presume to do that which God Himself will not do in seeking to control the minds of men. Thus they follow in the track of Romanism" (*Testimonies for the Church*, vol. 7, p. 181).

I love to see beautiful fruit on a tree, provided it grew there. I heard of a little boy who came down Christmas morning and was entranced with all the things that were on the tree—the apples, oranges, toys, and candy. He said, "Oh Daddy, let's plant the backyard full of this kind of tree."

Did you ever see a Christmas-tree Christian? Good fruit, but "tied on." Nothing wrong with the fruit, but it didn't grow from the inside. It wasn't a mark of individuality; it was a mark of conformity—just being like others.

Be sure you know why you do what you do, for why you do it is more important than what you do. We are building characters.

Here is another verse on the stars: "Lift up your eyes on high, and behold who hath created these things, that bringeth out their host by number: He calleth them all by names by the greatness of His might, for that He is strong in power; not one faileth" (Isa. 40:26).

> *The stars work together. Each one is right where it belongs, and yet they differ. If God can do that with the stars, can He do it with us?*

The stars work together. Each one is right where it belongs, and yet they differ. If God can do that with the stars, can He do it with us? If we listen to Him the way the stars listen, He will do it for us. That is one of the great lessons He wants us to learn as we lift up our eyes and behold those heavenly bodies.

The law that keeps the moon from running away from the earth is called gravity. It is the same law that keeps the earth in its orbit around the sun. Well, do you mean that the earth pulls the moon, and yet the earth, in turn, is held by the sun? That is right. And the sun obeys the law of gravitation, too. We are told that the sun is one of the millions of stars all traveling around the center of our galaxy, the Milky Way. But that is not the end of it. Let me give you a quote about this wonderful concept. Oh, I love this! Speaking of the redeemed:

> Unfettered by mortality, they wing their tireless flight to worlds afar—worlds that thrilled with sorrow at the spectacle of human woe and rang with songs of gladness at the tidings of a ransomed soul. With unutterable delight the children of earth enter into the joy and the wisdom of unfallen beings. They share the treasures of knowledge and understanding gained through ages upon ages in contemplation of God's handiwork. With undimmed vision they gaze upon the glory of creation—suns and stars and systems, all in their appointed order circling the throne of Deity. (The *Great Controversy*, p. 677)

Isn't that a wonderful picture? The center of the universe is the throne of God. And around that throne circle are great groups of stars like our Milky Way. But within each one of those systems, there is a center—each of those stars may have planets going around it, like the planets around our sun. Many of them may have moons like the moon circling around our earth. The point is that everything has a center that it revolves around. And the eventual center is the throne of God. What an order this is!

Our verse in Isaiah says, "He bringeth out their host by number." In mathematical order and precision. Yet one star differs from another star in glory. God has balanced the universe. Look at the planets in our system. Venus is almost the same size as our planet, but Jupiter is 1,300 times as large as ours. If you put Jupiter where Venus is and Venus where Jupiter is, we would have a mess. That is right. God has measured and balanced the gravitational pull of every object in the universe so that the whole thing fits together in order.

CHAPTER 3

Balance

I want you to imagine something for a moment. Here is the earth. Out in space is the moon. It has been going on its course around the earth. You and I are used to having it orbit us. But suppose that the earth was suddenly blotted out of existence. Where would the moon go? It would proceed in the same course that it was going on at the time that the earth was blotted out. The thing that makes it travel in that orbit is the earth's gravity—the earth is pulling it. And if you were to suddenly remove that, instead of curving around in orbit, it would just keep going straight. Do you know how long it would keep going in that direction? If it didn't hit something else, it would keep going forever. At least that is what scientists tell us. Gravity must be quite a strong pull.

Let's take another illustration. Here is a gun. You shoot a bullet out of it. A certain distance from here, that bullet will fall to the ground. What pulls it to the ground? Gravity. Suppose that the force of gravitation was removed right at the time we shoot that gun. What would the bullet do? It would keep going straight forever. It is gravitation that stops it by pulling it down.

I want to ask a question. If gravitation is that strong, that powerful, why doesn't it pull the moon down to the earth? The hand of God pushes the moon, and the power of God pulls it into the earth. And those two are exactly balanced. If God were to impart more momentum to the moon than it has, it would leave the earth's gravitational pull and go off into space somewhere. If the Lord were to decrease the momentum, it would keep getting closer to the earth as it made the orbit and finally smash.

There is a lovely balance of two forces—the pull of gravitation and the momentum that God has imparted to that moon to keep it going. Momentum is what makes the moon move. But what makes it move in the right direction is that it has just enough gravitational pull to keep it where it belongs. This is one of the most wonderful lessons in Christian leadership that I know about. This same lesson is running all through the universe.

We could use the same illustration with the earth and the sun. This earth is traveling around the sun. Besides turning over on its axis every twenty-four hours, every year, it makes a journey around the sun. Why doesn't it go off into space somewhere? What holds it? The gravitational pull of the sun. Just as the earth is holding the moon, the sun is holding the earth with the moon.

But if all there were to the earth's travel was that gravitational pull, where would the sun pull it? Into itself. We would be part of a bonfire. Aren't you glad that God's hand guides this planet in its march around the sun? There are doubtless many ways the Lord could have arranged this, but this is the way He did arrange it.

I want you to think of this gravitational pull as the power that keeps you and me from running off on a tangent. That is the purpose of organization. That is the purpose of direction.

But there is something that government is not designed to do. It is not designed to supply momentum. It is not designed to supply the power that keeps us moving. We need to get that individually from the Lord. And if we don't, then government may have to supply that with a bayonet or a paycheck.

Are there some people who move because there is a bayonet to their back? Are there some people who move because of a paycheck in front of them? But there is no bayonet behind the moon, and there is no paycheck in front of it. The hand of God is moving it on. It's a wonderful thing to be on a path that you keep going in, not because of fear or favor, not because you are being pushed from behind or pulled ahead by some selfish interest.

What is the third word in this little verse? Love. "If ye love Me, keep My commandments" (John 14:15). What the hand of God does for the moon in pushing it ahead, the love of God does for you and me in causing us to keep His commandments.

"For the love of Christ constraineth us" (2 Cor. 5:14). What does "constrain" mean? It makes us do things. "Constrain" does not mean "restrain." To restrain means to hold back. The love of Christ to the Christian is like the motor in an automobile that makes it go—like the great engine in a ship that turns the propeller and keeps it going.

Along with the love of Christ, we need a love for the bodies He has appointed to influence us. Should a child be influenced by the home that he is a member of? Yes. Are there some directions that God will give the child through the parents? Does a student in a school get all his directions directly from God? No. How does he get some of them? Through the teacher. He shouldn't have to get the motivation from the teacher; he gets that from God. But he gets some directions. And those directions are to help him keep in orbit.

Suppose we go out to our job. Does God tell each one of us directly what job to do and how to do it? No. Whom does God have for that? Leaders, supervisors, foremen, and superintendents.

Now we come to the church, which is the greatest organization in the world. You and I are members of the church. Suppose we think of ourselves as the moon, and we think of the church as the earth. Should the church have an influence on our lives? Yes. Should the church be the only thing we depend upon to know our duty and keep going? No. We have an individual experience with God.

Well, if I have an individual experience with God, then I don't need the church, do I? If there is no gravity keeping the moon in orbit, it goes out of orbit and goes off on a tangent. "Raging waves of the sea, foaming out their own shame; wandering stars, to whom is reserved the blackness of darkness for ever" (Jude 13).

The moon shines only with reflected light. The planets shine only with reflected light. And if one of these planets or moons should get out of place and go off through the universe, it would soon be so far away from the sun or any other light, luminous object that it would simply be in darkness. This is what happens to the individual who gets out of orbit. Now, to show you that this is what Jude is talking about, notice the eighth verse. Here are the people he is describing as wandering stars: "Likewise also these filthy dreamers defile the flesh, despise dominion, and speak evil of dignities" (Jude 8).

What is dominion? Government, control. There are individuals who despise control—they don't want to submit to direction. They don't want to be in orbit around some larger object or organization. They want to choose their own course, plot their own career, and carry it out. Jude says they are wandering stars. Instead of shining like the stars we read about in the last chapter, they are in darkness.

> *I hope that as a result of reading this book, you will make up your mind that you want momentum enough in love for God to keep going, and you want an understanding of and respect for the authorities He has established in the institution and in the church, that it will keep pulling you and keeping you in orbit.*

I hope that as a result of reading this book, you will make up your mind that you want momentum enough in love for God to keep going, and you want an understanding of and respect for the authorities He has established in the institution and in the church, that it will keep pulling you and keeping you in orbit. If the moon could think like some people, it would say, "Why can't I go where I am headed? Why do I have to be pulled at continually?" The answer is to stay in orbit.

Viewed from one angle, the moon is being interfered with every minute by the gravitational pull from the earth. But viewed from the other angle, that is the only way to keep it where it belongs. If you were the moon, what would you think about it? Some people might say, "Now see here, which am I going to do? My momentum is pushing me that way, and the earth is pulling me this way. Which way do I go?" In God's infinite plan, it's a balance between the two.

In religious organizations, we have the supreme example of making the gravitational pull supreme in the Roman Catholic body. In certain religious organizations, we have just the opposite of that extreme. There are some individuals who think that you only need to pay attention to the local church. There are other individuals who feel that they are responsible alone to God for their religious experience. And you have all shades in between.

Now let's go to Revelation, the first chapter where it says that Jesus has seven stars in His right hand. What are they? Let's see: "The mystery of the seven stars which thou sawest in My right hand, and the seven golden candlesticks. The seven stars are the angels of the seven churches: and the seven candlesticks which thou sawest are the seven churches" (Rev. 1:20).

Do you know what the word "angel" means? It means messenger. John the Baptist was an angel as far as New Testament Greek is concerned. "Behold, I send my messenger before thy face" (Matt. 11:10). He was an angel—he was a messenger. So, the ones we call angels aren't the only angels; there are human angels, too—human messengers. The reason the beings we call angels are called angels is because they are God's messengers. But they are not the angels that are spoken of in this verse. You'll see that as you look at the second and third chapters of Revelation: "Unto the angel of the church of Ephesus write…" (Rev. 2:1).

Did John need to write a letter to a heavenly being? No. Now, who are the messengers of the church? I'll read it to you here in *Gospel Workers*:

> God's ministers are symbolized by the seven stars, which He who is the first and the last has under His special care and protection. The sweet influences that are to be abundant in the church are bound up with these ministers of God who are to represent the love of Christ. The stars of the heaven are under God's control. He fills them with light. He guides and directs their movements. If He did not, they would become fallen stars. They are but instruments in His hands, and all the good they accomplish is done through His power. (*Gospel Workers*, p. 13)

So, the seven stars represent the ministers, the messengers. Where do these stars get their light? From God. The moon and stars of the solar system, the planets, all shine by reflected light. The only way any human being can shine is with reflected light. The only way we can be in our places is to have some momentum that God supplies and some gravitational pull that He also supplies (always through a larger body). The earth is bigger than the moon. The sun is bigger than the earth. If it weren't, the pull would be the other way. If you have studied some of these things in science, you know that the moon does have some pull on the earth even though it is smaller. But the earth has more pull, and so its pull is greater.

> *Every member of the church affects the church. Every one of us has a gravitational pull on the church.*

Every member of the church affects the church. Every one of us has a gravitational pull on the church. But the gravitational pull of the church on the individual member is to be greater than the pull of the individual member on the church. The mass is greater than the one individual.

Suppose we have a million members, and I am just one out here. The gravitational pull is much greater with these millions in the mass than just this one out here.

I want to read another statement on this. I am thankful God has given us, both in the Bible and the Spirit of Prophecy, so many precious lessons on how to work together—how to be organized for efficient work: "The stars of heaven are all under law, each influencing the other to do the will of God" (*Testimonies for the Church*, vol. 9, p. 258).

You may remember the story in scientific history of how at least two of the planets were discovered before they were ever seen by an astronomer. The effect of their gravitational pull on nearby planets was studied. And, from that, the astronomer said there must be a planet out there in a certain direction, and it must be a certain size and a certain distance. And they figured that out. And finally, with more powerful telescopes, they discovered the planet. But they knew it was out there. I think that is true of both Neptune and Pluto—the outlying members of our solar system.

This illustrates what this says: "The stars of heaven are all under law, each influencing the other to do the will of God, yielding their common obedience to the law that controls their action" (*ibid.*).

> The name of the chapter is "The Spirit of Independence." Oh, how Satan would rejoice if he could succeed in his efforts to get in among this people and disorganize the work at a time when thorough organization is essential and will be the greatest power to keep out spurious uprisings and to refute claims not endorsed by the word of God! (*ibid.*, p. 257)

The greatest power to keep out spurious uprisings is thorough organization. But an organization is of no value to me if I do not recognize its authority and yield to its influence. The government of Spain has no influence over me at all. I have not put myself under it. It is also true with France and England.

I have chosen to put myself under the United States government. In certain ways, I yield to its gravitational pull every time we buy a gallon of gas. I have chosen to live in the United States and be subject to its laws.

Now when we come into church organization, we place ourselves under the direction of an organization whose head is in heaven. This is more than a human government; this is a divine government, and yet it's exercised through human beings. We have already seen that it isn't enough to do anything that we're told to do like Roman Catholics are supposed to do with the priest. Oh, no. But the answer is not just the opposite of that—to rush off on a tangent. We are to have such respect for the church that it will help to hold us in orbit without destroying our individuality.

> "Some have advanced the thought that as we near the close of time, every child of God will act independently of any religious organization" (*Testimonies for the Church*, vol. 9, p. 258). Did you ever hear that? I have. I have heard that the church is merely a temporary arrangement until we can all get the Spirit and get sufficiently educated, so we don't need men to teach us anymore. And there is a certain angle of it that sounds reasonable. In other words, children need parents. But after a while, they ought to grow up. Then they are supposed to be adults and know how to make choices for themselves. And so, the lesson is supposed to be that you need a church when you are a baby, but somewhere along the line, you ought to grow up to the place where you don't need the church to tell you anything anymore. It sounds reasonable. But there is something greater than reason. It is the Word of God. I think if a person is really grown up, he or she appreciates the opportunity of counseling with their parents. But there is a relationship we have to the church that is far greater than the responsibility that we might have to counsel with our parents when we are adults.

> "But I have been instructed by the Lord that in this work there is no such thing as every man's being independent. The stars of heaven are all under law, each influencing the other to do the will of God" (*ibid.*). Oh, friend, I want to learn this lesson. Don't you? And can I learn it without destroying my individuality? I don't have to go smashing down, pulled by nothing but gravitation. I can receive enough love from God to keep me looking to Him and moving toward Him all the time, and yet the thing that keeps me in orbit is

that balance between my individual guidance and the guidance I get from my brethren.

A good example of this is the apostle Paul. He met Jesus on the road to Damascus. Jesus said to him, "Why are you persecuting Me?"
Paul answered, "Who are you?"
Jesus replied, "I am Jesus whom thou persecuteth."
Paul responded, "Lord, what wilt Thou have me to do?" Did Jesus tell him what to do? Let's see in Acts 9 and see: "And the Lord said unto him, Arise, and go into the city, and it shall be told thee what thou must do" (Acts 9:6).

Why didn't Jesus tell him what to do directly? Don't you think Paul would have listened to Jesus? Let me read the divine comment; we are not left to speculate on this. Paul cried out:

> 'Lord, what wilt Thou have me to do?' Jesus did not then and there tell him, as He might have done, the work that He had assigned him… Christ sends him to the very disciples whom he had been so bitterly persecuting, to learn of them… He answers the question of Paul in these words: 'Arise and go into the city, and it shall be told thee what thou must do.' Jesus could not only have healed Paul of his blindness, but He could have forgiven his sins and told him his duty by marking out his future course. From Christ all power and mercies were to flow; but He did not give Paul an experience, in his conversion to truth, independent of His church recently organized upon the earth…. (*Testimonies for the Church*, vol. 3, p. 430)

If Paul had gotten all his directions from Jesus that day, he might have been hard to live with for the church. Jesus deliberately got him to the point where he would listen and told him to go to those very people he had planned to put in jail and murder and ask them what he was supposed to do.

Thank the Lord that Paul did what he was told. It's a wonderful thing when the proud pharisee's heart is humbled, and he is willing to learn of the lowly disciple.

Will our hearts be humbled? Will we be willing to come into orbit and stay in orbit? This is Christian leadership.

> …He did not give Paul an experience, in his conversion to truth, independent of His church recently organized upon the earth. Jesus

directs him to His agents in the church for a further knowledge of duty. Thus He gives authority and sanction to His organized church. Christ directed Paul to His chosen servants, thus placing him in connection with His church. (*ibid.*)

What kind of church was it? An organized church. How could a disorganized church tell anyone what to do? How would the individual know who was speaking for Jesus? It has to be an organized church.

As you study the experience of Paul, you notice two things: there is no man in the New Testament who had so many problems in the church as Paul did. And there is no man who writes more about church organization and church loyalty as Paul did. Both of those are significant. You can study that for a long time. I hope you will. We are told that the people of God who stand in the crisis will have to have an experience like Paul. We have to have an experience of loving the church as Paul did, and we also have to have some convictions of duty that we get from God.

Let's go to Galatians, and you will see what I mean. This almost sounds to contradict what we have read so far, but it doesn't contradict it at all; it supplements it: "But I certify you, brethren, that the gospel which was preached of me is not after man. For I neither received it of man, neither was I taught it, but by the revelation of Jesus Christ" (Gal. 1:11, 12).

That sounds like he got it all directly from heaven. Both are true. If he hadn't had the revelation from heaven, not only on the road to Damascus but later, he would never have had the momentum to go ahead in the course he was going. On the other hand, if he hadn't been put into contact with the church, he would never have stayed in orbit. He would have become a wandering star. He needed both. He needed to be taught of God. He needed to be taught of the church. Do we need both?

Now let's look at Revelation 12:4. Satan's tail drew the third part of the stars of heaven and cast them to the earth. These stars were angels—one-third of them were drawn out of their orbits.

Remember what Jude says, "The angels which kept not their first estate, but left their own habitation" (Jude 1:6). Do you know why they got out of orbit?

The angels who fell were anxious to become independent of God. They were very beautiful, very glorious, but dependent on God for their happiness and for the light and intelligence they enjoyed. They fell from their high estate through insubordination. Christ and His church are inseparable. To neglect or despise those whom God has appointed to lead out and to bear the responsibilities connected with His work and with the advancement and spread of the truth is to reject the means which God has ordained for the help, encouragement, and strength of His people. To pass these by and think your light must come through no other channel than directly from God places you in a position where you are liable to deception and to be overthrown. (*Testimonies for the Church*, vol. 3, pp. 418, 419)

These angels fell through insubordination. They wanted to be independent. They wanted to go where they pleased when they pleased without being under the orders of Christ. They didn't realize they were choosing cruel bondage by going with Lucifer instead. They thought that obeying Christ would be bondage but obeying Lucifer would be liberty. Isn't that a strange infatuation?

It is happening today. I want to tell you that everyone in this universe is influenced by something and someone. If we are not under the mild rule of Christ and fitting into the orbit He established, then we are headed for the mist of darkness forever as we follow the influence of Lucifer and those who fell with him. Oh, I want to learn this lesson! Don't you?

Perhaps we might have a little illustration of how this works, and maybe you will understand why one-third of these angels couldn't take it anymore. If one-third of the people at Wildwood would all leave in one day, someone would say, "Where there is so much smoke, there must be some fire. There surely must be something wrong there." Was there really anything wrong in heaven?

"There is perfect order and harmony in the Holy City. All the angels that are commissioned to visit the earth hold a golden card, which they present to the angels at the gates of the city as they pass in and out" (*Early Writings*, p. 39).

Could you take that? Suppose you were about to go out through the gate here at Wildwood, and someone steps up and says, "Your card, please."

"What? You mean I have to show a card before I can get out of here? I won't have that."

Here is someone else coming in. Someone stops them at the gate and says, "Your card, please."

"You mean I can't get back in here without that card?"

Would you want to live in a place like that? The next sentence says: "Heaven is a good place. I long to be there. I long to be there and behold my lovely Jesus, who gave His life for me, and be changed into His glorious image" (ibid.).

The prophet of God wasn't discouraged when she saw it. She must have learned to love order. Do you love order? Do you like to be directed? Or are you like a horse or a mule that is always pulling off to one side?

Here is another reason why a third of the angels said they could not take it any longer:

> I have been shown the order, the perfect order of heaven, and have been enraptured as I listened to the perfect music there… There is one angel who always leads, who first touches the harp and strikes the note, then all join in the rich, perfect music of heaven. It cannot be described. It is melody, heavenly, divine, while from every countenance beams the image of Jesus, shining with glory unspeakable. (*Testimonies for the Church*, vol. 1, p. 146)

Do you mean that even in heaven they have to have leaders? That is what it says. Oh, friend, it is a wonderful thing to love teamwork, not as slaves but as free individuals. How do those two-thirds who stayed with Jesus put up with that program? They love God. For ages, they all loved God, and they were all happy together.

Then poor Lucifer, in that mystery that can never be explained, came to the point where he thought that he had a better way than heaven's order. That was for everyone to be free and independent, choose their own course, each one making its own orbit. One-third of the angels went with him, and two-thirds said, "No, we are staying with God. We love Him. We love His law."

Which group are you going to be with, friend? We are all going to wind up with one or the other. There were some vacancies made up in heaven. We are going to fill those vacancies if we learn the lessons they failed to learn. But can you imagine that it would make sense for you and me to fill the vacancies if we flunk the lessons they failed to learn? Can you see that we will be tested on this very point of whether we love order and organization?

Unless we learn the full lesson of perfect obedience and perfect cooperation, eventually, we will be in a mob that may destroy and drive the saints to the rocks and mountains. And it could be that someone reading this book would lead that mob like Judas led the mob that arrested Jesus. Unless I learn the lesson, that is where I will be. Unless I learn the lesson to love order, love organization, love direction, and love government, I will be with the mob. I want to keep in orbit.

CHAPTER 4

The Great Demonstration

The third chapter of Ephesians is one of the great mountaintops in Paul's epistles:

Unto me, who am less than the least of all saints, is this grace given, that I should preach among the Gentiles the unsearchable riches of Christ; And to make all men see what is the fellowship of the mystery, which from the beginning of the world hath been hid in God, who created all things by Jesus Christ: To the intent… (Eph. 3:8–10)

Now, watch. This is the purpose of the whole thing—the intention of God: To the intent that now unto the principalities and powers in heavenly places might be known by the church the manifold wisdom of God, According to the eternal purpose which he purposed in Christ Jesus our Lord. (Eph. 3:10–11)

Notice that God has had a purpose that is eternal. That means He had it from all eternity to all eternity. What is it? Paul says that this purpose is being worked out here in this world in the church. What for? So that the principalities and powers in heavenly places might know something—the manifold wisdom of God. This is an amazing statement!

The angels and their commanders are looking down here at what? The church. And it is God's purpose that through the church, by means of the church, all those commanders in heaven shall learn something which they have not yet fully grasped—the manifold wisdom of God.

That, dear friend, is the great motive for studying Christian leadership. That is why I say that if we can get hold of this, it will give us a most wonderful motivation and incentive to study and to apply these principles. This isn't merely to get some work done in an institution. This isn't just to get some

> *it is God's purpose that through the church, by means of the church, all those commanders in heaven shall learn something which they have not yet fully grasped—the manifold wisdom of God. That, dear friend, is the great motive for studying Christian leadership.*

unity in the church. This is to vindicate the character of God and demonstrate the wisdom of God for all the universe to see. The angels are studying Christian leadership as it is being worked out here in the church on earth. As they behold it, they marvel, adore, and wonder at the manifold wisdom of God.

Now, if you think I have drawn too much out of these verses, listen to what the different translations will bring out on these points. Here is the *Revised Standard Version*:

> And to make all men see what is the plan of the mystery hidden for ages in God who created all things; that through the church the manifold wisdom of God might now be made known to the principalities and powers in the heavenly places. This was according to the eternal purpose which he has realized in Christ Jesus our Lord. (Eph. 3:9–12)

If you were the devil, what would you do about it? Would you try to thwart that purpose? Oh, yes. That is what he is trying to do, but he will be disappointed. He is going to be amazed by the outcome.

This next translation is the *New English Bible*:

> It was hidden for long ages in God, the creator of the universe, in order that now, through the church, the wisdom of God in all its varied forms, might be made known to the rulers and authorities in the realms of heaven. This is in accord with His age-long purpose which he achieved in Christ Jesus our Lord. (Eph. 3:9, 10)

J. B. Philips New Testament translation:

> The purpose is that all the angelic powers should now see the complex wisdom of God's plan being worked out through the Church, in conformity to that timeless purpose which he centred in Jesus, our Lord. (Eph. 3:10)

Isn't that wonderful?

Making clear how the secret purpose is to be worked out which has been hidden away for ages in God the creator of all things, so that the many-sided wisdom of God may now through the church be made known to the rulers and authorities in heaven, fulfilling the eternal purpose which God carried out in Christ Jesus our Lord. (Eph. 3:9, 10, *Goodspeed New Testament*)

How can angels, who have been students of God's government for ages, learn anything about God's government by watching the church—by watching you and me?

We look at it, and we think, "Human beings aren't doing a very good job." Yet, Paul says that the angels are learning some things about the wisdom of God and the working out of His eternal purpose by watching the church.

Oh, if we could get heaven's viewpoint, friend! This next is Weymouth's translation: "…in order that the Church might now be used to display to the powers and authorities in the heavenly realms the innumerable aspects of God's wisdom" (Eph. 3:9, 10, *Weymouth New Testament*).

Oh, that is just thrilling, like a trumpet call! God's plan of government puts a high and infinite value on the individuality of every individual. Lucifer contends that there is no way to achieve absolute unity and still respect the individual. God says, "Yes, there is." It can be done through the love of God and the wisdom of God.

The church is His great laboratory in which He is working out that experiment.

> *How can angels, who have been students of God's government for ages, learn anything about God's government by watching the church—by watching you and me? We look at it, and we think, "Human beings aren't doing a very good job." Yet, Paul says that the angels are learning some things about the wisdom of God and the working out of His eternal purpose by watching the church.*

No wonder the dragon is wroth with the woman and goes to make war with the remnant of her seed, for it's in the remnant that this demonstration is to reach its full and final display.

The next is the *Twentieth Century New Testament*:

> I was appointed to tell the heathen the good news of the undreamt of wealth that exists in Christ and to make clear what is God's way of working out the secret purpose which for long ages has been lying hidden in the mind of the creator of all things. And the object of this is that God's many-sided wisdom should now through the church be made known to the angelic beings on high of every rank, in accordance with the purpose which He has had in view all through the ages and is now carried out in the person of Jesus, the Christ, our master. (Eph. 3:9, 10)

> *God's plan of government puts a high and infinite value on the individuality of every individual. Lucifer contends that there is no way to achieve absolute unity and still respect the individual. God says, "Yes, there is." It can be done through the love of God and the wisdom of God.*

He had it in mind all the time, and the church is to realize the fulfillment of His eternal purpose. Now from Moffatt's translation:

> And enlighten all men upon the new order of that divine secret which God the Creator of all concealed from eternity—intending to let the full sweep of the divine wisdom be disclosed now by the church to the angelic Rulers and Authorities in the heavenly sphere, in terms of the eternal purpose which he has realized in Christ Jesus our Lord. (Eph. 3:9, 10, *James Moffatt New Testament*)

Oh, isn't that wonderful—intending to let the full sweep of the divine wisdom be disclosed now by the church to the rulers in heavenly places?

How do we know this? We know it by faith. Take your own salvation. Can you grasp the fact that you are to be presented faultless at the coming of Jesus?

Suppose you were to look at your attainments for as long as you've been living the Christian life and make a chart of it. Now, project that onto the time ahead between now and the coming of Jesus, however long it might be. Do you think you'd be ready? Well, what makes you think you're going to be ready, then? Ah, it's faith in God's love and God's wisdom. "Being confident of this very thing, that he which hath begun a good work in you will finish it [marginal reading] until the day of Jesus Christ" (Phil. 1:6).

Watch this and don't miss it—the same faith that gives you a reason to believe that you will be saved is the basis for believing that the church will be saved. The same faith that makes you confident that you're going to reach that high standard makes you confident that the church will reach that high standard. It is the same faith—the faith of Jesus. He expressed that faith when He gave Himself for you and when He gave Himself for the church.

So, all these things we're studying, remember, they reach into your home, the institution, the schoolroom, your relationship to the church. All these principles, friend, are made in heaven, but they're being worked out and demonstrated in their fullness here on earth.

Watch this—while we look to heaven to learn how to carry these principles out, heaven is looking to earth to see these principles carried out in their fullness under the most unfavorable circumstances. If they work here and now, they could have worked anywhere and anytime in the past, and they will work anywhere and anytime in the future. On this point, the issue is joined. Satan says it can't be done. Christ says it can be done, and it will be done. For this, He gave His life.

> Watch this and don't miss it—the same faith that gives you a reason to believe that you will be saved is the basis for believing that the church will be saved. The same faith that makes you confident that you're going to reach that high standard makes you confident that the church will reach that high standard. It is the same faith—the faith of Jesus. He expressed that faith when He gave Himself for you and when He gave Himself for the church.

> *While we look to heaven to learn how to carry these principles out, heaven is looking to earth to see these principles carried out in their fullness under the most unfavorable circumstances. If they work here and now, they could have worked anywhere and anytime in the past, and they will work anywhere and anytime in the future.*

Satan has two lies, and they're like Siamese twins. It's just the opposite of these two great truths we've studied. One is that you can't reach that perfection that Jesus has called for. If you are ever saved, Jesus will have to not only overlook all your failures of the past, but He will have to overlook your failures right up to the time you're taken to heaven.

The other lie that goes with that is that the church will never reach that standard, that it's only in the eternal world that God's people will be thus united and reveal on earth the government of heaven. I repeat: both of those are lies of the devil. They're identical twins, and the answer to both of the devil's lies is these two great truths. By faith, I believe that Jesus is going to finish His work in my life. By faith, I believe that Jesus is going to do it for the church.

Now, let's see a quote from the Spirit of Prophecy on this Bible passage from Ephesians: "The church is God's appointed agency for the salvation of men. It was organized for service" (*Acts of the Apostles*, p. 9).

Tell me, is this talking about the invisible church or the visible church? Visible. By the way, if any of you find any place in the Spirit of Prophecy or the Bible that talks about the invisible church, I wish you'd bring it to my attention because I need that reference. But this is talking about a church that is organized.

Now watch:

> The church is God's appointed agency for the salvation of men. It was organized for service, and its mission is to carry the Gospel to the world. From the beginning it has been God's plan that through His church shall be reflected to the world His fullness and His sufficiency. The members of the church, those whom He has called out of darkness into His marvelous light, are to show forth His glory.

> The church is the repository of the riches of the grace of Christ; and through the church will eventually be made manifest, even to 'the principalities and powers in heavenly places,' the final and full display of the love of God. (*Acts of the Apostles*, p. 9)

Where is the love of God going to be revealed in final and full display? In the church. What kind of church? An organized church. After all, wouldn't you have to have an organized church to reveal a plan of government?

Always keep in mind that the same principles run through the home, the school, the institution, and the church. Everything that God is managing He manages according to these principles we're studying. He is going to make the final and full display of His wisdom and love in the organized, remnant church, revealing God's love as the universe has never yet seen it.

You remember that over 2,000 years ago, Jesus entered this world, and the whole universe bent low to marvel and adore. Through the man, Christ Jesus, God's wisdom and love were revealed.

Now watch—this time it's to be done, not just through one, but the 144,000 as a group will all be so united, welded, blended, and organized together that in their blended ministry, God's love and wisdom will be fully revealed. That is what this says: "…through the church will eventually be made manifest, even to 'the principalities and powers in heavenly places,' the final and full display of the love of God" (*Acts of the Apostles,* p. 9).

Isn't that wonderful? Then in the church, of which every home and every institution is a part, we're learning these same principles, and when the lessons get learned, and the demonstration is made, all the angels are going to marvel and adore and say, "Lucifer is a liar. God is true. Jesus is wonderful. His plan of government is wonderful."

Aren't we blessed to be called to have a part in such a demonstration?

This statement from *Acts of the Apostles*, page 9, is repeated in three other places, but each time in a different way. Here is one from the *Desire of Ages*:

> Christ designs that heaven's order, heaven's plan of government, heaven's divine harmony, shall be represented in His church on earth. Thus in His people He is glorified… The church, endowed with the righteousness of Christ, is His depositary, in which the riches of His mercy, His grace, and His love, are to appear in full and final display. (*Desire of Ages*, p. 680)

Now, the first reference I gave you from *Acts of the Apostles* said, "Final and full display." Here it says, "Full and final display." The reference from *Acts of the Apostles* says, "The church is the repository of the riches of the grace of Christ." *Desire of Ages* says it's "His depositary." Look up these different words in the dictionary and get the different shades of meaning.

> "The church, being endowed with the righteousness of Christ, is His depository, in which the wealth of His mercy, His love, His grace, is to appear in full and final display" (*Testimonies to Ministers*, p. 18). What does "final" mean? This is the end. What does "full" mean? Nothing is lacking. The will of God is done in the church on earth as it is done in the church in heaven. That must happen before the end can come, for the honor of the throne of God.

I thank God, He is going to get it done. Praise His wonderful name! Now, let's get a little picture of how this is done in heaven so that we can understand how it's to be done on earth. "I have been shown the order, the perfect order, of heaven, and have been enraptured as I listened to the perfect music there.... There is one angel who always leads, who first touches the harp and strikes the note, then all join in the rich, perfect music of heaven" (*Testimonies for the Church*, vol. 1, p. 146).

Notice the emphasis on two things. One is how beautiful the music is. It is in perfect harmony. The other is that there is leadership. I understand that one-third of the angels couldn't stand it any longer and pulled out. Was it a controversy over government, leadership, and carrying out orders? Is all going to get settled down here in the church on earth in spite of all its problems? "There is perfect order and harmony in the Holy City. All the angels that are commissioned to visit the earth hold a golden card, which they present to the angels at the gates of the city as they pass in and out. Heaven is a good place. I long to be there..." (*Early Writings*, p. 39).

Would you like to be there? Would you be willing to present your card? I've tried to picture it, friend. If some of us were given the privilege of going up there, and God says to us, "I have an errand for you today. Would you be willing to go back to the earth today and carry out this errand for me?"

"Yes, Lord, I would just be delighted."

So, we get all ready and start out, just so anxious to get down to the earth and do what God told us to do. But we're so busy that, being human and full of our mission, we forget to present our golden card as we go out the gate. What might the angel at the gate say?

"Where is your card?"

"Why, I don't have to show my card. God told me what to do. I'm on an errand from headquarters. Don't delay me."

Could it happen? It wouldn't happen in heaven, but it happens on earth. We haven't yet achieved heaven's order on earth.

I know that there are some people that are so wise, educated, and sophisticated that they would smile or sneer at this idea of angels having a golden card. I believe just what this says. I'm just that simple-minded, and I trust with a childlike faith. Let me read it again: "There is perfect order and harmony in the Holy City. All the angels that are commissioned to visit the earth hold a golden card, which they present to the angels at the gates of the city as they pass in and out. Heaven is a good place. I long to be there…" (Early Writings, p. 39).

I will tell you, friend, how you and I can find out whether or not we'd enjoy a place like that. God lets us have a bit of discipline, order, and organization right here, and if we've learned to tolerate it, we get a C grade. If you've learned to smile when you have to fit into it, that is probably a B grade. But if you've learned to actually understand it and appreciate it and enjoy it, that is A-plus. "To the intent that now unto the principalities and powers in heavenly places might be made known through the church the manifold wisdom of God" (Eph. 3:10).

I want to show you how angels are creatures with free will. They're angelic, but they have their limitations, and I want you to notice some of their experiences. The following quote is about Jesus praying in Gethsemane: "The angels cast their crowns and harps from them and with the deepest interest silently watched Jesus. They wished to surround the Son of God, but the commanding angels suffered them not, lest, as they should behold His betrayal, they should deliver Him…" (*Early Writings*, p. 167).

All the angels see Jesus in Gethsemane, and what do they want to do? They want to surround Him. But the commanding angels, plural, say what? "No! You must not do that."

But why did the commanding angels say that they should not surround Jesus? Lest as they saw His betrayal, they should deliver Him. Now, suppose you're one of the rank and file of the angels, one of the privates, you might say, and you and all the other angels around you hear Jesus praying. You want to answer His prayer and go to help Him.

A tall commanding angel holds up his hand and says, "No!"

"But hear Jesus praying. He wants help. We can help Him. What is the matter?"

"The plan must be carried out, and there is a danger that, as the betrayal takes place, if we were too close to Jesus, one of you might interfere."

"Do you mean you can't trust us?"

Did you ever hear students say that? Did you ever hear church members say that? Did you ever feel that way? Somehow the angels have learned to live with this, and if we're going to live with them, we're going to need live with it, too. But the amazing thing is that in this world, you and I are going to get so far in this science that the angels looking at us will learn more about this heaven's plan of government than they've ever known in all the ages of the past. We have quite an assignment, don't we?

Here is another look at the order of the angels. This is in the judgment hall when Christ was mocked and derided: "It was difficult for the angels to endure the sight. They would have delivered Jesus, but the commanding angels forbade them..." (*Early Writings*, p. 170).

What did they want to do? Deliver Jesus. They didn't want to do some bad thing. They wanted to do something they thought was good. God did not supernaturally endow them with wisdom so that they could see it would be better to leave Jesus alone.

Those angels (here is the crux of the matter) were dependent upon orders from above, not directly from God, but from whom? Other angels. Some people think that all leaders are for is to try to convince those under them of the reasons for compliance. So, some parents patiently and meekly

> *Every coin has two sides. The infinite value of individuality is one side of the coin, and the infinite importance of organization, order, and government is the other side. And it's love that makes those two sides together in one coin. Those two principles fit together in this beautiful demonstration in heaven and on earth. And it's going to get done, friend.*

reason with their children to try to get them to see something, but if they can't see it, they don't enforce their directives. What if the angels had had that philosophy back there in Gethsemane and in the judgment hall? Those angels would have darted to the rescue. "...the commanding angels suffered them not..." (*Early Writings*, p. 167). Thank God, they had learned to submit to that for which they saw no reason.

This next scene is from the crucifixion:

> The angels who hovered over the scene of Christ's crucifixion were moved to indignation as the rulers derided Him and said, 'If He be the Son God, let Him deliver Himself.' They wished there to come to the rescue of Jesus and deliver Him, but they were not suffered to do so. (*Early Writings*, p. 177)

Three times in twelve hours, the angels wanted to do something, and each time the commanding angel said, "No." And each time, the angels did what? Obeyed. It's wonderful, friend. I long to learn more about that.

"Harmony and union existing among men of varied dispositions is the strongest witness that can be borne that God has sent His Son into the world to save sinners" (*Testimonies for the Church*, vol. 8, p. 243). In other words, if we act as the angels do in following our leaders, that will be the most powerful witness that Jesus has come in the flesh. "But God cannot make them one in Christ unless they are willing to give up their own way for His way" (*Testimonies for the Church*, vol. 8, p. 243).

Are you willing to give up your own way?

"Ah but," someone says, "Brother Frazee, I thought you spent most of the last lesson talking to us about individuality and how we're not to let anyone regiment us and press out our individuality."

That is right. How does it fit? It fits wonderfully. They're two parts of the same coin. Did you ever see a coin with only one side? Every coin has two sides. The infinite value of individuality is one side of the coin, and the infinite importance of organization, order, and government is the other side. And it's love that makes those two sides together in one coin. Those two principles fit together in this beautiful demonstration in heaven and on earth. And it's going to get done, friend.

> God has a church on earth who are lifting up the downtrodden law, and presenting to the world the Lamb of God that taketh away the sins

of the world. The church is the depositary of the wealth of the riches of the grace of Christ, and through the church, eventually will be made manifest the final and full display of the love of God to the world that is to be lightened with its glory. (*Testimonies to Ministers*, p. 50)

This is the loud cry glory—this demonstration of unity, love, and of a whole church working together under the leadership of Jesus but using His human instrumentalities. Just as there are angel commanders in heaven, there are human leaders on earth in the church. "The prayer of Christ that His church may be one as He was one with His Father will finally be answered" (*Testimonies to Ministers*, p. 50).

Now, this doesn't mean that everyone who is in the church now will be in the church then. There were many who left Egypt who never saw the palm trees and fig orchards and vineyards of Canaan. Their bones lay bleaching on the desert sands. But there was a movement that left Egypt, crossed the Jordan, and entered the promised land.

There was a movement that left Babylon in 1844 and set out for the glorious inheritance. Thank God, friend, though our desert wanderings are already many times longer than Israel's, the movement that left Babylon is going to go through the gates of the city of God. It's going to go through as a movement. It is not going to go through as a scattered and broken program so that nobody can tell who's in the church and who isn't. No, no.

We need to be delivered from all human interpretations of the Spirit of Prophecy which weaken confidence in the triumph of this church—the organized church. We need to be delivered from every form, vestige, and hint of it.

I know there are questions people ask. They say, "Well, how is the church going to function as an organized church when there is a boycott and when many of the leaders are in prison and when our people are scattered?"

I don't pretend to be able to answer all those questions. I don't have to. I just take my stand on the written word. There is a church now, and there is going to be a church then. The demonstration is not merely that God is going to come and pick up an individual here and another one over there. He is coming to get His church. It's through the church—reference after reference that we've read stresses the fact—that this demonstration is going to be made.

Now, I'm going to quote from *Selected Messages*. This is talking about the crisis under the Sunday law, as the preceding paragraph plainly shows:

> Satan will work his miracles to deceive; he will set up his power as supreme. The church may appear as about to fall, but it does not fall. It remains, while the sinners in Zion will be sifted out—the chaff separated from the precious wheat. This is a terrible ordeal, but nevertheless it must take place. (*Selected Messages*, Book 2, p. 380)

Let's look at this quote more closely. There is coming a great crisis over the Sunday law, and it's going to be so terrible that it's going to look as though the church may be about to fall. When it happens, don't think that all we've read and studied thus far is wrong. Don't think that you were mistaken in the idea that the church is going through because this sentence that tells us that it may look as though the church is about to fall quickly adds that it does not fall, "…but it does not fall. It remains…" (*ibid.*).

What remains? The church remains. I hear people talk about the church being all broken up into pieces. This says, "It remains."

"It remains, while the sinners in Zion will be sifted out…" (*ibid.*).

How in the world could you sift sinners out of something that had already gone to pieces? There would be no need for a sieve. The sieve stays, and those who stay in the sieve remain, but the sinners in Zion are going to be sifted out. "…the chaff separated from the precious wheat" (*ibid.*).

Then, when the sifting gets through, what will be left in the sieve? Wheat. What'll be left outside? Chaff. "This is a terrible ordeal, but nevertheless it must take place" (*ibid.*).

Because this is truth and because these lessons we've studied are truth, we have this wonderful assurance: "There is no need to doubt, to be fearful that the work will not succeed. God is at the head of the work, and He will set everything in order. If matters need adjusting at the head of the work, God will attend to that, and work to right every wrong" (*ibid.*, p. 390).

From time to time, we see a crisis develop, and some people wonder how the church is going to go through this problem or that problem and this disappointment or that disappointment. Human leaders sometimes do things that disappoint God and disappoint the church, but God has His way of handling those things. We've seen Him do it again and again, in high places as well as low. So, notice: "If matters need adjusting at the head of the work, God will attend to that, and work to right every wrong. Let us have faith that God is going to carry the noble ship which bears the people of God safely into port" (*ibid.*).

This implies that God can do that without you and me taking it into our hands. He can adjust things that need handling at the head of the work. But now, I want to read you a statement that says it. We don't have to infer it. It just says it. This is wonderful:

> God has committed His work…to chosen servants. He has laid the burden of the work upon them. Angels of God are commissioned to have oversight of the work; and if it does not move right, those who are at the head of the work will be corrected, and things will move in God's order without interference of this or that individual. (*Testimonies for the Church, vol. 1*, p. 204)

When I got hold of that, I couldn't help but think, "Praise the Lord! So, I don't have to imitate Uzzah, do I?" I don't have to put forth my hand to steady the ark lest it falls off the cart. (See 2 Sam. 6.)

Now, we will go back to Ephesians, the third chapter, and I want you to look again at this wonderful statement. When I come to the tenth verse, I'm going to change the wording just a little and paraphrase in harmony with all these that we've studied from the other translations:

> Unto me, who am less than the least of all saints, is this grace given, that I should preach among the Gentiles the unsearchable riches of Christ; And to make all men see what is the fellowship of the mystery, which from the beginning of the world hath been hid in God, who created all things by Jesus Christ: To the intent that now unto the principalities and powers in heavenly places might be [made] known [through] the church the manifold wisdom of God, According to the eternal purpose which he purposed in Christ Jesus our Lord. (Eph. 3:8–11)

Do you see, then, dear friend, that the eternal purpose of God is at stake in all this? If this failed in the church, it would be a reproach to God through all eternity. That must not be.

So, I repeat, as I said at the beginning of this chapter, the study of these principles of Christian leadership isn't just so we can have happy homes, although it does that. It isn't just so we can have a smooth-running institution, although it should accomplish that. It isn't just so that we can get along as we should in the church, although that certainly is included.

But it is to the intent that now the manifold wisdom of God might be revealed in this wonderful experiment to all the angelic commanders in the government of God. That the angels might see worked out, down here in this world, through human beings that have had all the disadvantages of sin, the miracle of love. That they might see the church work together as a company of soldiers, not moved by force but by love, yielding to commands with alacrity, not because they're afraid of what would happen if they didn't, but because they love to obey, they love order, they love government, and they love the kingdom of God in heaven and on earth.

Let us pray, friend, that God will give us this experience. What do you say? Let's kneel and pray together.

Precious Lord, we rejoice in the glorious vision that has been disclosed, coming down to us through the open door of the Most Holy Place. Oh, keep our vision riveted there, whither the forerunner has for us entered. May the body here on earth respond moment by moment to those impulses of love and wisdom that come from the divine head in heaven. We ask it in Jesus' name, amen.

> *the study of these principles of Christian leadership isn't just so we can have happy homes, although it does that. It isn't just so we can have a smooth-running institution, although it should accomplish that. It isn't just so that we can get along as we should in the church, although that certainly is included. But it is to the intent that now the manifold wisdom of God might be revealed in this wonderful experiment to all the angelic commanders in the government of God.*

CHAPTER 5

Order and Authority

"Our Father which art in heaven, Hallowed be thy name. Thy kingdom come. Thy will be done in earth, as it is in heaven" (Matt. 6:9–10). We're praying for what to come? The kingdom. A kingdom is another name for government. What does "government" mean? Can you imagine a government without someone being told what to do? There are people whose idea of paradise would be to get somewhere where they were never told what to do.

Unfortunately, in many cases, that is due to the fact that some of those who give directions fail to reveal the spirit of heaven. So, we want to recognize that that is a weakness in many human forms, whether in the state, institutions, homes, or sometimes it even creeps into the church. Nobody likes to be barked at in the army or anywhere else. If a child has been brought up being barked at, and he went to the army or someplace where he was barked at some more, he comes to associate government, order, and direction with something that is distasteful. That is too bad.

And so, one of the great lessons that we have to learn in Christian leadership is how to separate those two things: government (order, directions, commands), which is a part of God's plan, and dictatorship (harshness, meanness, barking), which is not a part of God's plan.

The tree that Satan invited our first parents to eat of was called the tree of the knowledge of good… well, why not eat of it if it's the knowledge of good? It's good *and* evil. Satan, in his principles of government, has some good things, but he has them all mixed up. I would hate to have even a soybean roast that was all flavored with bacon and ham. And so, we want to be sure that we don't throw all the good out with the bad. We want to be equally sure that we don't retain any of the bad in trying to keep the good.

Instead of trying to recover sewage water and use it over again, it is best to get our water fresh from the fountain. Then we don't have to either filter it or chlorinate it. We can just get it where we know it's pure.

> We are praying that God's kingdom will come and His will be done in earth as it is in heaven. Our study of Christian leadership, then, is not a study so much of how things are done on earth as to how they are done in heaven and how they, therefore, should be done on earth.

We are praying that *God's* kingdom will come and *His* will be done in earth *as* it is in heaven. Our study of Christian leadership, then, is not a study so much of how things *are* done on earth as to how they *are* done in heaven and how they, therefore, *should be* done on earth. They can be. "Let all things be done decently and in order" (1 Cor. 14:40).

As we studied in an earlier chapter, order is a place for everything and everything in its place and a place for every person and every person in his place. "Order is heaven's first law..." (*Counsels on Health*, p. 101).

Now, in Psalm 119, let's see what attitude the converted heart has toward God's law. "O how love I thy law! it is my meditation all the day" (Ps. 119:97).

I'm just in love with God's way of doing things. I love His law. Do you? If we love His law, we love order. If we love His law, we love order because order is heaven's first law.

What is the first commandment of the Decalogue? "Thou shalt have no other gods before me" (Exod. 20:3).

The first thing to get settled is order—a place for everything and everything in its place, a place for every person and every person in his or her place. The first place to be settled is the place of authority. God is to be first. But, since He is given humankind choice, we can throw all that into disorder.

If I let Satan be my god, if I let a human priest be my god, or my wife, husband, any individual, or anything, then I'm in disorder. I've gotten everything out of order. That is all this confusion. That is Babylon.

So, the first thing in the Ten Commandments to get settled is order, and that means getting everyone in his and her place. When we put God in His place, the first place, then everything else comes from that. That is the first thing to get settled.

I want to make this book very practical from beginning to end. When you start a job, the first thing to find out is not what needs to be done. The first thing to find out is who is in charge. Say that you start a construction job, and you see many people working on a building, and you think, "I guess I'll get a hammer and start driving nails." That is just the way many people's minds work. That is not the thing to do at all.

The first thing to do if you want to be helpful is to say, "Who is in charge here?" If someone says, "There is no one particular, just pitch in and help anywhere you can." Personally, I would feel like walking off of a job like that because that is disorder, and order is heaven's first law.

A mob gets along quite well without organization. That is what a mob is—a group of people without organization. But an army always has to be organized and move in order, and that is the difference between an army and a mob.

Paul says everything is to be done decently and in order. We read over in *Counsels on Health* that order is heaven's first law, and we found that principle in the Ten Commandments. Because to have order, someone must give orders.

For everyone to be in his or her place, someone must be able to say what is my place and your place. Then the first question to be settled is, who is making the assignments?

Someone says, "I'm afraid of that. That sounds like a dictatorship. I don't want anybody to tell let me where my place is. I think I can pick that out myself." Study with me, friend, and see if, perhaps, by beholding, we'll become changed because we want to get ready to go to heaven, and order is heaven's first law.

We're not only to tolerate order but we are to love it:

> Ministers should love order and should discipline themselves, and then they can successfully discipline the church of God and teach them to work harmoniously like a well-drilled company of soldiers. If discipline and order are necessary for successful action on the battlefield, the same are as much more needful in the warfare in which we are engaged as the object to be gained is of greater value and more elevated in character.... (*Testimonies for the Church, vol. 1*, p. 649)

Think of it! Armies in battle have to move under direction and order, but this says it's even *more* important in God's program. So, we're told we should discipline ourselves to love order. "Those who have had no respect for order or discipline in this life would have no respect for the order which is observed in heaven. They can never be admitted into heaven, for all worthy of an entrance there will love order and respect discipline" (*Child Guidance*, p. 229).

I wonder if I dare get really personal. Did you ever witness a phenomenon like this—a meeting is going on, and people are invited, sometimes urged, sometimes begged, sometimes pled with, to come up and take the front seats so that latecomers and visitors coming in won't have to interrupt the meeting and be embarrassed by coming right up.

Now, don't misunderstand me. I wouldn't want to hurt anybody's feelings, and I know that there are reasons why some people have to be near the door. I recognize that. But, if everyone really has to be that near the door, I think the speaker ought to get back there with them.

Suppose I go to an institution. What do I go there for? "Well," someone says, "if I go to an institution, I go to get a job." Oh no, not in God's program. You go to fit into His wonderful order and to get something done for God. What position will you fill? If you believe in heaven's order, you will fill the place for which you were born. There can't be any higher place than that. If it's to wash the dishes, and that is the plan that God has arranged for you, that will be your highest delight. Whether it's what the world calls up or down, you know you fit into heaven's plan, and you will love it. You will love organization, order, being directed in what you do, and being told where to sit and what work to do.

"Oh," someone says, "this is too much. This wouldn't work." Don't forget, one-third of the angels in heaven thought it was too much. So if our hearts either resent or question these things, we have plenty of company—the millions of angels that have already thought this thing through and come to the conclusion that it's just too much to expect.

So, they pulled out and started their program, and they've been at it ever since. But it's more like cats and dogs than anything else. They have a lot of quarrels and squabbles. They fight and scratch and everything like that. You and I don't want that. We want peace and happiness. Jesus says that the way to have that is to have order. Order is heaven's first law, and we are to love it. "Those who have had no respect for order or discipline in this life would have no respect for the order which is observed in heaven. They can never be admitted into heaven, for all worthy of an entrance there will love order and respect discipline" (*Child Guidance,* p. 229).

The setting of this statement is about how parents should train their children. One of the greatest lessons that parents have to teach their children is to know what order is and to love it. Of course, you can't love something you don't know anything about. A lot of children growing up today don't know anything about it, so they couldn't love it. They never saw it. But God wants us in our homes to give our children a good many servings of the order of heaven so that—watch this point—when they come to the age of maturity, they can make the choice that the good angels made in heaven 6,000 years ago. When those angels came to that point in heaven, how many of them chose to stay with God and support His plan of government? Two-thirds. And how many of them said, "No. We can't stand it. We can't take it. We don't like it"? One-third.

> *Jesus came into this world and allowed His creatures to murder Him, but He would not surrender these principles. Why? They were written in His heart.*

Dear parents, while that broke God's heart, it didn't change His mind, principles, law, nor His plan of government. If my vision of these principles is so weak and shaky that, when a child rebels, that makes me say, "Well, I guess it doesn't work," where is my faith in the Word of God?

What a strange universe if the law of the Creator is to be set aside because some angel or some child rebels against it. That would surely be chaos. We as leaders, parents, and teachers must be so sure of our principles that, like the martyrs, we would die for them and not surrender them.

Jesus came into this world and allowed His creatures to murder Him, but He would not surrender these principles. Why? They were written in His heart.

"I delight to do thy will, O my God: yea, thy law is…"

Where?

"...within my heart" (Ps. 40:8).

Thank God, it is written not merely on the stone. It is written in my soul. Oh, that God may write in our hearts that love for and that delight in order and organization.

This is something different from the selfish pleasure of having our nerves tickled. Some people's idea of happiness is to get their ears tickled with music. Some people want their palates tickled with certain flavors. So on through the various things that tickle the senses.

> To have an intelligent appreciation of and love for order, organization, and government is the reflection of the divine. Humankind was made in God's image. When we think as God thinks, we will love what God loves, and therefore, we will act as God acts.

I think about two big chimpanzees that I saw up in the zoo at Brookfield near Chicago. One chimpanzee had his hands out through the bars, and he was clapping his hands to the people. He wanted them to throw him nuts and candy. The mate was over in the corner with a grin on her face as only a chimpanzee could grin. She had an all-day sucker in her mouth. She was having a good time.

My dear friend, if our idea of a good time is an all-day sucker and a few peanuts, we're not very far above the chimpanzee level. Am I right? Yes. If that is all it takes to satisfy us. To put it mildly, the pleasure and delight we're studying about in the law of God is something higher than the chimpanzee. To have an intelligent appreciation of and love for order, organization, and government is the reflection of the divine. Humankind was made in God's image. When we think as God thinks, we will love what God loves, and therefore, we will act as God acts.

Some people think that all of this would be much more simple and easier to carry out if God would just give all the orders Himself.

God could drop your orders down on a golden card every morning. He could have it that way for every creature in the universe. Wouldn't you like that? Just think of waking up in the morning, and there is a golden card by your bed. It tells you just exactly what to do all day long, so you don't have to be bothered by anyone telling you what to do.

Children, wouldn't that be wonderful? Instead of obeying your parents, you would just obey God, and God always does it right. I think that even some leaders and parents would be glad to get out of the job of having to give orders.

Personally, I think it would be wonderful if I knew every hour just what to do infallibly. I wonder why God doesn't do it that way. I'll tell you why, friend. God probably has several reasons, but the biggest reason is this. He wants us to be not merely happy but supremely happy, and the greatest happiness in the universe is through love. Love must find expression. Love is an intense desire to please.

There are two ways of pleasing that we're studying right now. There are more than two, but these are the two that we will study now on how to please. One is in telling someone to do something. If you think I misspoke, I didn't. I meant just that. The second way of expressing love is by doing what has been requested or commanded.

You can probably see that second point easily:

"If ye love me keep my commandments" (John 14:15).

"For this is the love of God, that we keep his commandments…" (1 John 5:3).

We can all see that obeying God, or whoever asks us to do something, is an expression of our love. But what about that first point? I said that one of the expressions of love is to tell people to do something. "…from his right hand went a fiery law for them" (Deut. 33:2). Then, it says, "Yea, he loved the people…" (Deut. 33:3). So, you see, the thought is that He gave them that law because He loved them.

So, law and love are related. They are related as effect and cause. Which is the cause—law or love?

What a strange thing it would be if there were a law that didn't have love for its cause—not in the government of God. Of course, in the dictatorships of this world, there is no love either way, but in God's government, love is always primary. Law is the effect, not the cause, and that is implied in what we read in Deuteronomy.

Now, I want to read it in plain English here in *Child Guidance*. By the way, if you want a textbook on Christian leadership, *Child Guidance* is a wonderful one, but so is *Testimonies to Ministers* and the book *Education*, and a number of these others. "The law of God, in the home life and in the government of nations, flows from a heart of infinite love" (*Child Guidance*, p. 259).

What picture do you get with the word "flows"? A river or some water moving. What is the fountain it flows from? Love. But notice that it says that the law is what is flowing.

> If I love God, and love is the greatest happiness, what would I like to do? I would like to please God. Now, who knows better what will please God—God or me? Then, if I love God and I want to please Him, the best way that God can please me is to tell me what I can do to please Him. That is it, friend.

Let's put it this way. God only ever told anyone to do anything because He loved them. Tussle with this problem for a moment—why would love find expression in telling someone to do something? Some may say, "If someone wants to please *me*, let them just lay off ordering me around."

Do you mean that the way to please someone is to (NOT) tell him what to do? That is a problem to think through. I'll tell you why, friend, because He wants to please them. The Maker knows best how to please people. God knows best how to please me.

Do you really think God knows more about how to please you than you do? If you do, you'll be right there trying to find out what He wants you to do instead of Him hunting you up.

Well, that is what the angels who stayed with God do. They never have to have a sergeant at arms round them up. They're always on time or, if possible, a little before to find out what their orders are. Why? Because they know that God knows better what will please them than they do.

But there is a second reason, and this is better yet. See if you don't agree with me. If I love God, and love is the greatest happiness, what would I like to do? I would like to please God.

Now, who knows better what will please God—God or me? Then, if I love God and I want to please Him, the best way that God can please *me* is to tell me what I can do to please *Him*. That is it, friend.

So, you see, God has two reasons for expressing love through telling me what to do. In the first place, He knows better than I do what will please *me*, and in the second place, He knows better than I do what I can do to please *Him*. And so, when He tells me what to do, He is fulfilling both of those points.

Incidentally, they're always the same because His greatest desire is to make me happy. So you see, it's just love back and forth, and there is no end to it. It gets better all the time. That is why heaven is never going to get monotonous, wearisome, or worn out. Love forever and forever, and love is expressed in telling people what to do, and they do it because love wants to please.

But we were asking why it is that God doesn't just tell everyone directly what to do. As I say, He wants to share this happiness with us. He wants a great many other people to get the joy of giving commands. So, He lets parents have children, He lets teachers have students, and He lets supervisors have helpers so that they can give commands as God gives them, for the same purpose, and thereby enter into a phase of happiness that would be left all for God if He did all the commanding. Do you see that?

> *God has two reasons for expressing love through telling me what to do. In the first place, He knows better than I do what will please me, and in the second place, He knows better than I do what I can do to please Him. And so, when He tells me what to do, He is fulfilling both of those points. Incidentally, they're always the same because His greatest desire is to make me happy. So you see, it's just love back and forth, and there is no end to it. It gets better all the time.*

Now the second part is just as important. If I got all my orders directly from God, then I would spend all my time aiming to please Him alone without any contact with others on that point. But oh, I'm so glad that God gave me a father and a mother to please! I'm so glad God gave me some teachers to please. I'm so glad God gave me some supervisors to please. I'm glad He gave me some church elders, pastors, and conference presidents to please.

There are all kinds of pleasures in God's government. Every leader, teacher, and parent gets the joy of giving orders like God gives them, and for the same reasons. Every employee, child, student, and church member gets the joy of obeying, like the angels who obey God, in the desire to please. Meditate on this until the reality of it gets deep in your souls, for this is the science of heaven.

But I want to ask you something. Will that make any difference in the *way* we give orders? Oh, yes. Notice: "Fathers and mothers, in the home you are to represent God's disposition" (*Child Guidance*, p. 259). And that is for the businessman, the church elder, and the minister in the church. That is for the teacher in the schoolroom, the supervisor on duty in the hospital, the work superintendent out in the shop, or on the farm, or wherever. Whoever gives orders is to do it in God's way because he or she is representing not merely God's authority but God's disposition. That is what we are supposed to do. I wonder if you would like a little more of His disposition.

> "Fathers and mothers, in the home you are to represent God's disposition. You are to require obedience, not with a storm of words, but in a kind, loving manner" (*ibid.*). Oh, isn't that nice? I could take another helping of that. Well, there is plenty more, friend. Let's have some more. What do you say?

But this doesn't mean some soft, mollycoddled thing because it says, "You are to require obedience..." (*ibid.*). So, it is to flow *in* love because it flows *from* love. That is right. And so, wouldn't it be nice if every time we give a command, we stop and think, "Does this flow from love? Am I giving this command for the good of the people that I'm commanding? Am I doing it to please them?"

"Oh," you say, "how would you ever get the work done on that program?" Now, wait a minute. Is it to get the work done or to get us done?

The dictators in this world get some things done. The Soviet Union got to the moon before the United States did. We'd better copy the Soviet

Union, then. Maybe we can get something done. No. We're going way beyond the moon. We're heading for something higher.

Love is the joy of heaven, and it's the joy of eternity, and if we've got to sell out love to buy efficiency, I don't have any for sale. I'll keep the love. But I'll tell you a secret. Love is the greatest power in the universe, and God is going to demonstrate right down here in His church on earth the power of love in getting people to work together in such a way that the whole universe is going to be thrilled and filled with admiration and adoration of God. Let's get with it. What do you say?

Then we are to cultivate love in thinking about what to command. But let's go a little step further: "Let every soul be subject unto the higher powers. For there is no power but of God: the powers that be are ordained of God" (Rom. 13:1).

Authority comes from God. If you read these first seven verses of Romans 13, you will see that Paul is talking particularly about civil government. He is talking about the government under which the people to whom he was writing were living. This is a letter written to the Romans who lived in Rome. Paul is telling them to be subject to the higher powers.

They must have had a wonderfully good government up there in Rome. Or did they? No. They had what we would call a tyrannical government. Nevertheless, Paul said to obey it. Paul continues: "Wherefore ye must needs be subject, not only for wrath, but also for conscience sake. For this cause pay ye tribute [taxes] also for they are God's ministers, attending continually upon this very thing" (Rom. 13:5, 6).

Were Caesar and his officers really God's ministers? Yes, Paul said so. God has arranged it for us. There are angels that have command of other angels. Down here in this world, God has put authority in the church, in the state, in the home, in the institution, and you and I, as members of God's

> *Love is the greatest power in the universe, and God is going to demonstrate right down here in His church on earth the power of love in getting people to work together in such a way that the whole universe is going to be thrilled and filled with admiration and adoration of God.*

family, are to render what obedience. Our obedience is to be prompted by love.

The unconverted person may sometimes comply out of fear of the police officer's club or a possible jail sentence. But you and I are on a higher plane. We're obeying it through what love? Love not only for God but love for the authority of the government. A Christian is the truest citizen.

And so, never forget the implication of what Paul is saying in the first seven verses of Romans 13. In an institution and in the church, even if a leader makes a mistake, that doesn't release me from loyalty to the institution or of the church and obedience to the directions that God has authorized them to give. That is vital that we understand that.

> While God is using poor, weak human beings to give orders, and poor, weak human beings to respond to orders, He has guaranteed to so manage things that affect you, and that no mistake that anyone else makes can keep you from the joy of fitting in with God's plan in this world and in the next.

You say, "Yes, but what about a church that goes beyond its rightful authority?" That is another subject. But now, we're studying this matter of order and authority, and we see that God has delegated authority. He has delegated authority to poor, weak people that make mistakes. I'm so glad that He is willing to use poor, weak human beings in His plan because if He hadn't, I never could have gotten into it.

I've had some experience in both phases of this thing—in taking orders and in giving orders. Friend, I've made a very poor record in both phases of it, and yet, God still lets me go to school in both phases of delegated authority. I'm seeking to learn more and more to give orders *from* love and *in* love, and I'm seeking to learn to obey orders in love and because of love in my heart for God and for those whom He instructs me to obey. Shall we practice it, dear friend?

Everyone reading this book has an opportunity to practice both phases. Everyone has someone and several "someones" from whom they get orders. Usually, it's a different person at work than it is from the one at school and church. What a happy thing it is to come to Sabbath school and have the superintendent say, "We'll sing number 331 this morning," and to have our hearts in happy cooperation.

What a pitiful thing it is to say, "Oh, why did they have to pick that one out!" Do you know what the matter is? Some of us as children started to cultivate this attitude very early, "I don't like this, and I don't like that." Do you know where children got that attitude? They got it from daddy. Too many daddies will sit at the table and, right in the presence of the children, tell the wife and mother, "You know, I don't like that."

"Thy kingdom come. Thy will be done in earth, as it is in heaven" Matthew 6:10. One closing thought, and this is the best news of all. While God is using poor, weak human beings to give orders, and poor, weak human beings to respond to orders, He has guaranteed to so manage things that affect *you*, and that no mistake that anyone else makes can keep you from the joy of fitting in with God's plan in this world and in the next. That is the wonderful thing.

The Great Shepherd is looking after every one of us every minute, and He makes all things work together for good to those who love the Lord.

> The Great Shepherd is looking after every one of us every minute, and He makes all things work together for good to those who love the Lord.

Do you love Him? Then, all things are working together for good. "But I can't see it." Look at Joseph. He obeys his father and goes to carry some food to his brothers, and he lands in a pit, then on a slave marketer's camel, and then as a slave in Potiphar's house. And then, he remains faithful and obedient. He obeys Potiphar and does a good job for him. He obeys God and resists Potiphar's wife's immoral advances, and as the result, he gets thrown into a dungeon.

It doesn't look like all things are working together for good to Joseph, does it? It doesn't look like it pays to cooperate with God's plan. But Joseph just keeps right on. At the right time, Joseph, having learned these principles of Christian leadership, is put in charge of all of Egypt. His brothers and father come, and there is a great family reunion. It's all a wonderful type of great reunion that is coming soon in the kingdom of God.

It's going to be wonderful, friend, to have Judah, Simeon, Levi, Issachar, Naphtali, Gad, and Assur, along with Benjamin and Joseph, all there in the kingdom of God together. Let's go. What do you say?

We thank Thee, Lord, for these wonderful principles of Thy government in heaven and in earth. Now we give Thee our permission to discipline us in whatever way we need so that we'll learn not only to tolerate direction but to love order with all our hearts. We thank Thee for it, in Jesus' name, amen.

CHAPTER 6

Authority from Heaven

It may have come as a new thought to some that the Bible is a textbook in administration and management, but I think we are finding it so. Our opening text for today's study is in Matthew 28:

> And Jesus came and spake unto them, saying, All power is given unto Me in heaven and in earth. Go ye therefore, and teach all nations, baptizing them in the name of the Father, and of the Son, and of the Holy Ghost. Teaching them to observe all things whatsoever I have commanded you: and, lo I am with you always, even unto the end of the world. (Matt. 28:18–20)

The word "power" means authority. That is what I want to study with you. Much of Christian leadership is the proper exercise of authority. Jesus says that He has all authority.

If you ever have any authority, where will you have to get it? Jesus. If He doesn't give you any, how much have you got? None. All the authority in the universe comes from God. That is what our text says.

Sometimes we read things, and we don't stop to think about what they say. Or sometimes we hear what they say, and we think it's just too much. A little girl heard her parents discussing something. And finally, she piped up and said, "Daddy, if God didn't mean what He said, why didn't He say what He meant?"

Is it really true that all authority in heaven and in earth comes from God? Is that where the authority in the institution comes from? Is that where the authority in the church comes from? Is that where the authority in government comes from? Let's find out.

"Let every soul be subject unto the higher powers. For there is no power but of God: the powers that be are ordained of God" (Rom. 13:1). Do you believe that? A police officer is at an intersection, and he beckons you to come. Traffic is coming the other way. He holds up his hands: "No." Whose authority is that officer exercising? The authority of God. This is what Paul is discussing in Romans 13—civil government:

> Whosoever therefore resisteth the power, resisteth the ordinance of God: and they that resisteth shall receive to themselves damnation. For rulers are not a terror to good works, but to the evil. Wilt thou then not be afraid of the power? do that which is good, and thou shalt have praise of the same: For he is the minister of God to thee for good. (Rom. 13:2–4)

Is he talking about the ordained minister? No, Paul is talking about the officer. And remember this, the government that Paul was writing about was a government that persecuted Christians and had many unjust and cruel laws.

Nevertheless, Paul said, "Be subject." There were two reasons he gave for being subject—for wrath and for conscience's sake. What does "wrath" mean? It means that you will get into trouble if you don't obey the law. People get put in jail for breaking the law. That is why Paul says to be careful and respect that authority. But respect that authority not only for that reason but for conscience's sake.

Then I ask, will a Christian obey the law even if he could be sure that he wouldn't get caught if he disobeyed? Yes, for conscience's sake. This doesn't mean he will disobey God because that's a higher power. The three Hebrews said "No" to Nebuchadnezzar. They were following this principle of being subject to the higher power. "For this cause pay ye tribute also: for they are God's ministers, attending continually upon this very thing" (Rom. 13:6). God's ministers are on the job twenty-four hours a day, maintaining the peace of the community. So, pay taxes to support them. Obey the law.

There is no power, no authority but from God. Does a work supervisor exercise the authority of God? If he doesn't, he does not have any because there is no power but that which is of God. Does the church elder or the pastor have some authority? If they do, they got it from God. And if they don't get it from God, how much do they have? Not a bit.

So, all authority that is exercised comes from God. There immediately follows two conclusions. One is that you and I should submit when we meet authority.

If the authority we meet contradicts the higher authority, it is not true authority. Let me illustrate. I go down the road, and a police officer stops me. Does he have the right to stop me? Yes. He says, "Let me see your driver's license." Does he have that right? Yes.

Then he asks, "What did you have for breakfast this morning?" Then he proceeds to tell me what I must eat for breakfast tomorrow morning. Does he have the authority to do that? No. I must listen to him and respect him, and obey him when he stops me and asks for my driver's license. But if he tries to tell me what to eat for breakfast, he is outside of his authority.

It is all right to listen to him. I can be respectful. But when I go home and sit at the table, he doesn't have any authority whatever as to what I eat. Am I despising authority if I eat something different from what he told me? Not the slightest. I am not violating any principle. I am not disregarding any law. I am not showing disrespect for authority, for he did not have any in that area.

When Nebuchadnezzar told those three Hebrews to come to the plain of Dura, did he have the authority to do that? Yes. Did they come? Yes. But when he told them to bow down before the image, did he have the authority to do that? Not a bit. So, when he said to kneel down, they stood up. Before the day was over, he acknowledged that he was out of place. It took some more time to learn the lesson, but he finally learned it—that the Most High ruleth in the kingdom of men. But that wasn't all he learned.

By the way, Nebuchadnezzar himself wrote the fourth chapter of Daniel. Daniel, of course, copied it out and put it in his book. But he was simply copying one of the royal decrees. You can prove that from the first verse and the last verse. Several times in the chapter, he states, "Until thou know that the most High ruleth in the kingdom of men, and giveth it to whomsoever he will." God rules, but He delegates authority. There is something else that Nebuchadnezzar learned: "This matter is by the decree of the watchers, and the demand by the word of the holy ones: to the intent that the living may know that the Most High ruleth in the kingdom of men, and giveth it to whomsoever he will, and setteth up over it the basest of men" (Dan. 4:17).

Do we have to obey them if they are base? Yes. Who put them there? God put them there. It may be a Caesar whose hands are covered with blood. It may be a Nebuchadnezzar who has burned down the temple. Still, who put him there? The Most High.

> *The basis of cooperation with authority is not our admiration of the one who has the authority; it's a matter of conscience. We respect the authority that they exercise because it is the authority of God. And we read there in Romans, "Whosoever resisteth the power resisteth the ordinance of God." I want to learn this.*

Just because the church elder isn't quite as sweet a man as I wish he were doesn't mean that I don't care what he says. Just because the teacher in the school isn't as Christlike as I wish he was, that doesn't absolve me as a student or release me from obedience. It is too bad for people to exercise authority in a mean way or a selfish way or a rough way. But remember that the subjects are not released from their obligation to obedience merely because the one who exercises the authority is not as God-like as he ought to be. He or she still has authority. If that were not so, very little authority would be left in the world today.

If workers had to wait until they had perfect supervisors before they obeyed them, there wouldn't be much obedience. If church members had to wait until the leaders in Washington and the leaders in the conference and the leaders in the local church did everything just right before they respected and cooperated with them, there would not be much cooperation at all.

You can see that the basis of cooperation with authority is not our admiration of the one who has the authority; it's a matter of conscience. We respect the authority that they exercise because it is the authority of God. And we read there in Romans, "Whosoever resisteth the power resisteth the ordinance of God." I want to learn this.

That is one side of the coin. Do you know what the other side is? Let's go to Genesis 18, and we'll find the other side of the coin. Every coin has two sides, you know. In this verse, God is talking about Abraham: "For I know him, that he will command his children and his household after him, and they shall keep the way of the Lord, to do justice and judgment; that the Lord may bring upon Abraham that which he hath spoken of him" (Gen. 18:19).

This text deals with the responsibility of the one who has been given authority. God said that He knew Abraham. He could count on him. He had given him authority, and he would exercise it.

Will he suggest? Will he beg? Will he hint? Will he maneuver? All of those things have been used as substitutes for commanding.

Let me read something interesting: "It is heart saddening to see the imbecility of parents in the exercise of their God-given authority" (*Child Guidance*, p. 237).

What a statement!

Notice the responsibility of the one in authority: "We are just as responsible for evils that we might have checked in others by exercise of parental or pastoral authority as if the axe had been our own" (*ibid.*, p. 236).

> *Everywhere you go you are going to meet authority. And it all came from God. And what comes from God works together.*

Two kinds of authority are mentioned, parental and pastoral. Oh, but they don't have any authority. Do you mean I am supposed to listen to the pastor and church elder? Yes. Don't be afraid of this. We never need to be afraid of what the Master says.

Someone says, "This sounds to me like it's next door to popery." It's next door to the popery, but it's not popery. When I say it's next door to popery, I'm thinking of the statement that truth and error lie close together (*Testimonies for the Church, vol. 8, p.* 290). Some people are so afraid of popery that they are a thousand miles away from it. And so, they're at least 500 miles away from law and order. They are way over in anarchy and chaos.

Fundamental to the success of God's government in heaven and in earth is the exercise of authority. In the first chapter, we learned to pray the part of the Lord's Prayer that says, "Thy kingdom come, thy will be done in earth as it is in heaven."

"I may have to put up with authority while I am in the home. But believe me, I'll be glad when I grow up, and I don't have to." I can remember more than once, both before I got to my teens and during my teens, that I looked forward with real expectation to the time when I could be my own boss and make my own decisions. But I found that to "grow up" means that you have more people telling you what to do than when you were little. Life is simple when you're little—you only have one or two people telling you what to do. But adult life carries with it the responsibility of listening to authorities in government (federal, state, county, and city) and listening to authorities in the church (general, union, local conference, local church).

How do you do it? One little thing that will help you very much is to remember what I said about the police officer stopping you and ending up telling you what to eat for breakfast. Don't worry about the last part, but be sure you carry your driver's license and show it when he or she asks you for it. If you keep that simple principle in mind, you can find your way through a lot of authorities in institutions and everywhere else.

Everywhere you go you are going to meet authority. And it all came from God. And what comes from God works together, my friend. Oh, I am so glad about that! The reason that we stress this matter of respecting and being subject to authority is that before we are fitted to command, we must learn to obey. But the great lesson in this book is not how to obey, it is how to command. I want you to learn how to command.

Command and dictate are not synonyms in this context. To command means to give orders in such a way that you get your helpers to move with you to get the job done. "Incline your ear, and come unto Me: hear, and your soul shall live; and I will make an everlasting covenant with you, even the sure mercies of David. Behold, I have given him for a witness to the people, a leader and commander to the people" (Isa. 55:3, 4).

Who gave David the job of being the leader and commander? God did. Just like He gave Nebuchadnezzar the job of being king over Babylon. Notice those two words from that verse—a "leader" and "commander."

During the reign of David, his son, Absalom, put his arm around the people and said, "Oh, if I were only king." The Bible says that Absalom stole the hearts of the men of Israel. Who did they belong to? David. Who gave them to him? God. It is a dangerous thing to steal the respect and obedience of someone that God has already given to someone else. Absalom ended up in the grave.

There was another son of David who got that idea. His story is full of meaning concerning the exercise of authority: "Then Adonijah the son of

Haggith exalted himself, saying, I will be king: and he prepared him chariots and horseman, and fifty men to run before him" (1 Kings 1:5).

If you read on, you will find out what happened to him. He didn't last long either. He followed his brother Absalom to an ignominious end.

But the sixth verse, if it weren't so serious, would almost make you laugh. You feel sorry for David, who had been given the job of being king, leader, and commander to the people, and look how he fell on the job with his son: "And his father had not displeased him at any time in saying, Why hast thou done so? and he also was a very goodly man; and his mother bare him after Absalom" (1 Kings 1:6).

David never displeased little Adonijah. Adonijah appreciated it so much that when he got to the place where he thought he could get away with it, he said, "I'll be king." And I suppose he thought that since his father had never crossed him up to that point, he wouldn't now.

But God, the overall King, was not ready for that. You read the chapter, and you'll see how God handled it. Oh, my friend, the pages of history are full of the records of the failure of parents to exercise their God-given authority and the resulting tragedies in the lives of their children, both when they were little and when they grew up.

Parents, God has given you authority. Supervisors in the institution, God has given you authority. Church officers, God has given you authority. "Never let your child hear you say, 'I cannot do anything with you'" (*Child Guidance*, p. 238).

What is that an admission of? Failure. It is an admission either that we think we don't have the authority or that we are not willing to exercise it.

I want to lay down a principle. It is such a far-reaching principle that I want you to listen very carefully while I state it. When a man is exercising God-given authority, he cannot abdicate. He may die standing for that authority, but he cannot surrender it.

Let me study that with you. Suppose there is a sheriff who is in charge of the jail and the prisoners there. A mob comes up. They say, "Give us that prisoner." They are going to lynch the prisoner. Can that sheriff surrender the prisoner? He can, but has he any right to? No. If he does, what has he done? He has violated his oath. He has abdicated. God gives him no authority to do that.

Suppose he says, "That mob looked menacing. There are a hundred men in the mob, and I am only one." Suppose the mob says, "You either give him, or we'll kill you." If I am the sheriff under those circumstances, must I give in? No. I can die, but I cannot yield.

I will tell you that if parents understood this, there would be fewer commands given. Let me read you a divine statement of the principle: "When it is necessary for parents to give a direct command, the penalty of disobedience should be as unvarying as are the laws of nature" (*Child Guidance*, p. 284).

If some young people had this kind of training, they wouldn't have some of the problems they have today. Very few have had this kind of training. Thank God, it is our privilege to learn the lesson now. But it is harder to learn it when you are twenty than when you were two years old. And it's harder still to learn it when you are thirty, and harder yet at forty, and so on. But if we are ever going to be with God and the angels, we will learn on this planet this question of authority. "For ever, O Lord, thy word is settled in heaven" (Ps, 119:89). And we are going to learn not only to respect authority but to exercise authority.

Did you know you are going to exercise authority in the world to come? That is right. We're to be kings and priests, and both of them exercise authority. So don't shy away from authority if it's given to you. Don't covet it if it isn't given to you. You'll get it soon enough.

Someone says, "It's a long time coming." It might be possible that the preparatory school hasn't finished you yet. Before we are fitted to command, we are to learn to obey.

Someone says, "I was afraid of that." As long as you're afraid of it, you're not through yet. We are to come to the place where we not merely tolerate it but love it. We love God's way—the way of authority, and we even learn to love the police.

By the way, you and I ought to love the police these days. Not very many people love them. They are the object of the hatred and ridicule of millions of people today, and the devil is behind it. If some poor fellow in a moment of frustration does a foolish thing, that is played up in the press and TV, taken up by multitudes of people. And careful thinking men and women recognize that behind a lot of this rising tide of crime is the disrespect for the law and the officers of the law.

Seventh-day Adventists, of all people, are to be people who stand for law and order—authority, in other words. And just as we learn to love both by receiving it and giving it, we learn authority both by yielding to it and exercising it.

If all this is true, do you think I ought to get out on the highway and direct traffic on the corner? Why not? I have no authority. It's that simple. I was not commissioned to do that. Do you think I should go to all the neighbors' children and intervene in their quarrels and tell Mary to sit down and behave herself? Why not? Nobody gave me that authority. There have been times I almost wished I had it. There have been other times I was so thankful that I didn't. But God has given me some authority, and that I cannot abdicate. That is the authority for which God holds me responsible. Even if it should kill me, I must still hold true.

I want you to go back in your thinking to an experience in Exodus. God had come down on Sinai and spoken His law, and all the people had promised obedience. God was the invisible leader, and Moses was the visible leader of Israel. Not long after the giving of the law, God called Moses to the mountain. He recognized the authority that was above him when he went up there. He stayed there as long as his higher Officer kept him.

Moses did what every officer should do. When he left the camp, he left his authority delegated to someone else. This is one of the important details of Christian leadership. Don't forget it. When you are not present to exercise your authority, delegate it to someone else. Moses left his authority with Aaron. All seemed to go well for a time. One morning, Aaron found a delegation of people. They said, "Make us gods." Why didn't they go do it themselves? They had a certain regard for authority. Like restless children, they were asking, or demanding, that the parents do something. They said that they didn't know what had happened to Moses. Things had been left in Aaron's hand, and they told him he had to do something.

Aaron sometimes thought that Moses exercised authority too firmly. So, Aaron was going to try a nicer plan. Do you know what Aaron actually did? He abdicated—he surrendered his authority. When a king abdicates, he steps aside and lets someone else take over. Aaron kept the title, but who was really running things? The people. That was democracy in action. If they had an election that afternoon, and Moses' and Aaron's names had been on the ballot, what percentage of the votes do you think Aaron would have gotten? A great majority. No question about it. "His natural desire to please and to yield to the people led him to sacrifice the honor of God" (*Testimonies for the Church*, vol. 3, p. 296).

Aaron tried to please the people. That is a wonderful thing, isn't it? It is a wonderful thing when it's the Second Commandment: "Thou shalt love thy neighbor as thyself" (Mark 12:31). What is the first? "Thou shalt love the Lord thy God with all thy heart" (verse 30). And Aaron was trying to keep the second when he had broken the first. That won't work. That was the problem. "Aaron had thought that Moses had been too unyielding to the wishes of the people" (*Testimonies for the Church*, vol. 3, p. 298).

Do you think Moses ran a Gallop poll every other day to see what his rating was in the camp? No. Did he govern by consensus? No. Where did he get his authority? He got it from God. His job was to administer that authority. It wasn't his; it was God's. And he was there to administer it.

> He [Aaron] thought that if Moses had been less firm, less decided at times, and that if he had made a compromise with the people and gratified their wishes, he would have had less trouble, and there would have been more peace and harmony in the camp of Israel. He, therefore, had been trying this new policy. (*ibid.*)

Aaron carried the camp with him. They had a wonderful time at parties, music, dancing, feasting, and lovemaking—just like a lot of people today. But Moses came down from the mount with the tables of the law. And when he saw and heard all that was going on, he broke the tables of the law. He was angry.

Was God angry with Moses for being angry with the people? No. God was angry, too. This was righteous anger. It wasn't that Moses lost his patience, was mean, or that he was selfish. He was indignant to see the honor of God so reproached, to see the law of God so broken by a people who had just heard the voice of the Creator speaking from Sinai.

Now, as you read the story in Exodus, Moses had the trumpet blown, and he said, "Who is on the Lord's side, come unto me." The tribe of Levi came. He was basically asking, "Who is there here in this camp who hasn't worshiped this calf? Who, in a time of universal apostasy, has kept his garments unspotted?" The sons of Levi came. That is interesting because Moses and Aaron were both from that tribe. Moses said to line up on his right side. He gave another trumpet call and told those who would repent and return to God to come and line up on the left side. They came weeping. Then he said to those on the right side to gird on their swords and go through the camp and kill all the rest.

Those who had kept themselves unspotted were used by God to exercise judgment. Did they have the authority to do it? Yes. Who gave it to them? Moses. Where did Moses get it? From God. I want to tell you something, friend. There are scenes ahead in this denomination that few people have any idea of. There is coming an exercise of church discipline that will make the ears of people tingle. They will rebel against it just like the people who thought Moses was severe. They will point to lovely-dispositioned people like Aaron and say, "That is the Spirit of Christ"—men who have sold us down the river in this world of conformity of feasting and merry-making and all the rest of this worldly stuff.

There is either going to be repentance or God is going to take a hand and, through men of His appointment, there is going to be a cleansing of the camp. Let me hasten to point out that the answer is not for someone to jump up and say, "That is what I'm doing!" Oh, no! Too many people run when they were never sent. Too many people like Absalom tell the people what wonderful things they would do if they were in leadership. Too many people like Adonijah say, "I will be king, and things will be okay." Not so. The only authority that anybody can rightly exercise is the authority of God, and God has His ways of delegating them.

CHAPTER 7

Theocracy

Let's think about the different types of government. What is the type of government in the United States? A democracy. What was the type of government they had in old Babylon when Nebuchadnezzar was in authority? A monarchy. There are other types.

What does "democracy" mean? Government by the people. Is this the best kind of government? No. What kind is it? Theocracy—government by God.

Is the government of the home democracy? Does the father have to run for election every year and watch to see whether he gets elected? Most people in America take it for granted that democracy is the best form of government. It has some advantages; it also has some disadvantages. But we must not get the idea that the ideal government is a democracy. The ideal government is a theocracy. This means that God rules.

Why do we have elections in church, then? If a reporter were to come in from one of the newspapers and watch a nominating committee appointed in the fall of the year, hear the reports given, and watch the church vote, wouldn't he conclude that the church is a democracy? It uses democratic forms and procedures. Church officers do not run for election, but democracy doesn't necessarily have to have people running for election. Democracy simply means that the people rule.

In the instances in the Bible where God revealed His will through one individual, that individual was usually a prophet. As you study the Bible, as a rule, you find that both priest and king, and those who were governed by them, sometimes rebelled against what the prophet said. But when they were in submission to God, they all listened when the prophet said. Why? They recognized that they were ruled by God.

We need wisdom in applying these principles in the institution and in the church. "Christ designs that heaven's order, heaven's plan of government, shall be represented in His church on earth" (*The Desire of Ages*, p. 680).

And in *Testimonies for the Church, volume* eight, page 140, we read that heaven's order is to be in every institution and every family. In everything that is to be managed or governed, you and I are to study how to represent the divine will. We are to study how to be under the divine theocracy. That is the point.

When Moses came down from the mount, he found the children of Israel all dancing around an idol. Their visible leader was Aaron. The people were with him because he listened to them. Shall we say that he believed in democracy? That was democracy in action.

Can democracy make a thing right that is wrong? No. A majority of the people of the United States are going to be in favor of the Sunday law of Revelation 13. In fact, turn to Revelation 13, and I want you to see something very interesting there. Do you see anything in Revelation 13 that shows that the United States government is a democracy? The first beast had ten horns. What is on them? Crowns. What isn't on the second beast? Crowns. In this case, the government is going to appeal to the people to make an image to the beast:

> 'Saying to them that dwell on the earth, that *they* should make an image to the beast.' Here is clearly presented a form of government in which the legislative power rests with *the people*, a most striking evidence that the United States is the nation denoted in the prophecy. (*The Great Controversy*, p. 443, emphasis added)

In a theocracy, God rules. God doesn't make mistakes. And a complete theocracy has the advantage of being guided by the wisdom of God. The best example of theocracy we have in the history of the world is Israel. And particularly in the exodus, under the visible leadership of Moses. But Moses, except once, recognized that he was not the real leader. On that occasion, he said, "Must we fetch water out of this rock?" He let the people look to him instead of God. But all the rest of the forty years, he looked to God, and the people did. That was a theocracy.

In *Testimonies for the Church*, volume eight, page 180 is a testimony to Dr. Kellogg. "The place assigned you by the Lord was under Him in the divine theocracy." It is too bad that he stepped out of that place.

The church is a theocracy. Then why do we have elections? This is a good question. Think about two people in India—a Seventh-day Adventist and a Hindu. They both might order a vegetarian meal, but they'd have two quite different reasons. The Hindu would not want to eat an ancestor. The Seventh-day Adventist would have an entirely different reason, although he is doing the same thing.

Therefore, when we see elections in the church or in a religious institution, we must never conclude that this is democracy in action. It is theocracy in action. And if we think it's democracy in action, then several things will follow that shouldn't. There may be parties that develop. They may not be labeled Democratic and Republican, but they are still factions. Also, in the democracies of this world, as it quite often happens, while one person is celebrating, the other is lamenting. This should never be in the church. It isn't in a theocracy.

> *Therefore, when we see elections in the church or in a religious institution, we must never conclude that this is democracy in action. It is theocracy in action.*

Does anybody lose in a church election? If anybody loses, then we are outside the theocracy in our thinking and in the way we are carrying on. Because in God's plan, nobody loses. We are told, "God's plan of life has a place for every human being" (*Education*, p. 226).

There will be just one place where I am supposed to be in heaven. Is there a special place for me here? If I am to be Sabbath School superintendent next year and someone else is occupying that place now, does he or she lose when I'm elected to take his or her place? Not if this is a theocracy. God has something else for that person to do which is for that time more important than to be Sabbath School superintendent again.

You will probably be sitting on a nominating committee. But remember, when you sit on a nominating committee, your business is not to get done what you want. Neither is it to get done what the people want (that is democracy). It is to get done what God wants. And your business is to find out what God wants. The purpose of appointing the nominating committee is not so the people can speak. It is so God can speak to those people on the committee. And the purpose of that committee is to get together and pray and seek the Lord to find out what heaven wants.

I would like to stress this point; this is so important. If people understand this, there will be no politicking, no trying to railroad certain ideas, or pushing to get certain people into office. Nothing like that. But, rather, there will be earnest prayer to find out what God wants. "The Lord has certain men to fill certain positions. God will teach His people to move carefully and to make wise choice of men who will not betray sacred trusts.... We are to present every case before God and in earnest prayer ask Him to choose for us" (*Testimonies for the Church*, vol. 9, page 264).

What should be the first prerequisite for a member of the nominating committee? Someone who knows how to pray and get answers to his or her prayers. We are not to choose one member of the Republican party and another from the Democratic party and another from the Socialist party and get them together and see what we can hatch up. No. People who know how to pray, who know God, are to get together and try to find out what God wants and who God wants in these different offices.

Then when they have their report ready, it goes to the whole church. Quite often, that report is laid over for a week. What do you suppose would be a good thing for the church members to do during that week? Pray. Pray to find out what God wants because this is a theocracy: "What we want is what You want, Lord."

There are cases in the Bible where they found out who God wanted by casting lots. Some today have suggested that that would be a good way. It would be a long way from democracy. And if God would condescend to use the casting of lots, then that would be a way of finding out what He wants.

> I have no faith in casting lots. We have in the Bible a plain 'Thus saith the Lord' in regard to all church duties... "I would say to the members of the church in _____, 'Read your Bibles with much prayer. Do not try to humble others, but humble yourselves before God, and deal gently with one another. To cast lots for the officers of the church is not in God's order. Let men of responsibility be called upon to select the officers of the church.'" (*Selected Messages*, Book 2, p. 328)

Remember, this is a theocracy, and theocracy means that God governs. So, the purpose of the nominating committee, and the purpose of the entire church as it votes, is to discover what God wants.

Now let's go a step further. Suppose I'm elected church elder, and something comes up in the middle of the year. As a church elder, I feel that principles are at stake in that matter. For example, it relates to what type of amusement we will have on Saturday night in the church auditorium. I'm dealing with a very practical problem. I'm the church elder in charge, and someone comes to me and says, "Brother, you are the elder of the church. We would like to use the auditorium next Saturday night for a certain program, and we would like your permission as the presiding officer of the church."

Suppose I ask, "What is it?" They tell me that it's a Hollywood movie. I ask, "You mean this is one of those Hollywood movies like they show downtown?"

They answer, "Yes, but this is several years old. It isn't bad like some of these they have now. It's a good movie."

Do I have a responsibility? Suppose I indicate by my questions and my attitude that I have some suggestions. And suppose they say, "We've talked to several of the church people about this, and everyone that we've talked to all say that this is just fine. They're glad we're going to do something for the young people."

If I can satisfy in my mind that a majority of the church want that movie, then can I go ahead and authorize it? If this is a democracy, do you see where I am? If it's a theocracy, do you see where I am not? I did not get my authority from the people; I got it from God. It is true the people voted, but all the people voted for who they thought God intended. That is all they voted for. They knew what they were doing. To state it in another way, they voted who they would accept that they believed God wanted.

Now a man who has been given authority cannot abdicate. As long as I have to make the decision, I would just have to say, "No. Of course, you can remove me from office. That is your privilege. But as long as the decision is mine, this is my decision."

Remember what God said about Abraham? "I know him. I can count on him. He is not like Aaron. He will stand up and be counted even if the count is one."

I have used some practical illustrations in order to make it "down to earth." You could use a hundred other illustrations in different areas. The point is that the person who has the decision to make has the authority and is responsible to God to exercise that authority. They are not to listen to the people to find out what to decide. Now, if they have some valuable counsel, fine. If they can give a reference in the Bible and the Spirit of Prophecy that will help to come to a decision, fine.

You also recognize that there are some decisions that are not made by individuals but by committees and boards. Here is a man who is the president of an institution but is outvoted on a policy. To my mind, it becomes something that man must seek the Lord for to see how vital is the matter involved. In many situations, all I could do would be to say, "Brethren, this is your privilege to vote as you have. You are voting your convictions. With the convictions that I have, it would be impossible for me to continue longer in this particular position." I would withdraw and find a place where I could fit into the Lord's work and be honest with my conscience and with the Lord. That is perfectly honorable. This happens from time to time. If it happened often, we would be closer to Canaan than we are.

Let me qualify this to be sure you understand. This doesn't mean that every time a committee votes contrary to my ideas that it's time for me to leave. If that is it, I would better not even join the committee in the first place. The only way that I can get the committee to agree with me all the time is for me to be the only one on the committee.

Let me illustrate this from a case in denominational history. Back in the 1870s, Sister White was writing a great deal about education. As the result of that, it was decided to start the first Seventh-day Adventist college. The prophet of God, having written about this, urged the brethren to select a place way out in the country. She even pointed out a particular place and said, "This would be a wonderful place for the institution." But they didn't get it. They said it was way too far out of Battle Creek. Then she selected a place a short distance from Battle Creek, but still at that time out in the country. But they said that was too far. Then, when the prophet was gone on a trip, they bought a few acres right across the street from the Battle Creek Sanitarium to build a college.

When Sister White came back, she wept, but she didn't withdraw. She didn't say, "You didn't listen when the Lord spoke, and you didn't listen when I pleaded, and now you will have to go your way, and I will go mine." She and her husband got in and helped in every way they could to make that college a success. A few years later, the things that she tried to forestall by having it out in the country developed.

You can read the first hundred pages of *Testimonies for the Church*, volume five, and you will see the state of things that came to pass. They got into such problems that the Battle Creek College was closed for a whole year. The prophet of God gave her counsel and made her pleas. And then, when the brethren wouldn't follow, she didn't withdraw. This needs a great deal of wisdom to know when to do one and when to do the other.

I want to turn to something else. It looks like something else, but it's just another side of the same thing. There are many good activities we can do, but there are only twenty-four hours a day, and some of them are for sleep. What do I do when someone comes to me and says, "Brother Frazee, will you do this?" And someone else comes to me and says, "Brother Frazee, will you do this?" And it happens that what this one wants and this one wants if I do them, have got to be done at the same time. Or, it may not be the same time by the clock, but it can be half a dozen different requests for your time.

Let me illustrate it with money. Suppose all you had in your pocket was a dollar, and three different people would come to you at the same time and try to sell you something that cost a dollar. How many of them could you respond to? Just one. The difference between the two things is this: you might find a dollar, but you can't find an hour. You might multiply money, but there is no way to multiply time. And, may I say it reverently, no matter how much you pray about it, you're still going to be shut up to twenty-four hours a day.

One of the most important things in Christian leadership is to learn, both on the receiving end and on the giving end, how to relate ourselves to this problem. We have learned that the great motive that keeps us moving is love. The motive that ties us to an organization is love.

Watch this problem. The more I love people, the more I want to do what they ask me to do. If I'm hard-boiled, the problem may be very easy. I can look anybody in the face and say, "Go find someone else to do that." But suppose I'm tenderhearted and loving and helpful and generous, and the people over here want me to help with this, and the people over there they want me to help with that. And maybe the different ones don't even know that the others have asked me. Then what do I do?

Do you know the answer? If you do, help some other folks who don't. I want to give you a part of the answer. This isn't all the answer, but this is a very important part of the answer. Suppose we have in the group ten people. If each one of those asks you to do something different, then you have ten different choices from which you have to choose. But suppose that you were to say on a given afternoon, "What would you like me to do?" and the first nine all told you to do exactly the same thing, but this one over here asked you to do something different. Would that make it a little easier to come to a conclusion? Yes. Why? Because there is nine times as much weight with the nine as there is there with the one.

> One of the most important things in Christian leadership is to learn, both on the receiving end and on the giving end, how to relate ourselves to this problem. We have learned that the great motive that keeps us moving is love. The motive that ties us to an organization is love.

You cannot please everyone. If you have been trying it, you may need to go in as a patient at the lifestyle center because trying to please everyone is a good way to develop ulcers and high blood pressure.

Don't misunderstand me. We should try to please everyone. But we should understand before we try it that we will never be able to do it. Paul says, "If it be possible, as much as lieth in you, live peaceably with all men" (Rom. 12:18).

Let's go back to our illustration of the moon and the earth. What keeps the moon going? Momentum. But if that were all that was keeping it going, where would it go? Off on a tangent. Why does it curve and keep going around the earth? Gravitation. But the only reason that it succeeds is that every atom on the earth is pulling in the same direction. It's pulling the moon toward the earth. Every atom in this world is saying to the moon, "Stay with us." That is gravitation.

It will be a wonderful thing when the church is as united in its appeal to the individual member as the matter of the earth is united in using the force of gravitation toward the moon.

Suppose that as an officer, I want to know what the group wants me to do. There are various ways I could do it. One way would be to take a pencil and a piece of paper and write out certain alternatives and then go around to everyone and ask each one, "What do you think I should do?" For one thing, that would take a long time.

There is an easier and simpler way to do it. And this is the way we do it in the institution. From time to time, we appoint committees and officers to act for the group in letting us know individually how we can fit into the plan. This is the essence of what organization is for.

You remember Jethro told Moses to appoint captains over thousands and hundreds and fifties and tens. He said the people could come to those officers to decide matters. The little matters, the captains over ten would decide. Greater matters will be brought to the captains over fifty and so on until the matters that can't be decided will be brought to Moses as the overall leader.

Who is standing behind the captain of ten? The captain of a hundred. Who is standing behind the captain of a hundred? The captain of a thousand, and so on to Moses. And who is standing behind Moses? God. This leads me to this point. If I really want to know how to fit into a program, I don't have the impossible or impractical task of going to everyone in the place and asking them what they think.

Suppose an individual comes to me and says, "Brother Frazee, I have something that I wish so much you would do tomorrow afternoon at 4:30."

What do I say? "Sorry, I have a previous engagement."

But suppose they say to me, "Yes, but this is so important. And I want you to do it so much. Won't you do it for me?"

One person is asking me to do something, but the entire group, through delegated committees and officers, has asked me to do something else. This is not democracy; this is a part of the organization God uses in His theocracy to help me to understand His will. And the weight of the counsel that the group gives is far more than any individual who makes up that group.

Now let's go a step further. Which do you think has more weight, the union conference or the local conference? The union conference. Why? It's a bigger mass. If the moon is the local conference, the earth is the union conference. But there is a still larger body behind the union conference—the General Conference. Sister White plainly states that that is the highest authority God has on the earth. It is not the highest authority in the universe. It does not claim to be or pretend to be. It's simply the highest authority God has on the earth. Should I, therefore, give greater weight to the councils of the General Conference than I give the local conference? Oh, yes. Now notice an interesting statement: "The Lord God of heaven has chosen experienced men to bear responsibilities in His cause. These men are to have special influence. If all are accorded the power given to these chosen men, a halt will have to be called" (*Testimonies for the Church*, vol. 9, p. 264).

So you see, while in the church, we are all equal as far as the value of our souls. We are not all equal in the value of our counsel and in the measure of authority. Do you see? God gave some men one talent, and to others two, and to others five.

> I have often been instructed by the Lord that no man's judgment should be surrendered to the judgment of any other one man. Never should the mind of one man or the minds of a few men be regarded as sufficient in wisdom and power to control the work and to say what plans shall be followed. But when, in a General Conference, the judgment of the brethren assembled from all parts of the field is exercised, private independence and private judgment must not be stubbornly maintained, but surrendered.... God has ordained that the representatives of His church from all parts of the earth, when assembled in a General Conference, shall have authority.... Let us give to the highest organized authority of the church that which we are prone to give to one man or to a small group of men. (*Testimonies for the Church*, vol. 9, pp. 260, 261)

These two pages will bear a great deal of study. They are the principles of the divine theocracy.

CHAPTER 8

Leadership with Love

I want us to think this afternoon about the two great manifestations of God's power—the earth and the moon. The moon is kept in place by the power of gravitation, and it is kept from falling into the earth by momentum.

The only way that you and I can keep from being pulled too close to that which exerts a strong force is by having such a sense of mission—that we are "on our way." It takes some momentum. 1 Corinthians 5:14 tells us that it is the love of Christ that gives momentum. "The love of Christ constraineth us." It pushes me on. It urges me on. I can't stop. I have got to keep going. Yet, in addition to pushing me forward, the love of God does something else as well that is just as much a manifestation of God's power, "And I, if I be lifted up from the earth, will draw all men unto Me" (John 12:32).

That is what the power of gravitation does. It's a drawing power; it's a pulling power. Within, we need a pushing power that drives us on—an individual conviction of duty. "The love of Christ constraineth us." But we also need to feel the drawing power of Jesus (through an institution, His church, through the home, through whatever group we are connected with) that helps to keep us in orbit. I would like to have you think of these two as represented by the push and the pull.

> *It is love that pushes me on to do the work I believe God has called me to do, and it is love that draws me to the institution, home, and church, and leads me to listen to counsel and accept direction.*

They are both love. It is love that pushes me on to do the work I believe God has called me to do, and it is love that draws me to the institution, home, and church, and leads me to listen to counsel and accept direction. Isn't love what draws you to the institution? "If ye love me, keep My commandments," Jesus says. Love prompts the response. So, I would like to have you think of these two manifestations of love—love giving us deep convictions within to serve God and do the work we believe He wants us to do, but love that leads us to be drawn, to cooperate with an institution and the church.

> *I would like to have you think of these two manifestations of love—love giving us deep convictions within to serve God and do the work we believe He wants us to do, but love that leads us to be drawn, to cooperate with an institution and the church.*

In order for God's plan to function, God must have human leaders who manifest this love. If we let a planet represent the church, and the influence of the church we think of as gravitation that holds the individual member in orbit, what is that power that reaches out and keeps that individual from going off on a tangent? It's the power of love. There must be love in his or her heart for the church, but there must be love in the heart of the church for him or her. And that love of the church for an individual is manifested through other individuals.

I want to study this matter of leadership. Without leadership, there can be no organization in God's government.

Are there leaders in heaven? Yes. God is the great leader. The Bible speaks of the principalities and powers in heavenly places. The angels are marshaled in companies, and they have commanders. We read about the organization of music in chapter 3. There is one angel that always leads. So, there are leaders in heaven. You remember that as the angels were marshaled in Gethsemane and watched Christ in His agony, they heard His prayer, and they wanted to go to His rescue. Why didn't they do it? A tall, commanding angel suffered them not. Isn't that interesting? Angels that never did anything wrong wanted to rescue Jesus, and the thing that kept them from doing so was a tall, commanding angel who said, "No." Did they obey? Yes. And it wasn't God who told them not to directly. It was that commanding angel who told them not to.

We all think that we would do what Jesus said, but it's sometimes hard to do what a supervisor or church elder says.

Let me clear up this point. Does any lower officer have the right to contradict his superior officer? No. When Nebuchadnezzar was king of Babylon, and he told the people to bow down and worship the golden image, he was going beyond his authority. He had no right to issue that command. Therefore, nobody had any duty to obey him. When the three Hebrews stood up while all the world bowed down, they were the most loyal citizens of Babylon that were on the plains of Dura that day. They were not in rebellion against authority. They weren't like these folks who have riots in the streets and on the campuses in our universities today. Nothing remotely like it. They were not fighting; they were loyally obeying a higher law. Nebuchadnezzar came to see that before the day was over, and He thanked God for them.

> *At forty years of age, Moses thought he was fully ready to take command of Israel and deliver them. Forty years later, he was reluctant, modest, and timid. But God found him ready. He had learned to obey. When is the time to learn to obey? Before we command.*

Will we need leaders in God's organization here on earth? Oh, yes. We will need leaders all the way through. And how to be a leader is another way of studying Christian leadership. But I want to study with you in this chapter some very important things with reference to leaders. "They must learn to obey before they are fitted to command" (*Gospel Workers*, p. 75).

If that were always carried out to the letter, some of us would never get much experience commanding. But this is the ideal. The nearer we achieve it, the better our work will be. If God has not given you all the leadership that you might think you are ready for, would this be a good thing to check?

Interestingly enough, at forty years of age, Moses thought he was fully ready to take command of Israel and deliver them. Forty years later, he was reluctant, modest, and timid. But God found him ready. He had learned to obey. When is the time to learn to obey? Before we command.

"Command," as used here, is not the thought of barking orders like the armies of this world. This is leadership. Let's put it another way; it is getting people to do things—the right thing, and to do it in cooperation with the leader and with other people.

How are you going to do that? The important thing is to get it done, isn't it? No, the important thing isn't to get it done; the important thing is how we get it done. We have gone over some of that. I want you to think of this power of gravitation as love, just as the pushing power that keeps the individual moving is the inward conviction of the love of Christ. It's a wonderful thing to have a father and mother whom you love so much that it's a joy to follow their lead. It is a wonderful thing to have brethren in the church whom you love so much that you love to follow their lead. So in the institution.

Next, I would like to study this not as it relates to our response to the leadership of others but as it relates to the leadership we exert.

You are put in charge of someone. How are you going to direct them? If all the individual has is a response to your personal leadership, he will crash into identification with you and will be out of order. Never seek to establish such a close identity between you and the people you lead that they lose their individuality.

The moon has individuality. Some people thought it was interesting enough to spend quite a bit of time and several billion dollars investigating it. It is an individual out there in space, yet it is doing something important for this world. It's held in place by that gravitational pull. If there was some way of increasing the gravitational pull of this earth, if you could turn a crank and make the pull stronger, the moon would crash into the earth. That wouldn't be good for either the moon or the earth.

Such gravitational pull happens quite often to teen girls. Some develop an admiration for a popular schoolmate and seek to imitate that girl's way of dressing, acting and talking. For the moment, this young follower has more gravitational pull between herself and the one she admires than is good for her. All she needs is more momentum. That will keep her in orbit. She needs a deeper conviction of the individual love of Jesus, a closer association with Christ, and needs to look to Him for direction.

There are people whose attitude toward church organization is, "Whatever the church says is all right." They will let the theologians study theology, and whatever is passed down, they will accept. They will let the people who are planning missionary work make all the plans, and they will just do what they are asked to do. When it is time to go ingathering, they will go. When it is time to give Bibles, they will give Bibles.

There are people who think that is the ideal church member. I will not give you all the references concerning that here, but that is not the ideal at all. God wants you to have an individual experience of knowing what God wants you to do.

Some go off on a tangent. They feel it is a bother to have to consult leaders. Yes, it is a bother—it takes time, it takes prayer, and it takes thought. And lazy minds don't like to think. It is easier to let the pope decide. Or it's easier to be an anarchist and say, "I am not going to pay attention to anybody. They can go their way, and I will go mine. I have a job to do, and I'm going to do it. If people like it, all right; if they don't, all right. I know what I am supposed to do."

Either one of those seems to be easier. Either one certainly takes less thought. But your job as a leader is to get cooperation without quenching or squelching individuality. And remember, you are to draw, not push.

> *"And when he putteth forth his own sheep, he goeth before them, and the sheep follow him: for they know his voice" (John 10:4).*

"My sheep hear My voice, and I know them, and they follow Me" (John 10:27). Sheep follow because they hear His voice. "And when he putteth forth his own sheep, he goeth before them, and the sheep follow him: for they know his voice" (John 10:4).

This verse gave two reasons why sheep follow. The first is that he goes before them. The second is they know his voice. He calls, and he leads. He leads by his voice, and He leads by his example. A leader is one who knows the way and shows the way and goes the way. That is what I want each one of you to be—a Christian leader. You must know the way; you must show the way, and you must go the way. This is the voice of love. This is the drawing power of love.

Have you ever been out in those parts of the United States where they have great bands of sheep? Do their sheep follow them? No. Those shepherds drive their sheep. They are not shepherds. They are sheepherders.

There is a difference. The shepherd whom Jesus was talking about goes before the sheep; these sheepherders go behind. The shepherd leads, these sheepherders drive, and they need a dog or two to help them. People who are following their method need a few dogs. I hope you won't use dogs. I hope you will never be some sheep herder's dog to bite people who will not come into line. It will bear some study and prayer. No, we do not want to be like the Western sheepherders. We want to be like the shepherds. This is what Jesus is talking about. The shepherd loves his sheep, and so the sheep love him.

You remember the rhyme about Mary's little lamb, "Everywhere that Mary went, the lamb was sure to go." I like that. What makes the lamb love Mary so much? Because Mary loves the lamb.

If you are to be a leader, you must be one who loves those whom you seek to lead. Talking about the same sheep but a different shepherd: "And a stranger will they not follow, but will flee from him: for they know not the voice of strangers" (John 10:5).

Someone who was traveling in the East a number of years ago came to a well where sheep were being watered. Several shepherds were there, and their flocks were all mixed up. The visitor wondered how they were ever going to sort them all out.

When they were done with their watering, and the shepherds had visited a little, one shepherd started off in one direction, and he gave a little call. In that great flock of sheep, this one and that one started going. Another shepherd started off in another direction and gave his call. Some of the sheep went with him. So with all of them.

> *This verse gave two reasons why sheep follow. The first is that he goes before them. The second is they know his voice. He calls, and he leads. He leads by his voice, and He leads by his example. A leader is one who knows the way and shows the way and goes the way. That is what I want each one of you to be—a Christian leader. You must know the way; you must show the way, and you must go the way. This is the voice of love. This is the drawing power of love.*

The shepherds didn't have to sort them out. The sheep sorted themselves out! Each individual sheep knew which shepherd loved him and cared for him. And as an animal could, it loved back. This is the drawing power of love. This is your job. Your job is not primarily to get the work done; it is to get people done.

The people who are responding to your loving leadership are learning to follow the Lamb whithersoever He goeth. Parents, our job is to bring our children to the point where they love to find out what we want so that they can do it. And when we have brought them to that point, they are ready to go to heaven and follow the heavenly Father to find out what He wants and to do it forevermore. That is our job.

All these experiences are laboratories in which this science is being learned and practiced. I appeal to you as Christian leaders, mature or in embryo, experienced or just learning, settle it in your hearts that your job is to draw people through love, not drive them with dogs.

By the way, would that concept have an effect on the tone of voice? If I am trying to drive cattle or drive sheep or drive people, is there a tone of voice that could go with that? Oh, yes. There are some tones of voice that would make me want to run to keep ahead of the person who was shouting. I wouldn't want to get close to feel the sting of the whip, the kick of the foot, or the bite of the dog. It takes an entirely different tone of voice to make me want to draw close to the one who is leading.

The Spirit of Prophecy tells parents never to scold. And as a friend of mine used to say, "Never, that is not very often, is it?"

> Christ is ready to teach the father and mother to be true educators. Those who learn in His school will never speak in a harsh, unsympathetic tone, for words spoken in this manner grate upon the ear, wear upon the nerves, cause mental suffering, and create a state of mind that makes it impossible to curb the temper of the child to whom such words are spoken.... If parents desire their children to be pleasant, they should never speak to them in a scolding manner. (*Child Guidance*, pp. 282, 286)

There is more precious instruction on page after page of this book. My point is that are we trying to drive? No, we are trying to draw. And this is so in everything that shall be managed—the institution, the home, the school, the church—anything. This is one of the reasons that I wouldn't work for the world. They are organized on a different system.

If I were a slave like Joseph, I might have had to respond to leadership that didn't understand this. But when Joseph finally became trusted and was put in charge of the other prisoners, did he use the methods that were used on him? No, he used the methods we are studying. We see him going around in the morning like a nurse making rounds. And he even notices the countenance of two of the prisoners who were sad. What ordinary jailer would notice whether the prisoners were sad or otherwise? Joseph was saturated with this spirit. He had drawing power. He got them to unburden their hearts, and he helped them.

Do you know where bees go? Where there is honey. Children like to be around people who love them. Older people like to be around people who love them.

"Well, Brother Frazee, if someone else will get the work done, I will be glad to sit down and be loving all day long. But after all, someone has to cook and wash dishes and hoe the corn and do all the rest."

If I thought any of this was just theory, I would not bother with this book. It's because I know that this is the most practical thing in the universe. The paradox of it is that although it seems to take time, and it does, to learn and follow this, in the end, it gets far more done than driving. This world has yet to see the demonstration. I want you and me to have a part in it.

> God has a church on earth who are lifting up the downtrodden law, and presenting to the world the Lamb of God that taketh away the sins of the world. The church is the depositary of the wealth of the riches of the grace of Christ, and through the church eventually will be made manifest the final and full display of the love of God to the world that is to be lightened with its glory. (*Testimonies to Ministers*, p. 50)

A final and full display of the love of God is to be given to this world, and it's to be given through the church, and the church is made up of people. The only way the church can be a revelation of this final and full display of love is for each member to be filled with it. And the greater the responsibility of your leadership, the greater must be your capacity to love. This is the thing.

Someone may be thinking, "Well, Brother Frazee, if I had a group of people who would respond to love, this might work. But you don't know what I have to put up with. You don't know how unresponsive the workers are."

No, I don't. And I didn't originate those quotes. But the One who did inspire it knows all about it. He knows all about the people you have to contend with. That is why He wrote this. This will work, and it's the only thing that will work if what you're trying to do is get people into heaven. Of course, if you are just trying to reach a goal and get a quota, you can do that with Hitler's method, Stalin's method, or Detroit's method. But we're not interested in that, are we?

Let me read you one of the most practical statements I know on this point. Sister White is writing to people about doing things for Christ. On this particular page, she is writing about taking orphans into the home and helping them, teaching them, and leading them. But this same principle works in everything we do, whether we are dealing with patients, or with our own children, or with students in the school, or helpers in the department. Listen to this. It will make you smile, but it will also make you think:

> *A final and full display of the love of God is to be given to this world, and it's to be given through the church, and the church is made up of people. The only way the church can be a revelation of this final and full display of love is for each member to be filled with it. And the greater the responsibility of your leadership, the greater must be your capacity to love. This is the thing.*

> You may have thought that if you could find a child without fault, you would take it, and care for it; but to perplex your mind with an erring child, to unlearn it many things and teach it anew, to teach it self-control is a work which you refuse to undertake. To teach the ignorant, to pity and to reform those who have ever been learning evil, is no slight task; but heaven has placed just such ones in your way. They are blessings in disguise. (*Testimonies for the Church*, vol. 2, p. 27)

Some of them are pretty well disguised. They are camouflaged so much that you would hardly recognize them as blessings. The greater the lack of response in the people you are trying to get to come with you and work, the less they are being drawn, the greater is this challenge in your heart to get down and plead with God for love. Along with love, you may want to pray for some good sense; the two are not antagonistic—they go together.

Of course, we labor under a handicap—we are usually contaminated with wrong ideas of what love is. If I should put some words on the blackboard and ask you to choose which one represents love, it would be quite interesting. Suppose I put hard and soft. Most people think of love as soft; love can be soft, but love can be hard. There are times when love needs to be hard.

When we are talking about love, we must not get the idea that love means, "Now I'm the leader, and I'm responsible for getting a job done, but I love everyone so much that I say to my group of workers, 'Well now, let's see, what would you all like to do this afternoon?'" Someone, being really honest, says, "I would like to go swimming." So I say, "All right, let's all go swimming." I could be popular for a while. There is a time to go swimming; there is also a time to work.

Love is the ability to get people to keep on working instead of going swimming when work is the thing to do (and to love to do it), partly because they are interested in getting the work done, but partly because they love the leader whose enthusiasm is helping them to see the joy in the thing that would otherwise be hard.

Who is sufficient for these things? Even Jesus had a hard time. One day, He showed His love for 5,000 people by feeding them. They all wanted to make Him king. Was He drawing them? Yes. And they were ready to follow Him anywhere, or so they thought. But twenty-four hours later, most of them had left Him. Was it the same Jesus? Was it the same love? And so, dear Christian leader, you will have some heartbreaks.

Love, the greatest power in the universe, will not reach every soul. The majority of this world is going down the broad road following the promptings of selfishness. Nothing that you can do, nothing that angels can do, nothing that all heaven can do, nothing that God Himself can do can make a selfish heart loving if it will not yield itself. So, do not set for yourself the impossible task of finding out how to reach everyone. God Himself has not been able to do it. One-third left Him in heaven.

When I say, "Don't set for yourself an impossible task," certainly try to reach everyone, but don't feel that you've made a failure if this child rebels—if that student can't see it; if this worker fails to cooperate. Be so certain of the plan you are following that you will go right ahead. Some folks will come back. The prodigal son did.

I would like to be very practical and immediate with the application of this lesson. I would like you now, this week, not sometime in the future, to be carrying out a laboratory experience in Christian leadership.

During deer season, hunters get a license from the state to hunt. If they get a license, are they sure to get a deer? No. All the license gives them is the opportunity to try and see what they can do.

If you are elected to an office, appointed to an office, or hired to be a supervisor, that is merely a license. It doesn't guarantee you will get a deer at all. Position doesn't make the man, and there is no committee that can make you a leader. By the same token, no committee can keep you from being a leader.

> *Position doesn't make the man, and there is no committee that can make you a leader. By the same token, no committee can keep you from being a leader. Jesus needs you, and I am going to show you how to begin.*

Jesus needs you, and I am going to show you how to begin. "Again I say unto you, That if two of you shall agree on earth as touching anything that they shall ask, it shall be done for them of My Father which is in heaven" (Matt. 18:19).

When I was a boy, one morning before school, following what I know were the impressions of the Holy Spirit, I went to school early, and I went down the road to meet a boy. When I met him, I started to walk back to school with him, and I said, "Robert, I've just been reading something in volume five of the *Testimonies,* page 112, 'One person with pure motives, intent on becoming intelligent that he may make the right use of his abilities, will be a power for good in the school. He will have a molding influence.' Robert, if one boy in the school can have a molding influence, what would happen if the two of us got together and prayed together for other boys in the school?"

Nobody told me to do that. No teacher suggested it. No church officer prompted it. It was the Holy Spirit putting within my heart that conviction. I had learned that principle by listening to some things that dear Elder Luther Warren used to tell in the young people's camp meeting when I was a boy about two or three getting together in little prayer bands. And so I said, "Robert, would you meet with me, and we'll have a little prayer band?"

> The way to begin in Christian leadership is to let the Holy Spirit prompt you to get one other person to respond to your leadership in prayer and working for other souls.

So we did. In a few days, a friend of his joined us, Irvin and then we had three. The Lord had put it in my heart, and I was the leader of that little band. Something happened that morning that, as I look back at it, I know there was a trail that led directly from that moment to this moment. And everything in my life in Christian leadership has been influenced by that. And I was just 14 years old.

I am not suggesting that any two lives are cut out alike; we're individuals. But the way to begin in Christian leadership is to let the Holy Spirit prompt you to get one other person to respond to your leadership in prayer and working for other souls.

Do you know what happened in that little prayer band of three? Pretty soon, we had four. And then we talked it over among ourselves, and the Lord put it in my heart, I said, "Let's have two bands now of two apiece." I asked Irvin if he would be the leader of the other one. So, Robert and I continued with our little prayer band, and Irvin and the new boy continued, and now we had two bands. Pretty soon, we had three bands, then four bands. And then, I gathered the leaders of those little bands together once a week and had a meeting with them, and each one had their band. Before the year was over, we had over half the school in prayer bands. No grown person had ever told us what to do. We were quietly following the prompting of the Holy Spirit. There was no announcement made of it. It was just quiet work among the students.

But believe me, there was some organization to it. We checked up with the leaders, "How are you getting along with your little band?" We tied them together with leaders' meetings. This was the laboratory in which I learned some of these principles of united prayer and group work, which have been with me all these years.

I say to you that God wants you to get down on your knees and say, "Lord, is there someone you want me to lead, not for some glory, not for some display, not for some reward, but just because I love You, and I love the ones You love? Is there someone that you want me to lead and love for You?" He will put someone on your heart. If He doesn't, pray until He does. And when He does, go to them.

There is someone who needs your leadership, who needs you to pray with them and encourage them. For many of you, the way you will get the most help is to go find someone who needs help more than you do.

When Jesus had hungry people and the disciples brought in their little supply, He didn't feed them. He told them to go feed those other people. The disciples didn't eat until all the others were fed, and they ended up having plenty. No matter how weak you feel, if you love Jesus, get down on your knees and ask Him to help you to lead, not an army, but one person.

CHAPTER 9

God Takes the Reins

As we continue our study of Christian leadership, let's remember this means how groups of people can work together successfully using heaven's methods instead of the world's methods. The world has made some wonderful showings in getting things done with groups. Sometimes with force and sometimes with rewards. Fear and favor are the two methods that get results. But in God's great plan of groups working together, the motive power that He desires to use is love.

I want to read a statement. I have read this statement for a long time, and not until recently have I seen in it what I believe the Lord wants us to see in it and what I am going to study with you. Talking about the loud cry, Sister White says:

> Let me tell you that the Lord will work in this last work in a manner very much out of the common order of things, and in a way that will be contrary to any human planning. There will be those among us who will always want to control the work of God, to dictate even what movements shall be made when the work goes forward under the direction of the angel who joins the third angel in the message to be given to the world. God will use ways and means by which it will be seen that He is taking the reins in His own hands. (*Testimonies to Ministers*, p. 300)

It would be interesting if we had an x-ray of some people's minds to see what that expression meant to them. Have you ever had reins in your hands? Reins are used to control and direct animals.

What a pleasure it is to ride on or behind an animal that responds easily to the pull of the reins. No amount of pleasure in driving an automobile or a tractor or an airplane can compare with the satisfaction of driving a horse. A machine responds. It has to. But an animal, that is something different. There is a personality there. It's true it isn't human, but the Lord has put something in those animals. There are horses that greatly love their masters and thus respond so nicely.

In the old days, as children grew up, they would often sit on their father's knee or by his side while he held the reins. They might put their hands on the reins. Father didn't always let go of the reins right away just because Johnny, Harry, or Alice had hold of them. They learned something about driving that way.

In the closing work, it's going to be seen that God is taking the reins into His own hands. For years, I have heard this statement quoted with the idea that soon, there won't be any human authority or direction. Soon everyone will just go here or there, and we won't need organization. My dear friends, I think there is something in it far deeper and more wonderful than that.

God will use ways and means by which it will be seen that He is taking the reins into His own hands. Reins indicate that there is something or someone that is being guided. Tell me, if God is going to take the reins into His own hands, where will I be? Will I be harnessed? Will I have some reins a hold of me? Or will I be running around in the pasture, showing how glorious it is that nobody tells me anything to do?

If God takes the reins into His own hands, I will be where those reins are pulling. I wonder if I need training in how to respond to the pull on the reins. I have gotten a great blessing in meditating on this. What is the last letter in the word "reins?" "S" What does that mean? More than one.

To successfully guide a mule or a horse, you must have two reins. Many times, it is with a steady light pressure on both reins that you drive. If you pull a little more on one, the noble animal goes around in that direction. If he gets out more than you intended, you pull on the other rein a little. That is driving a horse. God is going to take the reins into His own hands. I want to study these two reins that God uses with you.

Who is driving? God is. You remember that God taught Nebuchadnezzar that the Most High ruleth in the kingdom of men and giveth it to whomsoever He will. Nebuchadnezzar finally acknowledged that and wrote it down for the whole world. "He doeth according to His will in the army of heaven and among the inhabitants of the earth" (Dan. 4:35).

God has the reins. God is going to use two reins to direct me. For the purpose of our study, I would like to have you think of these two reins as God's guidance directly to me personally and God's guidance through an organization.

I am an individual in the world. God has a direct line to me. There are some things God will impress my heart with personally. That is why we praise God every day. That is why we study His Word every day.

There are some other things that God wants to do for me through an organization—through a group and through leaders. This bothers some people. They say they are in confusion all the time. God tells me to do one thing, and my brethren tell me to do something else. How do we solve that difficulty? Some of those people look forward to the time when they can be in heaven, and God will tell them everything to do.

We have already studied that. Up in heaven, the angels are marshaled in companies. For many of the things that the angels learned to do, they get their directions from other angels. When there is to be singing, there is an angel who leads. It isn't that God tells them what to sing, what pitch to start with, and in which key to sing. An angel does that. Those angels who respond have to believe that God is working through that angel.

Suppose I am a child growing up in a home. The Fifth Commandment says, "Honor thy father and thy mother," which is another way of saying that behind those parents, God is standing. If I am a boy in the home and my father says to me, "Bill, please fill the wood box this morning," suppose I would say, "If God told me to do that, I would."

There are some people who have such an exaggerated sense of personal guidance that they are just about like that. They have a hard time in the church, or in any institution, or with the government, or anywhere. They may be conscientious, but they just do not understand this subject.

It is one thing to tolerate reins; it is another thing to love them. I pray that God will help us to love these reins that God uses to guide us.

The purpose of having reins on an animal is to keep that animal on the road, going to the place where you want him to go, and keeping him off of any bypass. Suppose you are driving a horse, and for any number of reasons, the horse thinks it would like to go off on a side road. Maybe it is because you have always gone that road before or he may see something down that road that interests him.

I remember when I was plowing with a mule. When I got to the end of the row, the mule would be so anxious to go on home to the barn. But if I could succeed in getting him turned around, it was so hard to get him to go back down the row. But on the other end of the row facing the barn, it was easy to get him turned around. He had a desire that worked along with my plans. But to pull on that rein to get him turned around again away from the barn was hard.

We human beings have to be guided and directed by the Lord in the path of His providence, and He has reins, plural. One is the direct guidance of God to the individual, and the other is His guidance through others.

Some of our directions we get through a group. The whole church may send out through its authorized committees instructions about certain matters. In an institution, the board or executive committee may say, "These are the plans; this is what we are going to do." And I, as an individual, get my orders. But often, the directions that any of us get personally come not through the group as a whole speaking to us, but the group speaks through some individual.

For instance, I come to Sabbath School on Sabbath morning. Does the whole group tell me what to sing? No, the superintendent, song leader, or whoever is appointed tells me what to sing. Is that the group speaking to me? Yes, because the group has appointed him to do that.

It isn't just anyone who gets up and says, "Let's sing number 510 this morning." Wouldn't it be wonderful if everyone would say, "You know, that's just what I was impressed to sing!" Some people think that would be heaven. It might be a utopia, but it isn't heaven. In heaven, an angel says what we sing. And we all love to respond and join in.

So, we see the two reins: guidance directly from God and guidance through the group. But keep in mind that unless God has hold of this rein, this thing does not work. The same pair of hands have to hold both reins of a horse. Can you imagine what would happen if John had ahold of one rein and Harry had ahold of the other? The horse might get confused. So, let's remember this plan will never work unless God has hold of both reins. And that is what this promise is about. God will use ways and means by which it will be seen that He is taking the reins into His own hands. Oh, I want to be where God is pulling on both reins. What do you say? And if I am not, let me get to that place quickly.

That doesn't mean that we have to wait for perfection either in ourselves or in others. In Romans 13, Paul says concerning civil government: "Let every soul be subject unto the higher powers. For there is no power but of God; the powers that be are ordained of God," (Rom. 13:1).

God doesn't tell us what our taxes will be. The government tells us that. But is God using civil government with all its deficiencies? Yes, He is. He did back there in ancient Rome.

So in the home. The father may say, "Bill, please fill the wood box." Does that mean that the father is infallible? Oh, no. He might make mistakes sometimes. He might ask me to do too much. He might not ask me to do enough. But in any event, God is using my father and mother to help guide me. Making due allowances for their weakness, I must respect their position and believe that behind them is God. So it is with leadership in the church.

Let us see what the reins are, "I drew them with cords of a man, with bands of love" (Hosea 11:4).

That is Christian leadership—heaven's plan of leadership. The reins are love. Here is another beautiful illustration of it: "And when he putteth forth his own sheep, he goeth before them, and the sheep follow him: for they know his voice" (John 10:4).

That is beautiful! Do you know the difference between a shepherd and a sheepherder? Out in the West, I used to see great flocks of sheep driven past the place where I lived. The sheepherders were there. Sometimes they were on horses. They always had a few dogs with them. They drove the sheep. They had to be careful not to drive them too fast, but they were behind driving, not with reins, but with dogs and horses. That is the sheepherder. But Jesus says the shepherd goes before, and the sheep follow. They know His voice. They love Him.

Tell me, at church, at home, or at an institution, are you a shepherd or sheepherder? Do you go before, and do those who work with you love to follow? Or, do you simply get behind and bark the orders, and they jump either because they are afraid of you or want their paycheck? Is that a good question? It's very important. It's what we are studying about in Christian leadership.

Some people don't have enough force to drive others or enough love to lead them to do anything. They're not in this at all. But merely getting things done is not enough. The important thing is, how do we get things done? God is using the reins of love.

Look at it this way—why does God give me directions? Because He loves me. So, it is love that leads the Lord to direct me. And I know that, and I say, "Oh Lord, I am so glad You love me enough to tell me what to do." But watch. That love that leads God to tell me what to do leads me to do what He says. "If ye love Me, keep My commandments" (John 14:15). So it's love both ways. Love leads Him to pull; love leads me to respond.

It is no less true when the channel is through human agents. It is the love of God that is to be expressed by every parent in every command he gives. When you tell a little child what to do, the thing that must lead you every time is love.

Someone says, "That is idealistic. Nobody can do that."

Oh, yes. That is what we are going to do a million years from now, and all the time in between, if we will get into this program. If we are going to do it all through eternity, we might just as well get started now. Did you ever stop to think that there is no way to add anything to the joy in heaven on the other end? The only way you can get any more is to start earlier. And there is joy in this kind of relationship. Why wait until heaven to get the joy of giving orders through love?

God intends that every order that comes to me shall come to me through love. God's love is expressed to and through the group, down through the leader to me. But watch. Just as I recognize God's love in leading me individually, I recognize His goodness in giving me parents to guide me, teachers to instruct me, and supervisors to direct me. Work supervisors, church elders, Sabbath School superintendents, ministers, and conference presidents, I thank the Lord for every one of them. I need them. Each one of them is to be a channel for the revelation of God's love.

That isn't just to sing songs about love. It is to tell me what to do. God's love through them is to be revealed in telling me what to do. God will also reveal His love by helping me to respond back in cooperation. So it is the reins of love all the way through.

In John 10, the Shepherd leads through love, and the sheep respond. I want to give a sample of how love works in the home in a very practical way. Who is the head of the house? The husband. That is what the Bible says. Here, the prophet of God is talking to a husband:

> Your spirit is strong. When you take a position, you do not weigh the matter well and consider what must be the effect of your maintaining your views and in an independent manner weaving them into your prayers and conversation, when you know that your wife does not hold the same views that you do. Instead of respecting the feelings of your wife, and kindly avoiding, as a gentleman would, those subjects upon which you know you differ, you have been forward to dwell upon objectionable points, and have manifested a persistency in expressing your views regardless of any around you. You have felt that others had no right to see matters differently from yourself. These fruits do not grow upon the Christian tree. (*Testimonies for the Church*, vol. 2, p. 418)

You say, "How could a husband be the head of the house if he had to avoid pressing things that his wife didn't agree on? He is not the head; he is the tail."

No, he is the head. But what is he the head for? To have his way? Oh, no. What crude, immature, and meager ideas of authority some people have.

Someone told me about a common worker in the old days on the railroad who one day became the boss. When they got together the first morning under this new administration, he said to the gang, "Take that train off the tracks!"

So, they all got busy and got that car off the tracks. When they got it done, he said, "Put that car back on the tracks! I will show you who is boss around here."

Most of us would never do it that crudely. But I wonder if lurking in our minds, there is even one-tenth of one percent of that sort of thing. If there is, it is too much. Do you know there is some poison so potent that even a few parts in one million in water are enough to cause serious symptoms and even death? And this poison of selfishness and dictatorship is that kind of poison. It comes from Lucifer, not Jesus.

The prophet says to this man who is in a position of leadership, "Listen, when you are talking to your wife, don't be so bossy. And when you pray, don't pray about something that you know is disagreeable to her and that you're trying to ram down her throat. And don't bring up the conversation all the time."

I wonder if that would apply in a church or a Sabbath School. Suppose I have some pet subject that I am very interested in, but I know that my brethren don't see it as I do. But somehow, I am asked to take the 11 a.m. service or teach the Sabbath School class. Oh, there is my chance to ram it home! Well, haven't I the right to? After all, I've got the reins.

Who is supposed to take the reins into His own hands? God. If the reins are love, you see how that simplifies the whole matter. Don't misunderstand me. There are times when leaders have to give a straight message. Elijah did. John the Baptist did. That is not what I am talking about. I am talking about why we do things.

Let us ask God to deliver us forever from the idea that position is a chance to carry out our way to get things done the way we want. Position is a responsibility laid upon us to get things done God's way for love's sake, for the benefit of those we lead. Oh, what a difference that is! How smoothly that can make things run.

I thank God that He has warned us about dictatorship in the church. This same principle applies to any institution. We learned earlier that the same principles of government run through all these organizations.

Now, this particular one is about the church:

> Special instruction has been given me for God's people, for perilous times are upon us. In the world, destruction and violence are increasing. In the church, man power is gaining the ascendancy; those who have been chosen to occupy positions of trust think it their prerogative to rule. Men whom the Lord calls to important positions in His work are to cultivate a humble dependence upon Him. They are not to seek to embrace too much authority; for God has not called them to a work of ruling, but to plan and counsel with their fellow laborers. (*Testimonies for the Church*, vol. 9, p. 270)

Suppose that there is a horse that has been properly trained. How much of a pull or a yank on the reins does he need? He doesn't need any yank at all. All that horse needs is just the slightest little pull on the rein, just to let the horse know what his master wants. But sometimes, a horse has gotten insulted and abused because someone who was used to yanking methods got hold of the reins and began to pull and yank and spur that horse who is used to gentle methods. Poor horse.

God wants you and me in our leadership to cultivate gentle pulling on the reins. That does not mean being wishy-washy. That doesn't mean letting the horse go where it wants to go. It doesn't mean whispering in the ear of the horse and saying, "I wonder what you would like to do this afternoon."

A leader is supposed to have some plans. Not that there is anything wrong with counseling with those that we are over, but in general, a leader should have some plans and be able to go ahead with them. But he shouldn't have to bark like an army sergeant. He shouldn't have to drive like a sheepherder. He ought to be able, like the shepherd with the sheep, to lead and draw by the reins of love.

We read about this husband who wasn't sufficiently anxious to do things in harmony with his wife. I suppose that if he were of a mind to argue with the prophet, he would have said, "But look here, Sister White, after all, who is supposed to lead in the home, my wife or me?"

I think Sister White would have answered that she meant just what she said—of course, he was to lead, but he was to lead through love and consider the feelings of his wife. He should not yank at her. He should study how to lead, not to drive, and how to use the reins of love.

I come now to *Counsels to Writers and Editors*. This is a very valuable part of the inspired library that God has given. Beginning on page 75 is a very important chapter. It is practically addressed to A. T. Jones and E. J. Waggoner in 1887.

Those of you who are acquainted with the history of the church will remember that Jones and Waggoner were the men who, in 1888 (the year following this testimony that I will quote), brought to our General Conference a special message on righteousness by faith. There were some there who accepted that message and got a great blessing. There were some who opposed it. There were others who were in confusion.

Through the 1890s, righteousness by faith was quite a subject of discussion and agitation in the church. But the thing I want you to notice in this testimony is the effort God was making to try to get Jones and Waggoner to use the reins of love. If they had fully learned it, the history of this denomination might have been entirely different.

Don't misunderstand me. Those who rejected their message were not excused because Jones and Waggoner were imperfect in their presentation. God expected our brethren to listen to the message and weigh it on the evidence of Bible truth regardless of the way Jones and Waggoner presented it. But when you read this testimony, you will see that God was trying to get Jones and Waggoner to be gentle and to be considerate of their brethren and not to needlessly make division. God was seeking to get them in the line of these reins. He was seeking to get them to respond to the pull of love. He was seeking to make them leaders who were pulled by love and who would pull others by love.

With that background, let me read a little here now on page 75:

> Letters came to me from some attending the Healdsburg College in regard to Brother _____'s teaching in regard to the laws. I wrote immediately protesting against their doing contrary to the light which God had given us in regard to all differences of opinion, and I heard nothing in response to the letter. It may have never reached you. If you, my brethren, had the experience that my husband and myself have had in regard to these known differences being published in articles in our papers, you would never have pursued the course you have either in your ideas advanced before our students at the college. Neither would it have appeared in the Signs. Especially at this time should everything like differences be repressed. (*Counsels to Writers and Editors*, p. 75)

Right at this time, this was what was happening. This subject of the two laws, the *Signs of the Times* presented it in one way and the *Review and Herald* another. So when our people got their mail, what they got from California taught one thing and what they got from Michigan taught something else. There are some people today who would say, "Well, that is just fine. Everyone can hear all sides of it, and we can have a free discussion, and the more, the better."

I wonder why the prophet didn't think so. Her answer to the problem, this is what I want you to see, was not to tell the people in California or the people in Battle Creek that this is all the true light concerning the two laws. Oh, no. She taught them how to live together in love, even with some differences of opinion.

If we could all learn that lesson, friend, it would have completely saved us from some problems of past years. We will have some problems, however, and we must learn this lesson. I read on:

> These young men are more self-confident and less cautious than they should be. You must as far as difference is concerned be wise as serpents and harmless as doves. Even if you are fully convinced that your ideas of doctrine are sound, you do not show wisdom that that difference should be made apparent. I have no hesitancy in saying you have made a mistake here. You have departed from the positive directions God has given upon this matter, and only harm will be the result. This is not in God's order. You have now set the example for others to do as you have done, to feel at liberty to put in their various ideas and theories and bring them before the public because you have done this. This will bring in a state of things that you have not dreamed of. It is no small matter for you to come out in the Signs as you have done, and God has plainly revealed that such things should not be done. We must keep before the world a united front. (*ibid.*)

Then Sister White goes back to the days of the reformation and shows how the reformation was slowed down because some of its leaders got into arguments and discussions between themselves over some things. It threw some of the people into confusion. Now she refers to her own experience and the experience of her husband. This is wonderful. Listen: "My husband had some ideas on some points differing from the views taken by his brethren. I was shown that however true his views were, God did not call for him to put them in front before his brethren and create differences of ideas" (*ibid.*).

My dear friend, if there was ever anyone in this denomination that had the right to be called a leader, it was James White. But even James White was not to say, "Because I am a leader, everyone listen to me and do what I say." No. And there were some points of doctrine that he didn't see quite the same as his brethren, and Sister White says, "I was shown." What does that mean? God gave her a vision and told her to tell her husband, James White, that "however true his views were, God did not call for him to put them in front before his brethren and create differences of ideas."

While he might hold these views subordinate to himself, once they are made public, minds would seize upon them, and just because others believe differently would make these differences the whole burden of the message and get up contention and variance.

Some time ago, someone called me and said, "Brother Frazee, I have a tape I want to send you."

I said, "What is it?" And he told me. When he got through telling me, I had to say, "Brother, I have so many things to do that if I were to take time to listen to that tape, I would have to neglect some work the Lord has given me to do."

The tape was a defense of someone who thinks he has some views different from his brethren, and he wanted to urge and urge. Notice: "I was shown that however true his views were, God did not call for him to put them in front before his brethren and create differences of ideas" (*ibid.*).

Notice that this is not slavery. God did not say to James White, "You have got to believe the way your brethren believe whether you believe that way or not."

You can't believe just the way someone else believes if you don't believe that way, can you? No. Not at all. There can be varying views on different points but not on the great fundamentals. We all believe the seventh day is the Sabbath. We all believe Jesus is coming soon. We all believe Jesus is in the Most Holy Place of the heavenly Sanctuary. We believe that the dead are unconscious. We believe Sister White is God's messenger to the remnant. But every leader has some views which aren't quite like what some others have.

Anyone who studies the Bible is going to come to some tentative conclusions. Who is the king of the North in Daniel 11? I know. I am sure. Give me a chance, and I will prove it. Who are the seven kingdoms of Revelation 17? I know. I can tell you their names.

Do you know how many different lists there are of those seven kings? Quite a number. And this is not to say that we should never study it, but what a pity to take one of those questions and put them in front to make differences between brethren. God is leading a people. He has reins that He is pulling. One of the reins comes to your heart individually. But through the other rein, God is reaching you through your brethren. If you are a child, He is reaching you through your parents. If you are a student, He is reaching you through your teacher in the classroom. If you are a worker, He is reaching you through your supervisor in your work department. If you are a church member, He is reaching you through your Sabbath School superintendent, your Sabbath School teacher, your church elder, your pastor, your conference president, and on up to the General Conference. What a wonderful plan He has!

And who is it that has the reins? God. And the reins are love. If I have any position of responsibility, small or great, I am to get in the habit of pulling on the rein of love. I am to give my orders through love, and I am to seek to cultivate unity. I am to consider the wishes of those above me, the needs of those below me. It is all through love. I am not to think that I have a chance to ventilate my views to get my way. That is selfishness. In love, I am to seek to transmit the wishes of God the best that I know how.

In whatever place I find myself, I am to listen for the guidance of God through the leaders that He places over me. And I am also to listen to what God tells me personally through the Holy Spirit. Remember that both reins are needed in order to keep me on the road. I need both. Let us thank God for these reins of love and yield unreservedly to both of them. What do you say?

CHAPTER 10

Promotion from Above

In this chapter, we will study more about authority and our relationship to it. "God permits men to be placed in positions of responsibility. When they err, He has power to correct or to remove them. We should be careful not to take into our hands the work of judging that belongs to God" (*Ministry of Healing*, p. 484).

According to Daniel 4, who rules in the kingdom of men? The Most High, and He gives it to whomsoever He will. Verse 17 says He sets over it the basest of men. Not necessarily wicked men, but men who are low or might not be expected to be chosen. When they err, He has the power to correct or remove them. Which do you suppose He'd rather do? Correct them.

If you are chosen to fill a position of responsibility, might you need correction? But if you won't be corrected, someday you'll be removed. But now, looking at it from another angle. Here is someone who is above me in work. I say, "above." We use that word above and below in two different ways. Some people think of it in terms of favoritism or terms of desirability and power. But it's not in that sense that I would have you think of it. It's "above" merely in the sense that we look that way to get our directions.

When Moses had the camp of Israel organized, under him there were captains over thousands, and under them captains over hundreds, and under them captains over fifties, and under them captains over tens. The captain over the thousand was above the captain over the hundreds or fifties. But both of them were equally precious in the sight of God, and they were all brethren as far as their standing before God was concerned. But they differed in the measure of responsibility. That is what I am talking about.

So, who is it that, behind all committees and even political events, is watching over everything and permitting people to be put in responsibility? God. Dear friend, unless we understand this, we will get worried about a lot of things, and it will interfere with our work.

Remember a man by the name of Uzzah who was going along with the cart that some oxen were pulling? On the cart was the ark. What got on the ark? Uzzah's hand. Did it belong there? No.

God told him not to touch it, so he was killed. It was to teach us a lesson that God is able to care for His work.

Some things we should be careful to do; some things we should be careful not to do, like being careful not to take into our hands the work of judging that belongs to God.

Following this chapter's opening quotation, the next sentence says, "The conduct of David toward Saul has a lesson" (*Ministry of Healing*, p. 484). Did David know early in his life that he was going to be king of Israel? Yes, Samuel the prophet told him. Through divine revelation, David knew that he was going to be king.

Some people would be hard to live with if they knew they were going to be king. I have heard Brother George McClure say, "If some people were in David's place, they would say, 'Father, I will not be able to go back and take care of the sheep. The prophet has anointed me king, and I have got to get down to the palace and the court and learn how to take over.'"

But when Samuel went home after the anointing, David went back to his sheep. And he stayed there until the providence of God called him from the shepherd's work down to the king's court. God arranged that. And as soon as David got through with what he had to do down there, back he went to his sheep. Did God get David on the throne of Israel? Yes.

In the meantime, various things happened. As David grew into young manhood, first, he was flattered by the king and given opportunities. Then, as the devil stirred up Saul's mind, David had to flee for his life because Saul tried to kill him. He tried to kill him in the palace; he tried to kill him in the cave; he tried to kill him on various occasions. David, led by the Lord, was always one jump ahead of him.

Did there come opportunities in those experiences where David could have killed Saul? Did he have some friends who told him he should? Did some of his counselors suggest that this was the providence of God—that God had put Saul in his hands?

Now picture the situation. The prophet told David that he was to be king of Israel. Who is behind the prophet? God. Did David know that God had called him to be king? And here was the man who was standing in his robe. And was he doing a good job as king? No, he was making a mess of it. On top of that, he was trying to kill David. And those friends of David's put it all together and said, "See here, David, strike while the iron is hot. This is the hour of God's providence. Just strike Saul. That will get rid of a rebellious, devil-possessed king that is marring the work of God and put you on the throne—the one that God called years ago."

What did David say? "I will not put forth mine hand against … the Lord's anointed" (1 Sam. 24:10). The Lord could have given David the authority to kill Saul; the Lord could do anything that He wanted. If you study some of those cases in which the kings that God was through with were assassinated, I think you will find that, in most cases, it was some other devil-inspired men who did the job. God often uses sin to punish sin. But David was God's man. And God did not say to David to take the sword and kill the man who is in the road. Notice David's attitude. He said God would handle Saul. Either his time will come to die, or he will die in battle, or something.

Saul finally died in battle as a suicide. The Philistines would have gotten him if he hadn't. So, he merely hastened the end. The point is—God gave Saul every opportunity. Was David really ready to take the kingdom? I don't know whether he thought he was or not; his friends thought he was, but God knew he wasn't. David needed every one of those days of trial and patience to get ready for the task that was ahead.

In *Ministry of Healing*, it says, "The conduct of David toward Saul has a lesson" (p. 485). All of this is used to teach us the lesson that God is the one who permits people to be put in positions of responsibility.

Does God permit me to have the father I have and the mother I have? Did you ever, any time between when you were ten years old and twenty, wish you had some other father or mother? Well, it has happened. But I wonder who permitted you to have the father and the mother you have. God did.

You might have wished sometime, when you got into a hard problem, that you could find yourself under a supervisor who checks up on you. Human nature might wish that the supervisor was removed. Could God arrange it? Yes. Is the way to arrange it for me to rebel and make life so miserable for her or him that they resign or get sick so it changes? "There is no need to doubt, to be fearful that the work will not succeed. God is at the head of the work, and He will set everything in order. If matters need adjusting at the head of the work, God will attend to that, and work to right every wrong" (*Selected Messages*, Book 2, p. 390).

I wouldn't take anything for that paragraph. This helps me to know what attitude to take toward a number of things. I do not have to stand with those who leave the impression that the church never makes a mistake or that, if it makes a mistake, we are to shut our eyes to it or feel called upon to defend everything that the church or the leaders may do. No. We don't have to do that. But neither do we have to do what Uzzah did. God is at the head of the work. And He is going to work to right every wrong. Now, if God works to right every wrong, are there some wrongs that need righting? Yes. And who is going to do it? God. "If matters need adjusting at the head of the work, God will attend to that."

And so, as I relate myself to the authority above me, I can safely leave with God those whom He puts in positions of responsibility. What a mistake it would be for me to go to a conference session and say, "Well, if so-and-so is put in for president, I'll go along. But if the man they have in there now is put back in, I won't cooperate. I've had enough of him."

Let me tell you about an interesting experience that happened in 1902 in Fresno, California. Elder A. T. Jones was the president of the conference. He was a man who God had greatly used in 1888 and during the 1890s in preaching the message of righteousness by faith. In 1901, he had been asked to be the president of the California conference. Back in those days, they elected the president every year.

So, in 1902, as the brethren gathered for the meeting, they knew it was time for an election. Elder A. T. Jones, to put it mildly, was not mild. He was sometimes rough, quite forceful, and a pusher. And he pushed people as well as ideas. In fact, during the 1890s, Sister White had written him from Australia that, in a dream, she heard him preaching, and then a similitude was presented to her. She saw him offering the people a bowl of the most beautiful fruit. But she said his manner was such that nobody wanted the fruit. That is the kind of man he was. Now remember, God had used him mightily in the 1890s in spite of all that. It's another illustration of the fact that God permits people to be placed in positions of responsibility.

The ministers who had been working under his leadership from 1901 to 1902 had all they could take. They came to the meeting at Fresno determined that there was going to be a change. In their minds, they had selected one or two nice, sweet, Christian men who they wanted to be president instead of Brother Jones.

Sister White was there, and the Lord gave her instruction as to what to tell those people. She said, "It is the will of God that A. T. Jones should serve this conference as president for another year." Then she said that it was the will of God that Elder Jones should put away all magisterial manner, all the harshness. And she gave him an earnest reproof right in front of all the brethren. Imagine how you might have felt.

She also had to instruct the brethren who thought that Elder Jones should be put out. So, everyone got humbled by the time the meeting was over. Elder Jones broke down and wept, and he confessed that he had been unkind and rough and asked his brethren to forgive him. Sister White told the brethren that the men they had picked out to be president were nice, sweet men, but they did not have the push it would take to lead the conference into doing something for God.

Some of the brethren found James White hard to live with. He wanted to get things moving and done. Jesus was coming. He wanted to get the publishing work, the sanitarium, the college, and the conference all organized and running properly. He was pushing on and on. Some men thought that he rode pretty hard. Sister White was shown in vision that her husband sometimes did get harsh. But she was also shown in vision that he wasn't as bad as some people thought he was, or even as much as she sometimes feared. She was shown that it took a man with that kind of push and drive to get this movement off the ground. Oh, this question of authority is an interesting thing.

Well, back to A. T. Jones in 1902. He was elected. Sad to say, that was one of the last positions he ever filled. Within a few years, he was out campaigning against the general conference and the leaders of the church, advocating more freedom and less organization. It was right at this time that the crisis came. My point is that God took a man who was full of faults and allowed him to be put in as president of that conference. And when men thought they had all they could take, the God of heaven spoke through the gift of prophecy and said he was to be put in for another year, and they accepted.

If it hadn't been for the gift of prophecy, do you know where he'd have gone? Out. And I suppose there might have been men who, two or three or four years later, looked back and said, "Well, I wonder if the prophet knew what she was talking about. Look what happened to him." God did indeed know. He was giving Jones every opportunity, and He was using Jones while he was usable, to a point, as long as he could be used.

Oh friend, listen. When you see one of your leaders making a mistake, pray for them. If you can help them, help them. But never feel that it's your job to take a sword and cut their heads off or even jab them in the side. No, pray for them. Help them if you can. Remember, if the answer is that they need to be removed, God will do it when the right time comes. Wouldn't it be wonderful if this were fully understood and carried out all through the church? Yes. This is it. Even Jesus waited on Judas. Oh, what a lesson!

Let me come to a very practical point. Do you know one of the reasons that human nature sometimes rises up wanting to see someone removed? To make a place for me. In chapter 6, we noted how Absalom stole the hearts of the men of Israel. "Oh, that I were king!" He got to be king for a few days. He ruled in Jerusalem, and his poor father had to flee for his life. But did God take care of that? Yes.

So often, whether men realize it or not, and whether their helpers and the men who encourage them realize it or not, the desire to change someone in office is so that one of my friends or I can get the office. The first person who started that was Lucifer because he wanted Christ's place.

I've got good news for you: "If any are qualified for a higher position, the Lord will lay the burden, not alone on them, but on those who have tested them, who know their worth, and who can understandingly urge them forward" (*Ministry of Healing*, p. 477).

If I have a burden to take a higher position, that is not by itself evidence that I am supposed to be in that position. If God is managing it, He will lay the burden on the brethren—the people who know us, who have tested us, and can understandingly urge us forward.

Often, the person whom God chooses to bear responsibility has no burden to take it. One of the best examples of this is Moses. When God came to him at the burning bush and wanted to put him in the position of leadership, did Moses grab it? No. He gave all the reasons why he couldn't do it. Up to a point, his humility was beautiful. He carried it a bit too far. But God took care of that. So, the happy person is the one who waits for God's time; he doesn't worry.

We may never be called upon to take any higher position than we have right now. And if God's plan for you is to fill the little place you're occupying right now forever, isn't that all right? How foolish it would be to want anything more. Suppose a dogwood would try to grow as big as a pine tree—to stretch and stretch itself. Could it ever do it? And suppose the violet at the foot of the dogwood would even try to be as big as the dogwood. That would be something.

> "All who in this world render true service to God or man receive a preparatory training in the school of sorrow. The weightier the trust and the higher the service, the closer is the test and the more severe the discipline" (*Education*, p. 151). I was talking to a young person just a few days ago that I believe the Lord may be getting ready for some important service. I said to him, "You have not yet had your heart broken, but you will." I said, "Don't misunderstand me. You don't have to go out looking for trouble. You don't have to go around looking for sorrow and trials and disappointment. But remember, if God is getting you ready for what I think He is getting you ready for, you are going to have some sorrows that you have not yet anticipated. I can't tell you what they are. I don't know. It is nothing to worry about. Just remember when they happen what I told you."

I say the same thing to you. It will be something harder than having to eat burnt toast or having a roommate who gets on your nerves occasionally, or having someone else asked to sing instead of you. It will be something a lot more difficult than any of that—some really heartbreaking sorrows. And remember, it's all part of God's training for you to bear more responsibility. Let me read this again: "All who in this world render true service to God or man receive a preparatory training in the school of sorrow." This is not an elective; this is a required course. "The weightier the trust and the higher the service, the closer is the test and the more severe the discipline."

Look at James and Ellen White. Think of that little girl at the age of nine. The stone of an angry playmate is hurled through the air, and she turned just in time to get it full in the face. Why didn't God stop that stone? Why didn't He keep her from turning around just in time to get it right in her face? Where is God? Is He on the job? He is very much on the job. He is training little Ellen Harmon to be God's messenger to the remnant. And it takes sorrow.

Is that the end of it? Oh, no. Read her struggles with doubt. Read her burden to win souls when she is sick—one foot in the grave almost. And then read the disappointments after she received her call to the prophetic work—the sickness, the pain, the misunderstandings of brethren, the poverty. It's quite a story. Remember, none of this meant that God was angry with her or that she was wicked and that she was suffering because of her sin. True, some of it was suffering because of her ignorance because she didn't know how to eat and how to live. God taught her that eventually. But a lot of it was suffering for her good so that she could be a teacher of others.

Remember, sorrow is a required course in learning how to be a leader. Part of the sorrow and disappointment is to have to serve under leaders that you know aren't doing their job the way they ought to. This is our lesson, in the home sometimes, in the school sometimes, in the institution sometimes, and in the church sometimes. Let's learn it. I know God is going to help us do it.

"If we are capable of a larger service, a more important work, the Lord knows all about it, and it is His work to lift us up. How thankful we should be that we are not burdened with the responsibility of estimating our own ability and choosing our own place and position" (*Signs of the Times*, March 9, 1888). Thank the Lord that none of us has to run for office. You might be interested to know that the following are the words of Jeremiah to his secretary, Baruch, "And seekest thou great things for thyself? seek them not" (Jer. 45:5).

Are you hunting for big things for yourself? Don't do it. Choose the little things. Choose what God has chosen for you. In God's own time, if He sees you are needed in something that is bigger, He will arrange it. There is nothing you have to worry about. "For promotion cometh neither from the east, nor from the west, nor from the south. But God is the judge: He putteth down one, and setteth up another" (Ps. 75:6, 7).

The world has a proverb, and like many of the world's maxims, it is not good. The world's proverb on this is: "It is not so much what you know but who you know." Some people think it is that way in the church. That is a cynical attitude. It belongs to the kingdom of Satan. Never let even a tiny virus of that sort of thing lurk in your heart. Promotion does not come from the east, north, or south. Who is running things? God. And if He allows me to be put in the dungeon when I have been a good boy, God is still on the throne.

Did Joseph believe that? Did it work out? Oh, yes. I want you to see one of the reasons that God permitted it. Oh, this is wonderful, "He sent a man before them, even Joseph, who was sold for a servant" (Ps. 105:17).

Who is the "He" spoken of there? God. Do you mean God sent Joseph down there? It looked like his wicked brothers were the ones who sold him for a slave. But the Bible says God sent him down there.

> …Whose feet they hurt with fetters: he was laid in iron: Until the time that his word came: the word of the Lord tried him. The king sent and loosed him; even the ruler of the people, and let him go free. He made him lord of his house, and ruler of all his substance: To bind his princes at his pleasure; and teach his senators wisdom. (Ps. 105:17–22)

Someone has well observed that it's a good thing for a man who is going to have the power to bind princes at his pleasure to know how the binding feels. When Joseph sent a man to the stocks, he knew what it was like to be in the stocks himself.

After World War II, when some of those men who had led in Germany were put in prison, among them was a man who had been in charge of designing and producing the wooden shoes that all the prisoners wore. Now he was in prison wearing those shoes. He said, "If I had known that I was ever going to have to wear these, I would have made them more comfortable."

Oh friend, if you are having trouble getting along with someone who seems to make things hard for you, remember it's to teach you a lesson that you need so much that will help you sometime in the future to know how to deal wisely with someone else. Learn your lesson; don't break through the harness; don't break out of jail; stay there as Joseph did.

Paul and Silas didn't kill the jailer; they kept him from killing himself. And instead of having a jailbreak, they baptized the jailer. They go out at the right time. Meanwhile, they would have missed a glorious opportunity to win some souls if they had taken advantage of the situation and just run off.

Oh, what faith in the providence of God is wrapped up in all of these. So, whether it's forty years like Moses in the desert with the sheep, or thirteen years of bondage and then in prison like Joseph, whatever the term of servitude and trial and sorrow and oppression, remember God is going to graduate you the very first minute that He can. You can "flunk out," of course. You can "drop out." You can "skip it." But oh, what you'll miss!

We take flour and mix it with water and yeast. After it's raised, we put it into the oven. That flour and the other ingredients are having something happen to them that never happened before. It is hot in there. Suppose I am the bread. After about 15 minutes, I say, "I have stood this as long as I can; I have stood it as long as I am going to." Now, what am I good for? Can I go back to the flour bin? No. It is henceforth good for nothing. That is what Jesus said about the salt that had lost its savor.

How many dropouts are there over the country! Don't misunderstand me. Just going through some conventional course doesn't necessarily bake anyone. So much time in the oven by the clock, if the heat isn't on, will not accomplish much. Of what value would a certificate be if it only stated that you had spent time sitting in the oven with any heat? Ask God to help you to be willing to take the heat.

We are back to the point of individuals wanting to get someone else out so they can get in. I want you to see where it comes from:

> Lucifer desired God's power, but not His character. He sought for himself the highest place, and every being who is actuated by his spirit will do the same. Thus alienation, discord, and strife will be inevitable. Dominion becomes the prize of the strongest. The kingdom of Satan is the kingdom of force; every individual regards every other as an obstacle in the way of his own advancement, or a steppingstone on which he himself may climb to a higher place. (*The Desire of Ages*, p. 436)

Lucifer's way is to view my brother as a stone to either to be kicked out of the way so I can get somewhere or for me to step on to climb higher. I will either use him or kick him out. In either case, I use my foot. But if I'm a

Christian and I love him, I will be putting my arm around him. If I see any way to help him to accomplish more for God, I will do it. This is wonderful; this is the spirit of Jesus; this is the spirit of the angels.

There is a wonderful statement in *Desire of Ages* about what the angels are doing right now:

> The angels of glory find their joy in giving—giving love and tireless watchcare to souls that are fallen and unholy… by gentle and patient ministry they move upon the human spirit, to bring the lost into a fellowship with Christ which is even closer than they themselves can know. (*The Desire of Ages*, p. 21)

Think of it. The angels are working to get you closer to Jesus than they can ever get. They love it; they are standing in line, waiting for the opportunity. How much we want that spirit of heaven! "They [Christians] should rejoice in the superior reputation or prosperity of their brethren, even when their own character or achievements seem to be cast in the shade" (*Testimonies for the Church*, vol. 5, p. 242).

Test yourself. The next time you hear someone praising what someone else has done, particularly in a line of work that you're proficient in, see if perhaps there rises in your heart the thought to tell something bigger that you have done, or at least to match it. It's very human.

Turn to the Gospel of John, and let's see one of the supreme examples of this. Oh, this is beautiful! The third chapter of John, verses 27–30. This is talking about John the Baptist, who was the forerunner. Who picked him out? God did. He was appointed for his mission. For a while, the whole nation was stirred and came to his preaching. Thousands were baptized. If John had announced himself as the Messiah, multitudes would have rallied to his standard. But he knew that he was just a forerunner, and he never forgot it. And bless his dear heart, he was happy.

Then comes Jesus, and true to his mission, John points the people to Him. In harmony with John's suggestions, they began to follow Jesus instead of John. Some of John's closest disciples go with Jesus.

How would it be to see people that we have put our lives into training quit working with us, and go off to follow someone who hasn't been around as long? That is the test that John met. "A man can receive nothing, except it be given him from heaven" (John 3:27).

Do you believe that? Well, if you do, you will never have to worry about what you are getting or what someone else is getting. Who is passing out the positions? God.

> Ye yourselves bear me witness, that I said, I am not the Christ, but that I am sent before Him. He that hath the bride is the bridegroom: but the friend of the bridegroom, which standeth and heareth him, rejoiceth greatly because of the bridegroom's voice: this my joy is therefore fulfilled. (John 3:28, 29)

In that time, marriages weren't contracted as they are now. Sometimes, marriages were arranged between the parties—there was someone who acted as a "go-between." John the Baptist basically said, "That is my job. Jesus is the bridegroom. His church is the bride. I am just the one who has been arranging matters. The bride is not for me. I have just sought to introduce her to the bridegroom. So, my joy is in seeing the bridegroom and the bride brought together."

"He must increase, but I must decrease" (John 3:30).

In some parts of mathematics, we have not only plus numbers but minus numbers. In his own estimation, which way was John going? But what did Jesus say of him a few months later? Of all those who have been born in this world, there has never been one greater than John the Baptist. Ah friend, this is what heaven values.

Will you be a leader for God? Will you let Jesus place you in the position of His choosing? Will you endure the necessary discipline in the carpenter's shop, in the home at Nazareth, in the wilderness with the sheep, with the plow, in the dungeon—wherever the providence of God shall appoint? Will you stay in the oven until you are done? Will you refrain from taking the sword to chop off the head of the person who is making problems for you? Will you help that person every way you can, even if he or she seems to be in the way? If your answer to every one of these questions is "Yes," there are not enough people on earth nor devils in hell to keep back one day of God's appointment for you.

CHAPTER 11

Succession and Apprenticeship

The following verses are in Paul's last letter to Timothy—the last thing we have from Paul's pen written from that damp, cold dungeon in Rome. He was longing to see Timothy before he died, and he sent for him in this letter. But fearing that he might not arrive in time, he gave such instruction as he felt would help him the most. Notice the burden of Paul's heart in these two verses: "Thou therefore, my son, be strong in the grace that is in Christ Jesus. And the things that thou hast heard of me among many witnesses, the same commit thou to faithful men, who shall be able to teach others also" (2 Tim. 2:1, 2).

As he says further in the letter, Paul knew that he was about to die. He told Timothy to commit to faithful men the things he had heard from him. What does it mean to commit them to faithful men? Give to them, put in their charge, and turn things over to them as a sacred responsibility. These faithful were to teach others.

Here we have four links in a chain. It can well be that the man who taught you the Gospel was taught by someone, who was taught by someone, who was taught by someone, and so on until you reach the one who was taught by Timothy, who in turn was taught by Paul.

One of the interesting things in the hereafter is going to be to trace our spiritual genealogy. You may or may not know the one who is responsible for leading you to Christ. If you do, you probably don't know who taught and trained that one. In eternity, that will all be interesting to study.

Christian leadership is concerned not merely with getting today's job done but with training the teachers of tomorrow. Every Christian administrator is to be a teacher. A teacher needs students (disciples). Paul was a teacher, and Timothy was his disciple. Did Timothy have some disciples? Apparently, he did. That is what Paul wrote to him about. And those, in turn, were to have disciples. You remember the great commission:

> All power is given unto Me in heaven and in earth. Go ye therefore, and teach all nations, baptizing them in the name of the Father, and of the Son, and of the Holy Ghost: Teaching them to observe all things whatsoever I have commanded you: and, lo, I am with you always, even unto the end of the world. (Matt. 28:18–20)

The margin says, "make disciples of all nations." In Spanish, "discipulo," coming from the same Latin word from which we get "disciple," is used to mean a student in a school. A disciple is not merely someone who is baptized and joins the church. A disciple is a follower who is following for the purpose of learning. Jesus' disciples were in that category. They didn't just sit in a pew and go through some liturgy. They were training with Jesus.

I repeat, this is one of the greatest purposes of Christian leadership. I want to study this with you, for you are a link in the chain. You are being trained by someone, I hope. And I hope that you are already training someone else. If not, you should be praying about it.

In the home where you live, in the place where you work, and elsewhere is someone who needs to receive something that you have. You are to impart what you have received. You are to teach what you have been taught. You are to share what you have been given.

Physically, we are descended from our parents, grandparents, great-grandparents, and so on back to Noah and Adam. There is an unbroken line. The fact that we're here proves it. Spiritually, we know that the early church did exactly what Jesus told them to do. They went out and made disciples, who in turn, made more disciples, who in turn, made more disciples.

As in the physical, so in the spiritual. In a given case, a man may be the end of the line. I hope it will not be so with you. I hope that you will have a number of people when Jesus comes, that you have not only won to Christ but that you have trained to have a part in God's work. This is not reserved for the professors in universities alone. You can be a trainer of men and women. This is Christian leadership.

We want to note some examples of this. Let's take an Old Testament illustration. God is talking to Elijah the prophet: "Go, return on thy way to the wilderness of Damascus: and when thou comest, anoint Hazael to be king over Syria: And Jehu to be king over Israel: and Elisha the son of Shephat of Abelmeholah shalt thou anoint to be prophet in thy room" (1 Kings 19:15, 16).

What does it mean "in thy room?" In your place. Elijah had a position; he had a job. Why did God tell Elijah to select Elisha to be his successor? Because God was going to take Elijah to heaven. I don't think Elijah knew it that day, but he knew, as all of us ought to know, that he wasn't going to be around forever.

God said to Elijah, "I want you to go back to the land of Israel. There are some things along political lines that need to be taken care of. But I want you to arrange for a successor for yourself. You are not going to be here always. There is a young man that I want you to anoint to be prophet in your place." It is interesting who this young man was. It is also interesting what he was doing: "So he departed thence, and found Elisha the son of Shaphat, who was plowing with twelve yoke of oxen before him, and he with the twelfth: and Elijah passed by him, and cast his mantel upon him" (1 Kings 19:19).

When he went to find this young man who was to be his successor, he found him plowing. I wonder, would you see any connection between plowing and being a prophet? God did. God picked out a man who was plowing. It is interesting that he was plowing with twelve yoke of oxen before him. That is, there were twelve teams of oxen out in the field. He was working as his father's stand-in. Doubtless, he was born and reared on that farm. He knew the business.

Elijah came along, led by the Holy Spirit, and cast his mantle upon Elisha. What is a mantle? It was his outer cover. We would say his "overcoat." What was the meaning of this? That someday he, Elisha, would inherit Elijah's work. He actually took that mantle when Elijah went to heaven. Elijah didn't need it anymore when he went up in the golden chariot. But Elisha didn't get it the day that Elijah threw it over him. Elijah used it for a long time after that. What happened in Elisha's life between the day when the mantle was put upon him symbolically and when he actually got it to wear? He went with Elijah.

"Then he arose and went after Elijah…" (1 Kings 19:21). That meant he followed him; he went with him. Elijah led and Elisha followed "…and ministered unto him."

This is God's way of getting a young man ready to take an older man's place. This is heaven's ideal plan of training—by association—the apprenticeship method. I hope you will become an expert in receiving it and in giving it. "The prophetic call came to Elisha while, with his father's servants, he was plowing in the field. He had taken up the work that lay nearest" (*Prophets and Kings*, p. 218).

If you wanted to pick apples and a beautiful apple tree was in front of you, you wouldn't have to go far. There are people who will go into an orchard and pick an apple here and an apple there and end up way over on the far side, always looking for better ones. But Elisha took up the work that lay nearest.

He possessed both the capabilities of a leader among men and the meekness of one who is ready to serve. "By faithfulness in little things, Elisha was preparing for weightier trusts. Day by day, through practical experience, he gained a fitness for a broader, higher work" (ibid.).

I want you to see a divine statement of a triad of great principles.

> He that is faithful in that which is least is faithful also in much: and he that is unjust in the least is unjust also in much. If therefore ye have not been faithful in the unrighteous mammon, who will commit to your trust the true riches? And if ye have not been faithful in that which is another man's, who shall give you that which is your own? (Luke 16:10–12)

There are three things to be developed during your apprenticeship period. They are mentioned in these three verses. The test mentioned in the tenth verse is being faithful in little things. If you are in the divine plan of education and training, you will be tested first with little things. And if you are faithful in the little things, God says that you will be faithful in much. It follows as day follows night.

You could learn arithmetic just as well with pennies as you could with dollar bills. In Christian leadership, if God is training you for a big job, He will train you with a little job. Do not despise the day of small things.

The next thing mentioned as a test is to be faithful with the unrighteous mammon. If you are faithful in that, you will get true riches. The unrighteous mammon means material things. It does not mean something wicked. It is something material in contrast to the spiritual.

This is represented in what we've studied about Elisha. He was busy plowing. Plowing is a material thing; it deals with materials such as soil and crops. That is what Jesus is talking about.

Jesus went through the same apprenticeship in the carpenter shop. He spent many years there. He was being faithful in the material things. Moses, who perhaps didn't get so much of that in his Egyptian training, had to take a special apprenticeship taking care of sheep (material things) out in the desert.

So, the first test Jesus mentions is little things to prepare us for big things. The second one is faithfulness in material things in order to prepare us for responsibility in spiritual things.

Oh, I wish that every minister and Bible worker could first have a successful experience in doing practical work. It's so important. We could use the rest of this book just on the reasons for that. But you probably know some of them.

The twelfth verse is very interesting. "And if ye have not been faithful in that which is another man's, who shall give you that which is your own?" Joseph was faithful when he was in Potiphar's house. He was there as a slave, but he was faithful. He took care of it just like it was his own. Finally, he got his own—a royal mansion, but think of how long it took.

You are first to be faithful in that which is another person's. As children, we grow up in someone else's home—our parent's home. If we are not faithful in the parental home, who will give us one that is our own? I'll tell you who will, the devil. He is busy doing that. He is busy rushing people into the responsibilities of marriage and homemaking who have never been successful in their parent's homes.

Unfortunately today, in many of the homes out in the world, there is not much they can learn from the cigarette-smoking, alcohol-guzzling, fashion-following, money-mad, status-seeking parents that they have. So, God in His mercy lets young people who really want to get the kind of training we are studying be in someone else's home.

Apprenticeship training is something that we must desire in order to get the real benefit of it. Do you think there were other servants in Potiphar's house besides Joseph who never became prime minister of Egypt? Probably many of them. Do you think there were some other prisoners in the dungeon who never got called out to tell the king how to run the kingdom?

Yes. It takes something more than an opportunity to produce the results. Joseph addressed himself to the opportunity. He was faithful in that which was another man's.

If you live in someone else's home, be just as faithful in it as though it were your own; someday, you may have one. In the ministry or business that you're in, if you're not the head, be just as interested in it and faithful in your work as though you were the head; you may be someday. But friend, the great reason for being faithful is not that someday you might be in charge. No, the great reason for being faithful is to be faithful for Jesus' sake.

Don't let your experience as an apprentice be like a young man I saw who could recite the exact number of days that he had yet to serve. It was evident that every passing day was lived in anticipation of the time when he could get out.

I usually associate serving time with a penitentiary. It's all right to long to get out of jail. But what we are studying is not that. It's the joyful opportunity of associating with leadership as link in the chain let down from heaven. Someone who was trained by someone whom God appointed is training me, and I, in turn, am going to train someone else. The good news is that we don't have to wait until we have been fully trained before we start to train others. Just as fast as you learn something, impart it. Just as fast as something is shared with you, share it with others.

This was represented in the feeding of the five thousand. Jesus took the bread, blessed it, broke it, gave it to the disciples, and right away, they started passing it out. And did you know that the food multiplied not only in Jesus' hands but it multiplied in the disciples' hands? Peter fed more people with his basket of bread than there was enough bread to feed them when he started out. I know that what we have received is multiplied as we impart it; I've seen it happen again and again.

You say, "But Brother Frazee, I don't know enough to impart the little I have." Then I will give you two answers. First, if that is so, then make it your business to get with someone who can teach you and stick to them like a leech or a cocklebur. Find someone who knows more about prayer and soul-winning than you do, and don't let go of them.

Elijah put the mantle on Elisha, and then what did he do? He went off. And Elisha ran after him and said, "Before I go, can I run back home and tell my father and mother goodbye?" Elijah told him that he could go back again and that he didn't have to go with him. Elijah didn't get down and beg Elisha to come. He gave Elisha a broad hint that there was a chance for him. And then he fixed it up so that if Elisha really wanted it, he would have to make some effort.

But Elisha was so responsive to the Spirit's call and the personal call of Elijah that he had a farewell feast and used the wooden plow to make the fire and the oxen that he was plowing with to make the feast. He was literally burning his bridges behind him.

I can fancy some people saying, "Elisha, wait a minute. What are you going to do? Are you going to kill these oxen? Are you going to burn this plow? What are you doing that for? Play it safe. Hang up the plow in the barn. Turn the oxen out to graze. You may be back in a few weeks or next year."

Do you know what would have happened if he had hung up the plow in the barn and put the oxen out to graze? He would have needed them. That is right. He would have been back. But he knew God's call and answered it and literally burned his bridges behind him. This is wonderful.

Do you know what he was doing when he went with Elijah? He ministered unto him. Let me show you an interesting glimpse of the life of Elisha. After Elijah had gone to heaven and Elisha was carrying on the work, there were some kings who were about to go into battle, and they decided that they wanted some counsel from the Lord:

> But Jehoshaphat said, Is there not here a prophet of the Lord, that we may enquire of the Lord by him? And one of the king of Israel's servants answered and said, Here is Elisha the son of Shaphat, which poured water on the hands of Elijah. And Jehoshaphat said, The word of the Lord is with him. (2 Kings 3:11, 12)

That was his reputation. Elijah had gone to heaven, but here is the man who used to pour water on Elijah's hands. It is a wonderful thing to be the son of a prophet. In a sense, we can all be that as we listen to the words of the prophet for this generation. If we follow the counsels of the Spirit of Prophecy through Ellen White as faithfully as Elisha followed Elijah and listened to his words, we can learn many things like Elisha learned from Elijah.

God uses the word "prophet" sometimes in His Word, not merely to speak of someone who sees visions but of one who speaks for God. In that sense, all of us are to represent the Master. Not that we can be inspired and speak with the same authority, but that which we have received we can share with others.

Elijah and Elisha, as they were in their work together, reestablished the schools of the prophets. The young people who attended those schools were called sons of the prophets. It doesn't mean that they were their flesh and blood children, but there was a relationship between the students and teachers like that of children and their parents. That is why they were called the sons of the prophets. They were being trained by the apprenticeship method. And Elisha had the special training of close association with Elijah.

"It was no great work that was at first required of Elisha; commonplace duties still constituted his discipline" (*Prophets and Kings*, p. 222). What are commonplace duties? Ordinary things. Doing them over and over. Sometimes I hear some people say, "I think I have been in this department long enough. I know all this. I do not have to do this anymore."

Have you ever heard that? Don't misunderstand me. There is a time to move and learn something else. But what did we learn from the chapter ten? If God has called us to something else, He will lay the burden not only on us but on others who have tested us. My point is that Elisha could have said after six months or a year, "Elijah, don't you think I have poured water on your hands long enough? I know how to do that pretty well. Don't you think I need something a little higher and more important to do?"

Back there, they didn't have washbasins and hot and cold running water like we have today. Water was in jugs. So, it was a nice thing to have someone hold the jug and pour the water so you could wash.

If there is still something you need to learn, God has someone that you can be with to learn that. And remember, one of your greatest opportunities to learn it is in doing little things. Press close to men and women of God's appointment that you can help; this is your glorious opportunity to learn. Nothing that you can learn in classes or by reading books can take the place of this. "As the prophet's personal attendant, he continued to prove faithful in little things, while with daily strengthening purpose he devoted himself to the mission appointed him by God. Elisha's life after uniting with Elijah was not without temptations" (*ibid.*).

We studied from *Education*, page 151, that all who render service receive a preparatory training in sorrow. Elisha experienced that. He had more sorrow when he went with Elijah than he did at home. Did that prove he was in the wrong place? No. He was in the right place.

My dear friend, you may have more trials in ministry than you had at home. That is all right. There are more problems in high school mathematics than there are in the second grade, aren't there?

> Trials he had in abundance; but in every emergency he relied on God. He was tempted to think of the home that he had left, but to this temptation he gave no heed. Having put his hand to the plow, he was resolved not to turn back, and through test and trial he proved true to his trust. (*ibid.*)

We are living in an interesting time. People think it's something new, but it's like the days of Noah and like the days of Sodom and Gomorrah in that violence fills the land. One of the big things on many university campuses is that the new generation (the "now" generation) is going to take over and do things. Well, this is not the way that Elisha was with Elijah. This isn't the way that Timothy was with Paul. This isn't the way the disciples were with Jesus. The greatest way that young people can make their contribution is by pouring water on the hands of Elijah.

God let me grow up in a home where my father and my mother trained me by association. They taught me the Bible at home. They taught me to work in the home. Then the day came when, as a young man, a minister put his hand on my shoulder and said, "Bill, come with me and get trained in gospel-medical evangelism." I had a training at Loma Linda in the classwork of medical missionary work, in the treatment room, in nursing in the hospital, and in a bit of community missionary work that we did in connection with that. But now this man of God said to me, "Come with me."

What could I do? I could carry his briefcase. I could run his stereopticon machine [a type of two-headed projector used from the mid-1800s to the early 1900s]. I could learn to go to the homes and make visits. I could help have prayer bands with the young people. I could go with him to meetings and help meet people. As I did those things, I learned to do other things by watching him and helping him. His name was Elder John Tindall, and the years I spent with him, oh, how I treasure them!

I will tell you the truth. I did not want to leave him. It wasn't my choice, but the time came when the brethren, including Elder Tindall, felt that it was time for me to go out and hold an evangelistic campaign by myself. We were in San Francisco at the time. That is where I had been trained for several years—first by watching Elder Tindall, then helping him, and then finally, they told me to go across the bay to Oakland and hold a meeting. But I was still under Elder Tindall's direction and training. The time came when the brethren asked me to move out and train some more folks.

I appreciate those years. From the day I went with Elder Tindall, I was starting to train other young people in what I was learning from him and what I had already learned in my former training. When all I could do was have a prayer band with a young man, thank God, I did it.

I think of a young man I met early in my training in San Francisco before I had held a single meeting, or before I had preached any sermons when I was in the briefcase-carrying, stereopticon-running stage. This young man was just a few years younger than I was, and as Elder Tindall had put his hand on my shoulder, I put my hand on that young man's shoulder. I had prayer with him, and he finally became my assistant in young people's work. For years he has been in the ministry. The Lord has given him hundreds of souls baptized. I could tell you of others. My point is that I know because I've been through it, what a wonderful thing it is to be trained by someone who knows more than I do. And I also know what a wonderful thing it is to pass on to younger people the precious things we are learning. We are told that as long as life shall last, we are to be both learners and teachers.

Are you doing it? Are you pressing close every day to someone (maybe several "someones") who can impart something to you? And are you also seeking opportunities all the time, not merely to say a kind word, that is good, but to actually lay hold of someone that you can train for God? The way to begin is with this prayer-band ministry. Teach someone how to pray. Teach someone how to claim the promises of God. Teach them what you know about fellowship with Jesus. Teach them what you know about soul-winning. You say, "Well, I don't know very much." The way to get more is to impart what you have.

Take a pipe. Whether it's full of water or oil, what is the only way to get any more in it? You'll have to get some out. There is no other way. This is it. This is an essential part of this training by association. This is the way Timothy was with Paul. This is the way Elisha was with Elijah. This is the way the twelve disciples were with Jesus. This is the way you are to be—one hand getting, the other hand giving. This is the life. This is the most wonderful thing on this side of heaven! Do you know that, even in heaven, we are going to go on with this program? Let me read you something wonderful here in the book Education. The last chapter in this wonderful book is called "The School of the Hereafter."

> In our life here, earthly, sin-restricted though it is, the greatest joy and the highest education are in service. And in the future state, untrammeled by the limitations of sinful humanity, it is in service that our greatest joy and our highest education will be found—witnessing, and ever as we witness learning anew 'the riches of the glory of this mystery;' 'which is Christ in you, the hope of glory.' (*Education*, p. 309)

If we are learning and witnessing there, then we just as well might have heaven on earth. There is only one way to get more. There is no way to lengthen the other end because heaven is going to last forever. The only way to get more is to start sooner. So, put yourself into this.

You may need more emphasis on taking advantage of your opportunities to press close to those to whom you can be a good apprentice. Or, you need more emphasis on taking hold of some other people and training them. Maybe you need both. But whichever it is, add it, and add it now. Will you do it? And remember, don't forget how to begin: "Again I say unto you, That if two of you shall agree on earth as touching any thing that they shall ask, it shall be done for them of My Father which is in heaven" (Matt. 18:19).

The way you begin is by finding someone who can teach you something. The way you continue is, in turn, to lay hold of someone you can help. And the way you continue still further is by multiplying the number of your helpers who are helping you help others to learn to pray and to learn to do things for God.

I don't know how many talents you have, but I do know you have one. I don't know how many people you can compass, but I know you can get your arms around one. If you will begin to pray with and train one in the things God has taught you, you may leave with God how fast and how far you develop and how much your capacities increase. Will you do it? God bless you.

CHAPTER 12

The Golden Rule

Let us turn to the Sermon on the Mount. We are outside with Jesus, and we are going to hear Him speak to us. "Therefore all things whatsoever ye would that men should do to you, do ye even so to them: for this is the law and the prophets" (Matt. 7:12).

How are you to treat others? If you are a Christian administrator, you are to deal with those under you the way you would like to be treated if you were the helper. Suppose it's the other way around. Suppose you are the helper, and someone else is the leader. What is the golden rule then for you? Help them the way you would like to have someone help you if you were in the leader's place. So, this is a wonderful rule, and it works in both directions. I would like to study it with you as it relates to both directions, but particularly in the direction of the administrator and his attitude toward those working with him (and especially in this matter of securing the cooperation of those under him with plans and policies).

How do you do that? In the military, does a sergeant always come around and explain all the orders to you and ask if you would like to cooperate? I don't suppose that is done a great deal. But even in the army, efforts are made to communicate to the people in the ranks something of the reasons for at least some of the decisions. Of course, some are military secrets. But there is a military discipline in which individuals are supposed to cooperate whether they see any sense in it or not.

And lest we miss the blessing of certain angles of that, I would like to read a statement that may help us. "What general would undertake the command of an army while the officers under him refused to obey until they had satisfied themselves that his command was a reasonable one?" (*Evangelism*, 647, 648).

If the prophet were talking here only about a military situation, would there be any point in putting it in these inspired pages dealing with evangelism? No. You will see how the application is made.

Here is a general, and he is going to give commands to a group of officers, but he has to wait until they make up their minds whether what he has told them to do is a good idea or not. What might the enemy do in the meantime? Kill them all.

What does it mean to undertake the command of an army? Then if a general were confronted with a situation where the officers under him refused to obey until they were satisfied that it was the best plan, what would he have to do as the general? He would have to resign. He would have to tell the government, "Sorry, I can't be responsible for this battle. You'll either have to get someone who can secure the cooperation of these officers, or else you'll have to discharge them and get some sub-officers who will cooperate."

> What general would undertake the command of an army while the officers under him refused to obey until they had satisfied themselves that his command was a reasonable one? Such a course would mean loss to the entire army. It would weaken the hands of the soldiers. The question would arise in their minds, Is there not a better way? But even though there be a better way, the orders must be obeyed, or defeat and disaster would result. A moment's delay, and the advantage that would have been gained is lost. (*ibid.*)

In the *Review and Herald*, the servant of the Lord says: "The Lord will have a well-trained army, ready to be called into action at a word" ("Go, Preach the Gospel—No. 2," *The Review and Herald*, March 15, 1898). I like that. They will spring into action as the call comes ringing down the line.

> Every good soldier is implicit and prompt in the obedience he renders to his captain. The will of the commander is to be the will of the soldier. Sometimes the soldier may be surprised at the command given, but he is not to stop to inquire the reason for it. (*Evangelism*, page 648)

When, in the course of life, should that soldier learn this lesson of prompt obedience whether he sees a reason or not? Before he was three years old. "One of the first lessons a child needs to learn is the lesson of obedience. Before he is old enough to reason he may be taught to obey" (*Education*, p. 287).

In a similar sentence *in Counsels to Teachers*, page 111, it says, "Before he is old enough to reason, he must be taught to obey." So, if you are a parent, before your child is old enough to even reason with, he or she is to be taught to obey. And we are told that the lessons a child learns before he or she is three years of age affect the child more than what he or she learns afterward.

One of the greatest problems in the United States Army today is that many of the men who come into the army have never learned obedience. That makes it very hard for the officers. I think this is one of the reasons that the Lord lets some people be in the army, hoping that there they will learn obedience.

Joseph was quite an obedient boy to his father Jacob, but he got spoiled just a little. Do you think Potiphar spoiled him any? They didn't spoil him in the dungeon. God, in His providence, was training Joseph for leadership, but he first had to learn obedience—prompt obedience, faithful obedience—day after day, year after year.

Dear young men and women, thank God for every opportunity you have to learn obedience. And remember this, the test of your faith in these principles is when the command goes against your good judgment.

Now we're back to page 648 of *Evangelism*. The word we use when we're inquiring about the reason is "why." It's a good word used at the right time and in the right place. But do children sometimes use it when it's out of place?

> When the order of the captain crosses the wishes of the soldier, he is not to hesitate and complain, saying, I see no consistency in these plans. He must not frame excuses and leave his work undone. Such soldiers would not be accepted as fitted to engage in earthly conflicts, and much more will they not be accepted in Christ's army. When Christ commands, His soldiers must obey without hesitation. They must be faithful soldiers, or He cannot accept them. (*Evangelism*, p. 648)

Now comes this sentence, and I wish you would memorize it: "Freedom of choice is given to every soul, but after a man has enlisted, he is required to be as true as steel, come life or come death" (*ibid.*).

Is this slavery? No. Because there is freedom of choice. But my freedom of choice comes when I decide to enlist.

Suppose I go to General Motors, and I get a job. I apply for the job; they don't come and grab me in the night. I apply, and I am accepted; I am given a certain job.

One of the first things that happens to me is that I'm given some directions. Suppose I say, "Well, I don't like those directions. I would rather do it this another way."

And suppose they say, "Well, this is the way we do it here."

And I say, "There is no liberty around here."

In that case, I could use my liberty again by leaving. I exercise my liberty in that case by either continuing to stay or choosing to leave.

But I want to tell you something. While I'm on duty, if it's only for one hour, I owe it to my employer and to God to do what I am told to do. This is vital.

Christian leadership doesn't sacrifice that principle at all. It gives us far more weighty reasons for recognizing this principle, for we are dealing not merely with honesty with men but with God.

This is what made Joseph so valuable to Potiphar. Of course, in Joseph's case, he was a slave. He had been sold there. But he still recognized this wonderful principle that he was going to be true to his employer and loyal. And God did bless him in it.

There is an exception to what we have just studied, and that is being loyal to the higher power. No supervisor, no foreman, no leader has any authority to give a command that contradicts a command of God. When David, the king of Israel, commanded Joab to place Uriah in the battle where he would be killed, was Joab doing his duty when he obeyed the king? No. He was a murderer. So was David. It was terrible. And we are told that it was a sin for Joab to obey that command. But mark you, not because it conflicted with his judgment, not because it was unreasonable, but because it was a contradiction of a divine law. Do you see the difference?

I have seen individuals whose idea of ministry is that we are all in this thing together, and nobody is boss. And that means that we all do "what we wish, when we wish, the way we wish."

You can have something of a picnic that way, but you can't get much of a job done. We couldn't build a house that way. We couldn't run a lifestyle center that way or accomplish anything constructive.

On a picnic, people can rest or walk, go down to the lake or up a mountainside just as they feel moved, when they wish, with whom they wish, and as long as they wish. And each person can chart his or her own program. Even at a picnic, there are some things that get done a lot better when there is cooperating, such as providing a lunch and all eating together.

Having established the importance of prompt and cheerful and whole-soul response to directives, I wish to come back to this golden rule: "Therefore all things whatsoever ye would that men should do to you, do ye even so to them" (Matt. 7:12).

"It is better to request than to command" (*Education*, p. 290). Notice what this doesn't say. It does not say, "Never command." It doesn't say it's wrong to command. It says it's better to request than to command. Notice why it says it: "The one thus addressed has opportunity to prove himself loyal to right principles. His obedience is the result of choice rather than compulsion" (*ibid.*).

I hope that you, as you have the opportunity to be an administrator, study how to do this. It's the study of a lifetime to request people to do things instead of ordering them to do them, and yet in a way that gets it done.

I have seen some people who were appointed to lead out in something, and the attitude was, "What do you think we ought to do today?" Or, "How do you think we ought to do this?" And the attitude can be so lenient that the people who are supposed to help them wonder what it is they are going to do and how they are going to do it. That is going too far in that direction. There is a nice balance on this thing.

Let's take an example. Jesus is on the mountainside. He has been healing and teaching all day, and there are 10,000 people out there on the grass. I want you to see the skillful way in which the Savior handles the situation: "When Jesus then lifted up His eyes, and saw a great company come unto Him, He saith unto Philip, Whence shall we buy bread, that these may eat? And this He said to prove him: for He Himself knew what He would do" (John 6:5, 6).

Jesus said this to one of His helpers to prove him. There is a time to do this, but it's probably a good thing to have "something up your sleeve." It's better to request than to command.

How easy this is. Take the mother in the home. Here is a daughter helping her. "Mary, would you hand the dishcloth to me?" I hear people sometimes say, "Would you like to do this or that?" Well, it's according to what it means. There is something in the tone or the manner that tells far more than the words used. But, as a rule, it's better to request than to command.

As I said previously, study how to do it in a way that doesn't sacrifice leadership. Study how to do it in a way that doesn't leave your helpers in confusion. Study how to do it in a way that causes them to want to respond.

In a certain school several years ago, the principal taught the students by his own example a fine little phrase that I think is still used by a number of them. When the students or the teachers were asked to do something, they would say, "I will be most happy to." Don't you like that? Yes. It's good.

This is something that, in some situations, we will have to pray a lot about. Some of us are naturally inclined to be very capable as an army sergeant to bark orders and expect things to move. That is not the way the shepherd works; that is the way the sheepherder works, and he has to have a dog to run after the ones who won't obey. In other words, some of us are going to have to kneel down and pray for the Lord to give us the spine to stand up and take our place as leaders.

It helps us appreciate what we have already studied that before we're fitted to command, we must learn to obey the obedience of love. I think that every parent needs to appreciate the value of, as early as possible, giving children some choices where the child is left to decide for himself or herself, even though he or she knows what the preference of the parent is.

Notice what I said and what I didn't say. I didn't say that the parent is to let the three-year-old child decide whether he will run out in front of an automobile or not. How foolish it would be for a mother to say, "Danny, I'm going to tell you what will happen to you if you run out there, but you'll have to decide whether you do it or not."

We see the folly of that. But there are dangers that are confronting sixteen-year-olds today that are just as perilous as the moving automobile to a three-year-old. And the sixteen-year-old is just as unprepared to deal with the choice. The freedom that is being granted to teenagers today is proving the ruin of millions. Behind it is the fact that the parents who should have trained them were not trained themselves. They couldn't communicate that which they never received. The world is breaking up.

You and I have been called into a program of education in which we are learning the principles of heaven's order and organization. To request instead of command doesn't mean that the individual who is requested is put in the place where if he wants to, it's all right, and if he doesn't want to, that is all right, too. The one thus addressed has the opportunity to prove himself or herself loyal to right principles.

What is to be expected then when a request is made? Loyalty. "If ye love me," Jesus says, "keep my commandments" (John 14:15).

One of the most important places in carrying out this principle is when individuals are asked to do certain things in taking office. In an earlier chapter, I mentioned that you may be on a nominating committee before long. But whether it is a church nominating committee or whether you are working in a committee in an institution that allocates people in their work departments, listen carefully to this. This particular statement that I'm going to read is something that Sister White wrote back in 1895:

> The work of God has often been hindered by men considering that they had power to say, "Go here" or "Go there," "Do this" or "Do that," without consulting the individual himself, or respecting his convictions as a laborer together with God. God has promised His presence to every believer; and let those who are in positions of authority, presidents of conferences and board councils, and everyone who has to do with the human mind, respect the individuality of mind and conscience. These workers are in copartnership with Jesus Christ, and you may interpose yourself so as to interfere with God's plans; for the human agent is under His special authority and dictation. (*The Paulson Collection of E. G. White Letters, p.* 398)

It has been my practice when I was chairman of a nominating committee or acting as pastor of a church, and the nominating committee asks a certain individual to be the Sabbath School superintendent, for instance, to go to that person and say, "Here is something that I wish you would consider and pray over and find out what you feel is God's will. The committee has voted to ask you to be the Sabbath School superintendent. We want you to pray over this. Give it study and thought. If this is what the Lord wants you to do, and He has helped the committee to see it, He will help you to see it. Pray and study, and let us know how the Lord guides your mind."

Does this take time? Oh yes. Another way to do it would be for the committee to read off its report on Sabbath morning, and the person finds out for the first time about it when he or she hears the secretary read the report. And, of course, he or she might, as a good loyal soldier, go along and say, "Well, if that is what the brethren want, perhaps I had better do it."

If I were the individual in that case, I think I would dart a prayer to heaven right there when the report was being read and say, "Lord, what do you want me to do about this?" I would expect the Lord to give me a quick answer either to accept it, decline it or say, "Brethren, I'll have to have a little time before I can give you a yes or no answer." As administrators, do what this says: "respect the individuality of mind and conscience."

As you are reading this book, you likely are going to have many opportunities to follow this. Study how to let the individual have a part in the decision that affects him or her as much as possible. Sometimes, it will try your soul. There are times when a tiny little tail wants to wag the whole dog. When an individual seems to be perfectly willing to let a whole institution stand still while he tries to get things worked out so he is working just where he would like to work. And so, there are real trials in doing it this way. The easiest way, from some angles, is just to send the word down the line as they do in the US Army, and the man sees his name on the bulletin board that he is to be shipped out, or the sergeant tells him, and that is it.

You say, "Brother Frazee, I thought earlier you read something about it being like an army."

Yes, I did. I read that first, so we could get some balance when we read some of these other statements. There is a balance between them. If we are good, loyal soldiers, we will want to cooperate, but if we are good leaders, we will want the individual to have some conviction of duty in his own mind.

I will give you an illustration. Many years ago, when our work was small in the church, there was a General Conference session held at Battle Creek. Early in that session, there was a call for a missionary to go to Africa. The General Conference Committee voted that a certain minister, who was a member of the General Conference committee, should be the one to go. He told the brethren in the meeting he did not feel any particular burden to go to Africa, but he would pray over it.

As the meetings continued day by day, he was praying that the Lord would either lay the burden on him or on someone else and cause the brethren to see light in it. It came near the end of the session, and this minister could never get the consent of his own mind that the Lord had chosen him to go, yet there had been no other name discussed.

One morning the president of the General Conference came into the committee meeting and looked across the room to a certain brother and said, "There is the man I think the Lord is calling to Africa." It was another man. This other man told the brethren, "For several days, a conviction has been growing in my heart that the Lord might want me to go to Africa."

It was an easy matter to rescind the earlier action and vote to have this other brother go. Was it worth the time in prayer and waiting on God?

This is a wonderful principle, but it becomes ridiculous when we have to go through something like that just to find someone to wash the dishes after breakfast. Any of us should be ready and willing to wash the dishes if it is needed. This is a thing we settle when we enlist.

In between the little detail of getting the dishes washed and the great major decision of who is to go to Africa to open up the work in a foreign field, there are all kinds of decisions. Every administrator needs to know how to give more time and attention to the weighty decisions, and we who cooperate should be in the groove so that thousands of tiny decisions go like the snap of the fingers.

If we have enough love, it is easy to do. But remember, the greater the importance of what is being decided, the more we need to involve the individual concerned. This is the point. "Let those in positions of authority and everyone who has to do with the human mind respect the individuality of mind and conscience" (ibid., abbreviated).

If you had been in Moses' place and asked the children of Israel to move into the Red Sea, and the Red Sea did not open, what would you do? This is the risk we take in following divine principle. The only thing I would know what to do would be to ask the Lord what to do next. Nothing that is ever done through love for God is lost. You can't lose if you are seeking to do the will of God.

"No man is a proper judge of another man's duty" (*Testimonies to Ministers*, p. 348). This is not talking about parents with six-year-old children. This is talking about adults dealing with adults. If I am the pastor of the church, I can tell a brother that the church would like to have him be superintendent, but can we know infallibly what the Lord wants this brother to do? No. All we can do is suggest.

Look at it the other way around. Can this brother decide by himself to be superintendent, whether the church votes it or not? This is where we get offshoots. They are not willing to submit to organization. But it is a two-way street. And just as the individual does not have the right to make decisions of this kind by himself, the organization is wise if it follows the wonderful principle and consults the individual.

Even if you are dealing with a student, learn the joy of going to them and saying, "Study has been given to this, and it has been decided to invite you to go to such and such a branch to play the piano or teach a Sabbath School class, or just help with your presence." Instead of walking off as though it is settled, it might be quite a big thing to that individual. How are they going to learn the principle we are studying unless they get an occasion to follow it?

Say to them, "Maybe you know right away as you look to the Lord for guidance whether you can do it, or maybe you need to take time to pray and study over it." It will not hurt, and of course, it comes back to the question of what you do if they say they do not think they should. You are tested on whether you believe in this principle or not. That is the thing.

I believe in it. If I know my heart, I would say to any church member or any fellow worker that when he is invited to do something like that, and he comes back after prayer and study and says, "Brother, I don't think this is what God wants me to do."

I would say to him, "Very well, pray with us that the Lord will help us to find someone else." That is all I would know to do. I am sure we either missed the signals, and the Lord never intended him to take that job, or else the Lord does intend for him to do it, but he is in no state of mind to accept it.

He may have to take a submarine ride with a whale before he is ready. But I am not the whale. The Lord will arrange that. The Lord may have to put him through some experiences where he will be glad to do what God and his brethren want him to do. But if he is not ready, far be it for me to put pressure on him, to twist his arm. No. That is not my business. Remember, we are in a laboratory.

We are not dealing with theory. We are dealing with principles that we can go out and apply day by day. We have a lot of changes to make in order to carry out these principles.

It doesn't mean when you are on the job and need to lift a beam, you say, "Men, go home and have a prayer meeting and decide whether it is the proper thing for you to help lift this beam or not." No, they decided that when they reported for duty. But it does mean when someone is assigned to work with you, you need to know that he or she wants to work with you. I would hate to be giving orders to someone who did not want to get orders. I would hate to be in that position. I would rather do it myself.

We started this chapter with the Sermon on the Mount. Jesus gave the golden rule, treat other people the way you want them to treat you. Here is a closing sentence: "There is to be no slavery. The service of all is to be cheerful and willing" (*Medical Ministry*, p. 178).

> *Thank God we are not slaves. We are servants. We are helpers. We are not regimented. We move in exact order like a company of soldiers, but we move by love, not by force of pressure. Oh, how happy it is to do what we are asked to do because we love the work and love the one who is directing us. What a joy it is to give directions because we love the work and love the people who are helping us. Love is what makes it move.*

"No slavery." Slavery is enforced servitude. Thank God we are not slaves. We are servants. We are helpers. We are not regimented. We move in exact order like a company of soldiers, but we move by love, not by force of pressure. Oh, how happy it is to do what we are asked to do because we love the work and love the one who is directing us. What a joy it is to give directions because we love the work and love the people who are helping us. Love is what makes it move.

CHAPTER 13
Christian Discipline

We studied these two reins through which God leads an individual. One rein is the direct guidance of the Lord as if that person were the only person in all the world. The other channel of guidance is through a group. The church is the supreme example of this. The family is another very important illustration of this.

In most things, the parents are the ones who tell the child what to do. They, in turn, are to get their orders from God. But the orders that the child receives from his parents, if the parents are doing their job, constitute the guidance of God to the child. The child is being guided, not through the first rein, but through the second rein. As the child grows, the wise parent more and more leaves certain decisions to the child. But as long as the child is in the home, he is supposed to be under that second rein. "Just as long as children are under the roof of the parents, dependent upon them, they should be subject to their control. Parents should move with decision, requiring that their views of right be followed out" (*Child Guidance*, p. 240).

The answer of some children to that is, "But you're forcing me." No, they are not being forced; they are being required to yield obedience. That is what God required in heaven. Did He force those wicked angels to obey? They made their choice. They could stay and obey or choose to rebel and leave.

I want to study with you the steps in Christian discipline as they relate to the institution, the church, and the family. You understand that we are not dealing with infants or little children. We are dealing with people of moral responsibility. As long as we understand that there are people who are capable of being reasoned with, capable of making their own decisions, and living with those decisions, then we will see how these principles apply.

The classic presentation of these principles is in Matthew 18:15–18. Here is God guiding both through the group and to the individual directly. But both of those reins are to be drawn by God. Unless God has something to say about what the group decides, that rein can't help us very much.

Having said that, I should point out that even civil government, when it's in the hands of wicked men, is used by God to direct. When they led Paul out and cut his head off, he submitted. He didn't fight with the executioners.

Someone says, "Well, it wouldn't have done any good." But he wasn't trying to fight. He accepted the will of God as God allowed civil government to act. He wasn't in a bind over it. He was getting orders directly from God to preach the Gospel. If, through the other rein, God allowed them to punish him, that is all right. That was up to God.

This is a happy way to live. Let God run your life directly and through whatever group you are subject to.

> Moreover if thy brother shall trespass against thee, go and tell him his fault between thee and him alone: if he shall hear thee, thou hast gained thy brother. But if he will not hear thee, then take with thee one or two more, that in the mouth of two or three witnesses every word may be established. (Matt. 18:15, 16)

The purpose of this visit is not to lose your brother; it's to gain him. The purpose is not to disfellowship him; it's to keep him from being disfellowshipped. So, if your brother has made a mistake, it's your privilege, and it may be your duty to go and labor with him. If he hears you, you have gained your brother. Let's take a cross-reference on this: "If any man see his brother sin a sin which is not unto death, he shall ask, and he shall give him life for them that sin not unto death. There is a sin unto death: I do not say that he shall pray for it" (1 John 5:16).

We do not know when people have committed the unpardonable sin. But notice the early part of the verse. Here is a man who sees his brother sin a sin which is not unto death. That is a sin that can be repented of and forgiven. He breaks the Sabbath, or he loses his temper. What can the man that prays for the sinning man get? Life.

Having prayed, where does the brother go? In John, he went to God. In Matthew, he goes to his brother. There is a little word of two syllables in

Matthew that indicates how many people are to be present. "Alone." Many times, things like this are told alone, but not to the one who made the mistake. Sometimes it finally reaches him over a certain vine. You have heard of that vine, haven't you? The grapevine.

But Jesus doesn't say anything here about the grapevine. He makes it very clear that we are not to use the grapevine. Go and "...tell him his fault between thee and him alone." You say, "But oh, I couldn't do that."

Don't misunderstand me. I am not talking about getting so angry at someone that you tell them off. That isn't what Jesus is talking about. Your purpose isn't to tell the brother off; it is to *gain* him. This lesson is one of the most important in Christian leadership. If this is neglected, all the rest that I have given you won't work. This is one of the vitamins. There is nothing else that can take the place of it. "Brethren, if a man be overtaken in a fault, ye which are spiritual restore such an one in the spirit of meekness: considering thyself, lest thou also be tempted" (Gal. 6:1).

Is it possible that the one I help today may need to help me tomorrow? Yes. And I am to help him today the way I wish he would help me tomorrow if I need it.

We all need this kind of help. I have been preaching for God for scores of years, but I still need this kind of help. I still need people who love me enough to come to me and say to me, "Brother Frazee, you said this or that, and I think you made a mistake."

I get this from time to time. I have friends who love me that much. If any of you don't think I mean that, if you want to try it with me, I'll be glad to listen to you and accept your suggestions. This is a vital part of God's organization in every institution, in every church, and in the church as a whole. There is no way for human beings, with all their mistakes, to work together unless we do this. The substitute is gossip, friction, misunderstanding, stress, tension, and disappointment. I don't like any of those, do you? But this is both the preventive and the cure for all of them.

If there is some friction, you who are spiritual restore such a one in the spirit of meekness. In *Testimonies for the Church*, volume seven, pages 260–264, there is a wonderful chapter on church discipline. You'll find many of the principles we are studying presented there in a most wonderful way.

Do not tell others of the wrong. Suppose you are the administrator and someone is helping you, but your helper doesn't seem to gear in with you.

What are you going to do? Are you going to tell other people what a bad helper you have? Go and tell him his fault between you and him alone.

This applies not only to the leader who is working for and under the group as he deals with the individual, but it also applies to individuals one with another. You don't have to wait to be appointed a manager or a foreman, or an administrator. In fact, one of the best ways that you can develop the gift of administration is by listening to the voice of the Spirit, impressing you to help someone that you see needs help.

You don't have to be appointed or elected to do it. Helping a soul is something that can come directly from God to you, especially if you are involved in the matter.

Suppose this brother and I are two helpers working together, but he gets on my road. He does things that make my work hard. An easy thing would be to go to the foreman that we're both working for and say, "I wish you would either let me work somewhere else or let Larry work somewhere else. He is getting in my road all the time. He makes my work hard. I could do more without him than I could with him there."

That is one way to do it, but that is not the way we are reading about. Suppose it's a roommate, and the roommate gets on my nerves. He leaves things around the room, and I like everything in order. It could be any one of a dozen other things. So, I go to those in charge and say, "Is there any way that you could put me somewhere else? It's just a pain to me." Can I do that? Yes. That's one way, but that is not the way we're studying about.

It's a wonderful thing to so believe in divine providence that if I am in a problem of that kind, I know that it's by God's appointment. The very thing I would not have chosen, God has chosen. God has deliberately maneuvered things to get that fellow and me together, on the job or in the room, or wherever. Why? To help him and also to help me.

He needs the help I can give him. I need the help that helping him will give me. And the more I hate to do it, the more it proves I need the lesson.

We may think, "Oh, but if the pastor would only go and talk to him, that would help. He would listen to the pastor. He won't listen to me."

I've got good news for you, friend. If we follow this direction that we have just read, we are told by the One who knows that in nine cases out of ten, the results will be favorable. If you can succeed nine times out of ten on this, and you don't know which number this particular one is, isn't that encouraging? If a colporteur knew that he could sell in nine out of ten homes, that would be encouraging. And even if the first home that he went to turned him down, he would want to get right on to the next one.

> It is not necessary to bring everything that needs to be corrected before the manager. When you see a worker in error, go to him and talk with him kindly and tenderly, showing a sincere desire for his welfare. In nine cases out of ten your efforts will be successful. You will save a soul from death and hide a multitude of sins. (*Medical Ministry*, p. 181)

Do you know how you will get the sins hidden? He will confess them, and Jesus will cover them with His own blood. Let's do this. With love, with prayer, with tenderness, and with wisdom born of the presence of the Spirit, make the appeal.

A brother came to me a while ago and said, "Brother Frazee, I want to talk with you about something."

I said, "All right." We sat down.

He didn't take thirty minutes to come to the point. He was nice about it. He said, "Brother Frazee, sometimes I think you make it hard for some of the people you work with. You take things out of their hands, and you are not as kind and thoughtful as you ought to be."

He gave me some examples of what he meant. When he got through, I thanked him, and we had prayer together. I tried to learn something from it. Don't you think I ought to thank the Lord for that? Yes. I thank the Lord for a friend who was willing to call that to my attention. It doesn't detract in the least from the value of what I am saying to you that when I went to one of the men that he thought had been offended by something I had done, I found that that particular man was not offended by what I had done and that what the brother had talked to me about, he hadn't thought that was out of the way at all. That isn't the point. The point is that God saw something in my character that needed that lesson. I thank the Lord for it.

If you are going to have a part in Christian leadership, either on the giving or receiving hand, cultivate an appreciation of this simple step. If you see something that needs correcting, go to God in prayer. If you do any *more* than that, go to the person who is making the problem. The average success of doing this is nine out of ten, according to what we read. What do we do about the one out of ten? At that point, we do one of two things. We either leave the matter with God or we take one or two more.

On the matter of leaving it with God is this statement: "If sin is plain in a brother, breathe it not to another, but with love for the brother's soul, with a heart full of compassion, with the bowels of mercy, tell him the wrong, then leave the matter with him and the Lord. You have discharged your duty" (*Testimonies for the Church*, vol. 1, p. 165).

There are times when the first step is all you take, whether you get results or whether you don't. If there is another step to take, if it's something that needs to be carried further, then: "But if he will not hear thee, then take with thee one or two more, that in the mouth of two or three witnesses every word may be established" (Matt. 18:16).

Notice what this text says. You know that when you're making something in the kitchen like trying out a new recipe, it's important to follow the directions. You might look down the list and say, "Well, now I notice there is some yeast in the directions. But I don't happen to have any yeast today, but we'll just stir up all the rest and hope it turns out all right."

Every detail is important. So, let's look at what this verse says. If he will not hear thee—that is, if he doesn't *listen* to you, if he won't accept what you say—then, not before, take *with* thee one or two more.

Are you to take them off in a room somewhere and tell them what a hard time you have had trying to help the man? No. You are to take them to the man, that in the mouth of two or three witnesses, every word may be established. Established to whom? To the one at fault, to the erring one. He is the one you are trying to help. He is the one who has to be present.

It would be an interesting thing if you were on the receiving end of this. Suppose here comes Brother Smith, and he talks with you about a fault that he has seen you do. But you don't pay any attention. A few days later, he comes back again, and he is got Brother Jones and Brother Brown with him. The four of you sit down together, and, for the first time, these two other brethren hear what the thing is all about. Does that happen very often? No.

Somehow, we seem to deal with the faults of people as if they were birthmarks or a wooden leg that nothing could be done about except to talk about them, of course. Tell me, friend, if you are on the receiving end, would you be glad if two or three would help you face up to your problem?

If we are really in earnest in getting the work done and in going home with Jesus to heaven, won't we want all the help we can get?

Now think of it on the *giving* end. You have tried to help a brother. He wouldn't listen. You take two others. By the way, would you take the man's *enemies*? Would you try to think of someone who might have an influence on him? If it is a matter that is between you and him, would you think through it and find someone who would back you up?

These are to be two or three witnesses. Witnesses of what? Of my effort to help this brother. They are to listen as I present the thing. They are to listen as he answers back in explanation, perhaps in defense. They are witnesses.

It could happen that, after hearing it all, they turn around to me and say, "Brother Frazee, we hear what you're saying, but really we think you are the one who needs help."

Should I be ready to get that help? Should I have people that I have confidence in as well as the *brother* having confidence in? If nine out of ten can be reached with the first step, there are at least some who can be reached by the second step. That wouldn't leave very many for the third step. But there is a third step.

Jesus gave the second step because He knew that everyone wouldn't get help on the first step. Why did He give the third step? He knew that everyone wouldn't get help on the second step. Did you ever in all your life have someone come to you about a fault and pray with you and love you and try to help you, and when you wouldn't respond, bring one or two other people with them, and they labored together for your soul? I wonder why God put it in the Book?

Have you ever once in your life gone to someone and tried to help them with some fault, and then when they wouldn't hear you, in love, you've taken one or two others with you and labored for that soul? Even once at any time in your life? Are those fair questions?

I repeat, this is an essential element in Christian leadership, and unless it is carried out, all the rest that I have studied with you will break down. "And if he shall neglect to hear them, tell it unto the church: but if he neglect to hear the church, let him be unto thee as an heathen man and a publican" (Matt. 18:17).

Suppose you were so bullheaded and stubborn that even after someone had come and prayed with you and wept with you, you held them off. Then they bring one or two more, and they work and plead with you, but still, you will not listen. And now they get the whole church and you together, and the whole church unites in prayer and pleads with you. Wouldn't it take an awfully hard heart not to be melted by that?

This is Christian leadership in the church, in the institution, in the family. These are the principles of God's government. Is this the way things went in heaven when Lucifer rebelled? God and Christ and loyal angels worked to try to remedy things and tried to help those uncertain angels to take the right step.

There is a final step. If the brother neglects to hear the church, let him be unto thee as a heathen. What does that mean? That his name is no longer on the books. He was in the group, but now he is no longer a part of the group. Jesus did not use this as a term of reproach like calling a person a dog. He simply means that he is outside the church. Don't we work for heathen and send missionaries to them? So that is what He is talking about.

Who put this man outside the group? He put *himself* out when he refused to yield to the united entreaties of the group. Let me illustrate it. Suppose we have a church of a hundred members. One member dies and is buried. The church clerk takes the name off the books, thereby recording the fact that has already taken place.

We are to understand from this that when the church takes action that we call disfellowshipping, it is simply recognizing the action that the individual has taken in refusing to yield to the entreaty.

> If he will not hear them, then, and not till then, the matter is to be brought before the whole body of believers. Let the members of the church, as the representatives of Christ, unite in prayer and loving entreaty that the offender may be restored.... He who rejects this united overture has broken the tie that binds him to Christ, and thus has severed himself from the fellowship of the church. (*The Desire of Ages*, p. 441)

Who severed him? He severed himself. You have heard of people getting up and walking out of a meeting. Perhaps they were angry or disgusted with what was being done. And the man who resists and rejects the united appeal of the church has severed himself.

> No church officer should advise, no committee should recommend, nor should any church vote, that the name of a wrongdoer shall

be removed from the church books, until the instruction given by Christ has been faithfully followed. When this instruction has been followed, the church has cleared herself before God. The evil must then be made to appear as it is, and must be removed, that it may not become more and more widespread. The health and purity of the church must be preserved, that she may stand before God unsullied, clad in the robes of Christ's righteousness. (*Testimonies for the Church, vol. 7,* p. 262)

Notice what Jesus is talking about in Matthew 18. He is not talking about Sabbath-breaking. He is not talking about using tobacco or drinking whiskey. He is talking about if thy brother shall trespass against thee. We speak of grievous sins. One of the most grievous sins is disrupting the unity of the church of Christ.

Our difficulty is that we are used to it; we are like a man who has a dozen bones in his body all out of joint and has gotten used to the pain. How wonderful it's going to be when the prayer of Jesus is answered, and the whole church is united as closely as He and the Father are one!

I am sorry to say, but I have to face the fact that there are those who, when this step is taken, may say, "Well, don't worry about that. As long as your name is in the book of life in heaven, you don't have to worry about whether it's on some church book." Have you ever heard that?

> Let none speak lightly of the duty of the church to administer censure and rebuke. Neither let them criticize the action of the church when this painful task becomes necessary. Christ has given plain instruction regarding the duty of the church toward those who, while professing to be loyal members, are bringing dishonor to the cause of God by their course of action. Every plant which my heavenly Father hath not planted He says shall be rooted out. God has commanded that those who prove themselves unworthy of church fellowship shall be separated from His body. Those who speak against the exercise of this authority speak against the authority of Christ. (*The Review and Herald,* March 19, 1908)

It is a serious thing to disrespect the authority of the church in administering church discipline, yet every now and then, we hear it ridiculed or censured. Someone may say, "Don't you think the church makes mistakes sometimes?" Well, I have seen a few parents that I thought made mistakes in the disciplining of their children, but I still think it is better for parents to exercise authority. There are cases where policemen have done an unwise thing and arrested the wrong man or beaten the wrong man, but I am not on the side of the folks who riot. I am on the side of law and order.

We are told by inspiration that the spirit of this age is the spirit of rebellion and is manifested in the church as well as in the home and civil government. Of all people, the remnant are to be outstanding in their loyalty, for it is written, "The dragon was wroth with the woman, and went to make war with the remnant of her seed, which keep the commandments of God, and have the testimony of Jesus Christ" (Rev. 12:17). They are commandment *keepers*, not commandment breakers.

This includes being subject to authority in the church and in the state. Now let me give you an illustration of this.

Elder A. T. Jones was a man that God used mightily in this movement for many years. He and Elder Waggoner led out in the great righteousness by faith message in Minneapolis in 1888. All through the 1890s, at every General Conference, one or both of those men were giving a series of studies. They went from church to church, and God blessed them.

But they had some opposition, and they had faults of their own that needed correction. Sometimes their brethren tried to help them. Sometimes Sister White wrote trying to help them. The time finally came around 1904 and 1905 when a break developed between them and their brethren. Jones was more argumentative and rebellious in spirit, and he led in quite a rebellious agitation, accusing the conference officers of being arbitrary and dictatorial. He not only lost his credentials as a minister, but he was finally disfellowshipped from the church.

He wasn't disfellowshipped for breaking the Sabbath, for he was still keeping it. He wasn't disfellowshipped on some moral or dishonest charge. It wasn't because he was stealing money. It wasn't because he was breaking any law of the land. He was disfellowshipped because he was opposing and casting reproach on the church organization and its appointed leaders.

I want to read something from Sister White in perhaps her last appeal to Elder Jones by letter in 1911. This is in the *Ellen G. White Letter*, #104, 1911. You can find some of this in *Through Crisis to Victory*. It is the story of the 1888 message and the work thereafter. In the appendix of that book there is a history of Waggoner and of A. T. Jones. In it you will find some of these messages. I want to read this to you, this last appeal of the prophet of God to this poor man who had people labor with him and the church labor with him and yet persisted in his rebellion. Listen:

> If you are truly seeking to become one in spirit and faith with the remnant people of God, if you will confess your sins and give evidence of genuine repentance and conversion you have the privilege of uniting with us. We should rejoice greatly if you would be really converted. The Lord will not receive you as a faithful minister to be trusted with His flock unless you throw your lot in with His people, to confirm them in the faith, not to rule them according to human ideas. If you wish to renew your covenant with God by confession and re-entrance and re-baptism, we shall rejoice with you. (*Ellen G. White letter 104,* 1911)

He had broken his covenant with the church. We are baptized not only into Christ, we are baptized into the church (see 1 Cor. 12:13).

> When you are converted, your self-sufficiency will disappear and you will become meek and lowly in heart. When you see and repent of your mistakes you will be a great blessing in helping others. If there is a work of reformation going on in your heart, if you are convinced of your error, we shall say the way is open. Come. (ibid.)

The dear Lord through His prophet was following Jones with appeals several years after he had been disfellowshipped. But the lesson is clear that the church had to take action. And remember that the issue was over the question we are studying—would he yield to the appeals of his brethren?

I heard one of our men who was present at the 1909 General Conference tell of the final appeal that was made. The president of the General Conference was seated on one side of a table near the pulpit, and Elder Jones was on the other side. They discussed things back and forth. The General Conference was in session.

As the president of the General Conference, Elder Daniels pled with that man, he stretched his hand out across the table and said, "Come, brother Jones. Come with us."

Brother Jones arose and started, then drew back. Elder Daniels appealed again and stretched out his hand. Jones started and drew back. Ah, my friend, what a sad thing it is to resist the united appeals of the body of Christ!

With many a heart, this problem is because they haven't learned this lesson in the home. I want to give you a reference on this same principle as it applies to the home. Remember, we are not dealing with infants. You can't disfellowship an infant or a child. That is why we have spanking. That is why we have a lot of other methods of disciplining youngsters. But you can't spank the adult in the church. And there comes a time when a child in the home is too old to spank.

> Some indulgent, ease-loving parents fear to exercise wholesome authority over their unruly sons, lest they run away from home. It would be better for some to do this than to remain at home to live upon the bounties provided by the parents, and at the same time trample upon all authority, both human and divine. (*Child Guidance*, p. 241)

I am so thankful that this is in the inspired volumes. I am sure that there are many people who have the idea that it is better to keep a young person at home at any cost, hoping that he or she will get some good out of it. But this says no.

> It might be a most profitable experience for such children to have to the full that independence which they think so desirable, to learn that it costs exertion to live. Let the parent say to the boy who threatens to run away from home, 'My son, if you are determined to leave home rather than comply with just and proper rules, we will not hinder you. If you think to find the world more friendly than the parents who have cared for you from infancy, you must learn your mistake for yourself. When you wish to come to your father's house, to be subject to his authority, you will be welcome. Obligations are mutual. While you have food and clothing and parental care, you are in return under obligation to submit to home rules and wholesome discipline.' ...Such a course would check the downward career of thousands. (ibid.)

So this matter of love in Christian administration is not some soft putty. One-third of the angels in heaven on this program of Christian leadership made the final decision and severed themselves from the group. Lucifer promised them a wonderful time, which they have been having for 6,000 years. But I don't want any part with them. Do you?

I love God. I love His government. I love His church. I love His pattern of home life. I am sorry for every rebellious spirit that I have had in my heart. Believe me, I know what it is. I have had it to contend with ever since I can remember. But I am so glad I had parents who were firm with me. I am so glad that I have learned in the church of Christ to appreciate more and more church organization and church discipline.

Remember that people make mistakes, but that gives no license for rebellion on the part of anyone. Let's learn these three great steps in Matthew 18. Let's learn to participate in helping other people to come in line.

CHAPTER 14
Counsel and Committee Work, Part 1

You will remember that when Jesus told the story of the talents, He illustrated the fact that some men have more and larger talents than others, but did He leave anybody without any talents? Everyone has some talent.

And so, in God's organization, whether it's in the home or the school, the church, the institution, there is a place for everyone. And, of course, what we all want is to find our place and fill it, and as we've already noted, there is no greater work for me in all the world than simply to fill my place. Isn't that right? Yes.

And, if we know what our place is and fill it and are happy in it, then there is no bribe that can induce us to abandon it and no threat that can scare us into leaving it.

Now, much of the science of Christian leadership centers on the relationship between a manager—those from whom he gets his orders and those to whom he gives direction. I want to study that with you.

Now, by a manager, I mean more, of course, than someone who bears that title. Everyone who makes decisions involving the spending of time or money is a manager. He may be managing like a man in the parable two talents, five or ten, but you take in an institution—whoever decides on the spending of money is a manager.

And in the home, whoever handles the buying of the groceries—if that involves making decisions of taking so much money and spending it for so many meals to feed so many people, that calls for what? Management.

A Sabbath school superintendent is a manager. He or she is taking the time of quite a number of people and organizing and directing the use of that time, so we might use many illustrations, but whoever is deciding on the use of time and money (either one or both) is a manager.

A manager gets instructions from someone. Every manager should get instructions, of course, from God, but in an institution, a manager is responsible to someone. If he or she is the head of the department, he or she may be responsible to the general manager or to someone who is assisting the general manager in oversight, depending on the size of the institution.

In a church, the chairman of the deacons, for instance, is a manager, but he is responsible to the church board, and he looks to the church board for direction. In a conference, a conference president is a manager or director, but he looks to the conference committee for direction, and so we might go on with various illustrations.

Now, just as a manager looks to, usually—unless he owns a business himself and simply is responsible directly to himself—a manager usually looks to a group, as we've said, but a manager has someone that helps him. He might have one, he might have a large number of people that he is directing that are helping him, and it's the manager's business to see that the time of those individuals is used to the best advantage.

You remember, Sister White tells the experience of a man who was the owner of a large mill, and he found one day as he was going through his plant, a foreman down making some simple repairs on some machinery, while several men that were experienced in that line, under the direction of the foreman, stood by watching him.

And after the owner had looked at it a while, he called the man into the office, after he had asked and was sure that he understood the matter, and he said to him, I'm going to have to discharge you. He said, "I can't afford to pay several men's wages to employ you to teach them how to be idle." He said, "It's your business to keep them busy. That is what you're employed for."

And in the book *Gospel Workers*, Sister White applies that to the pastor of a church. She says it may apply in some instances and not in others. My point is that the work of a manager is to direct those under him and keep them busy profitably for the good of the enterprise.

That, of course, calls for helpers who wish to be directed. It's a hard thing to direct people who don't want to be directed, isn't it? In some countries, they solve that by putting a bayonet at the back. It helps get things done. In other countries, they sometimes solve that problem by increasing the paycheck.

And so whether you beat the horse or offer him some corn ahead, either way, you may get him to move, but we've already studied that the great motive in the kingdom of God, whether in heaven or on earth, is what? Love.

It's a wonderful thing when managers direct the work in love and when helpers seek direction and are glad for it and respond to it because they love God, because they love the group, and because they appreciate the privilege of working with the manager.

It ought to be a privilege to work with any supervisor, any foreman, any manager, any administrator that has been put there by the Lord and by his brethren. Shouldn't it, friends? That doesn't mean that they're perfect. I haven't met any yet that are all perfect, but we're all aiming for that, and God uses men and women along the way.

Now, I would like to study with you about the relationship between the manager and committee work. Unless we understand clearly the purpose of committee work and the purpose of management, we may get confused. We may mix up the responsibilities, and we may think a manager is out of place because he or she makes certain decisions, or on the other hand, a manager may fail to make decisions.

I think I can illustrate this best by speaking of the matter of driving an automobile. Now, suppose we're thinking about having an excursion.

A committee usually plans an outing of this kind. They sit down together and study what day the excursion shall be and where it shall be and provide for certain key people that will need to take responsibility in various lines.

Now, among those responsibilities will be the job of getting the student body and the teachers to the place of the excursion.

Now, we might have a committee of three or five or more or less to decide where to go, and that committee might also decide who would drive, or the general manager or someone else might simply ask someone to drive, but my point is this. When you get in that truck, and the thing is ready to start, how large a committee do you want to actually do the driving? A committee of one.

But now, I want to ask you something. If you had people who were wise enough and experienced enough, wouldn't it add to the efficiency of the driving if you had one person ahold of the wheel and another one ahold of the brake, and another one with his or her foot on the gas? What do you think about that? Would you vote for that?

Would you get in the car? I don't think so. Would you accept the position of taking hold of the wheel if someone else had the brake and another one had the gas? You'd better not.

Now, that is so absurd that you wonder, perhaps, why I'm taking any time on it, but as simple as that is when you make it concrete with an automobile, it's very difficult for some people to grasp that when it comes to institutional work, and they see someone making decisions, and they say, "Well, why didn't he take that to the committee?" Why, indeed. Is a committee to be in session twenty-four hours a day or even eight hours a day to decide on the hour-by-hour things that have to be decided? Why, no. That is what we need what for? Managers. That is what we need managers for.

And I want to tell you something. A committee, as a committee, never does anything. All a committee can do is talk and listen and vote, and then someone has to take what has been decided and go what? Implement it, carry it out, and that calls for a manager.

For instance, on the board of Wildwood Sanitarium, we can sit down and decide whether or not to build a sanitarium. That may take a number of board meetings over a period. Larger groups may be called together for counsel, but when that is all been done, someone may lean back and say, "Well, now, that is fine. That is all voted now. Thank the Lord, we have a sanitarium."

But do we? Why, no. All we have is some drawings that someone made, and we have a vote committing the institution to do that, but who will build it? The committee? Not a bit of it.

Some members of the committee may act in building the sanitarium, but they will not act as a committee. They will act as a part of (to use a construction term) a crew—and when that crew gets there, will they have a committee meeting every morning? I hope not. No, no. That group of people will not get together and poll one another to decide on that particular morning who's going to drive nails and who's going to saw boards and who's going to do this and that.

That would be inefficient, wasteful of time, and also, in the very act of dividing responsibility, it would make it impossible to require responsibility. The board needs to be able to look to *someone* who can tell the board how much is being done, what is anticipated in the need of time and money, and when that doesn't happen, the board can say, not in any critical or faultfinding or mean way, but in a meaning*ful* way, "Well, brother, what about this? You thought that we could get this done at a certain time, and it isn't done. What is the explanation? What can we plan for the future?"

And he may come up with a very reasonable explanation. The board may accept it. Again, the board may have to say, "Well, now, brother, thank you for the effort you made. Apparently, we need a man who is a better manager who can accomplish more with a given amount of time and money, so we're asking you to step aside and let someone else drive." Do you see what I mean?

And that is no reflection upon a person's integrity or his Christian experience. Jesus, as I say, illustrated it very well when, in the parable, he pictured one man as receiving one talent, another two and another five, and you remember in the story, as Luke tells it, the man that had the most talents given him and improved them well—he was made ruler over ten cities. He became an administrator of a district, didn't he?

Now, don't misunderstand me. That doesn't mean that the man who has what we call a larger responsibility is a better man in the sense of being a better Christian. Neither does it mean that he is worthy of greater honor. Oh, no. If you study the record there in Matthew 25, you find that what the master said to the man with a few talents was just the same as what he said to the man with a larger number of talents: "Well done good and faithful servant; thou hast been faithful over a few things, I will make thee ruler over many things: enter thou into the joy of thy Lord" (Matt. 25:23).

So we're never to feel dejected or discouraged because we're not asked to take as big a job as someone else. Really, friends, it's a great blessing that we're not asked to take too big a job. Probably, the job we have will keep us busy if we look at it instead of looking far afield at some other thing. There is plenty to be done where we are.

But now, back to the manager in his relationship to the group that gives him directions and to the helpers that look to him for direction. The manager, I repeat, must be a man that is willing to make decisions.

Let's come back to the illustration of driving. Here now is the man driving the car. Maybe he has 30 people on the bus, and he is driving along.

Whose judgment must he use as he drives that car? He has to use his own. That is right.

Now, he may have some good drivers sitting in the car with him. It could be they're even better drivers than he is. They might venture a word of suggestion, but if any of them attempt to actually control the driving of the car, it would be much better for them to do what? Take the wheel because in an emergency, the man who is trying to drive under someone else's direction really is in a hard place, and he is liable to do the wrong thing and blame it on the man who is directing him, whereas the man who is directing him will blame it on who? The driver. Who is responsible? The driver, of course, and every administrator should recognize that principle.

If I have a helper and I direct him in what to do—in the details of what to do—then he is not a manager. I'm the manager, and that may be the proper relationship, see.

Suppose I'm laying blocks here, and I have a helper that brings me the mortar. Who is directing him? I am. If I'm the mason and he is my helper, I'm directing him. What decisions does he need to make? None, except to be there on time and do what he is asked to do in a faithful way. Is that right? Yes.

But, suppose now that I'm the superintendent, and I turn a certain wall over to an experienced mason, and I say to him, "Very well, Jack. I would like to have you take charge of building this wall. Here are three helpers who are to help you." And he goes ahead with that wall.

If I stand there all day long, telling him how to do his work, there is one man too many there, right? Either I need to get out of the way or he does. Is that right? And this principle of administration runs through all the work. So, if you are asked to take any responsibility in directing others, be sure just how much responsibility is being committed to you and then use it.

But now, suppose that with the amount of time, either your own or helpers who are committed to you and the amount of money that may be committed to you to spend—suppose in spite of all you can do, you haven't been able to do what you thought you could do and what others thought you could do. Then what?

I want to read you something interesting, folks. Now, this was written by the servant of the Lord way back many years ago, nearly a hundred years ago, and the men to whom it was written are all dead, but the principles are timeless and timely, wonderful, and they will help you and me to learn Christian leadership.

Sister White wrote this particular testimony to brethren A, B, and C. One of these men later became president of the GeneraC conference, but at the time that she wrote this testimony, he had had a bit of experience, but he lacked a great deal, and Sister White wrote this testimony. It's entitled "Leadership," which is another name for management. "The great reason Brethren B and C are at this time deficient in the experience they should now have is because they have not been self-reliant. They have shunned responsibilities because in assuming them their deficiencies would be brought to the light" (*Testimonies for the Church,* vol. 3, page 493).

Now, someone is going to get more help from this one sentence than from all the rest of the lesson. Let me read it again: "They have shunned responsibilities because in assuming them their deficiencies would be brought to the light" (*ibid.*)

They were invited to take a job of management of something, but, oh, they were afraid that if they took it, what would happen? They wouldn't do a perfect job, and that would show their deficiency. "They have been too willing to have my husband lead out and bear responsibilities…" (*ibid.*)

That was Elder James White. "…and have allowed him to be mind and judgment for them" (*Testimonies for the Church,* vol. 3, p. 493).

In other words, they didn't want to occupy this position. They were willing to help Brother White, but they wanted him to do what? Make the decisions and take responsibility.

Well, do you suppose that they reasoned something like this, "Brother White knows more about this than I do, and this is the work of God, and it's very important that we don't make any mistakes. So I'll ask Brother White. He knows, and I'll just do what he decides." Does that make sense? Yes, it makes sense from one angle, but it doesn't make men, it doesn't make managers, and when James White gets sick or dies, who is there to take his place?

That isn't all. James White is not omnipresent. He can't be everyplace, and the work of God is going to be quite narrow if one man has to make all the decisions. So God wants to multiply counselors, but the main way men learn to swim is to what? Swim.

Did you ever burn any bread? Yes. Well, that teaches you that you should never do it again. You should let the mother do it or the teacher do it because they probably won't burn it. They did their burning thirty years ago.

Back to our reference:

> They have shunned responsibilities because in assuming them their deficiencies would be brought to the light. They have been too willing to have my husband lead out and bear responsibilities, and have allowed him to be mind and judgment for them. These brethren are weak where they should be strong. They have not dared to follow their own independent judgment, lest they should make mistakes and be blamed for it. (*ibid.*)

I don't want to get blamed, and I'm so anxious to keep from being blamed that I won't use independent judgment. I'll get other people to make those decisions, and then, if it doesn't turn out right, I can just turn and say, "Well, of course, that wasn't my decision. Someone else decided that. So, of course, then, he is to blame."

"They have not dared to follow their own independent judgment, lest they should make mistakes and be blamed for it" (*ibid.*). But now, watch: "...while they have stood ready to be tempted and to make my husband responsible if they thought they could see mistakes in his course" (*ibid.*).

Ah, they didn't want anybody to blame *them*, but they were willing to blame the manager, and that very spirit of blaming the manager kept them from wanting to take any manager's responsibility.

Did you ever hear of a game or see it played where they have a ball or a bean bag, and everyone gets to throw it at someone?

Now, some people think that is what the manager's for—if anything doesn't go right, throw something at the manager. A variation of that song is, "Why don't *they* do something about it." "They," of course, means the manager.

And that is another reason that God wants many people to get experience in management. The man that is busy carrying his own responsibility doesn't feel very much like throwing something at someone else. Also, he gets an experience that enables him to be a good counselor.

Now, back to these brethren: "They have not lifted the burdens with him. They have referred continually to my husband, making him bear the responsibilities which they should have shared with him, until they are weak in those qualifications wherein they should be strong" (*Testimonies for the Church*, vol. 3, p. 493).

Now, let me hasten to add that someone may say, "Well, that is just what is the matter. I wish I had a chance to be a manager." Did you ever see someone that wished so much they could get hold of the wheel and drive? It happens quite often at about the age of fourteen. I wonder if any of us can remember when we were fourteen, and we just were so anxious to get hold of that wheel of the car and, of course, the accelerator and the brake, too.

And there are people that think they could do it and, occasionally, you find a fourteen-year-old that can. However, his or her judgment may not be the best, and the insurance companies recognize that, and they charge extra-high rates for that. You all know that, don't you?

So, we need a balance on this thing, and back to lessons that we had earlier, we can trust the Lord and our brethren to help us know when to accept higher responsibilities, but the lesson is on the importance of being willing to take responsibility and go ahead and make decisions, even if some of them are not the best and we get blamed for them.

"It is even more excusable to make a wrong decision sometimes than to be continually in a wavering position, to be hesitating, sometimes inclined in one direction, then in another" (*Testimonies for the Church*, vol. 3, p. 497). So, you see, the man who makes decisions is going to make some of them that are going to be what? They're going to be wrong.

I remember reading a number of years ago that Babe Ruth, who at one time was the great American baseball idol because he hit so many home runs, struck out oftener than a large number of other baseball players, but nobody ever remembered that. They remembered his home runs.

And remember this, friends, any degree of management that is given you, if you succeed, thank God, people will eventually forget your failures. But the man who fears taking responsibility because he is afraid of making mistakes is making the greatest mistake of all. Is that right? Yes.

God is looking, the church is looking, and every institution is looking for people who can make decisions and make a success of it. Remember, the two great things involved in this are how to use time and how to use money.

Some people are so thorough that it takes them forever to do something. I know a man who does nearly perfect work. But the problem is that there are all kinds of jobs waiting for his attention, but he will not be hurried, believe me, not at all. Whatever he does is going to be done perfectly, even if a dozen other people have to wait week after week after week for something.

So, we must be willing to temper that desire for perfect work with the importance of getting things done. We must be willing to take responsibility even though we make mistakes. We must be willing to make some decisions, even though they're not always the best ones, and trust God and our brethren to get us back in line if we get too far out of line, to remove us if our mistakes are too great, and we can start over again. God is at the helm, and He is leading people to a successful experience.

Now, I want to ask you a question. If individuals need to make decisions hour by hour and day by day as to the use of time and money, what do we need committees for anyway? To appoint the manager. To counsel the manager. To appoint helpers under the manager. To give general direction.

Now, there is where we need wisdom to distinguish between general direction and specific direction. We've illustrated it already a few times. We've indicated how a committee might decide where the outing was going to be. But, if the committee had to tell each person how to make the cookies and be in there in the kitchen to be sure that he or she put the right amount of each one in, that would be carrying committee work way too far. Wouldn't it? Yes. There is where we turn it over to management.

The committee can vote to build a sanitarium, and the committee can approve plans, but the committee will not sit there and draw all the little lines in the plan. Will it? No. But after they've laid general plans, someone will draw those, bring them back, the committee will look at them, and say, "What about this, what about that?" and that will be all polished up, the one who's drawing the plans will make new plans conforming with what is been voted, but when those plans are finally approved, again, the committee doesn't carry them out. That goes to managers with helpers, who, as a team, will carry it through.

Now, in administrative work, there is always room for difference of opinion as to some details, whether they go to committees or whether they are done by the manager. Never forget that. And no matter where you are in the thing, if you're a manager, no matter how many decisions you make, someone will think you should have made more, and someone will think you made too many.

You can listen to that as far as it can teach you something; you can weigh the matter, but never think that you can please everyone. Some people's minds run to having everything settled by committee. Some people could get along well, they think, without any committees at all, and they think committees are a waste of time, and somewhere in between is that middle road.

Now, if you are *really* in the middle of the road, you will get suggestions from both sides. There'll be some people that think you ought to take more counsel with the committee, and there will be others that think you ought to make more decisions yourself, so just live with that, and be prepared to live with that all your life as long as you're in this work.

Volume two of *Testimonies for the Church*, page 673, says that we cannot carry out exact rules if we meet the cases of all. Here is another place where we need managers. No committee can frame policies and rules that can take care of every situation.

One of the best ways of expressing this particular thing came from the dean of the Harvard Law School several years ago. He said, "My business is to break rules. Any clerk can keep them."

Now at first, that sounds bad, doesn't it, for the dean of the law school to say, "My business is to break rules? Any clerk can keep them." But this is what he meant. The law needs some human moderator that can deal with individuals and meet their needs and meet their situations.

Let me illustrate it. Suppose the college has a rule that nobody can register more than one week late. It probably has to have a rule somewhere, whether it's a day or a week or ten days or two weeks or thirty days—whatever it may be, there is a rule set there, and it's published. There it is on the calendar or on the bulletin.

But here comes a student, sooner or later, that has a very good reason why he is late, and there needs to be some officer of the institution that can sit down with that individual, examine his problem, see whether he has got the brains, as we say, to enter the course later than the ordinary time and still make it, see whether he had a valid reason he wasn't there, and all those things, and be able to do something about it.

Now, in that particular thing, the dean might have to take that back to an admissions committee, but here I come to another very important relationship between administrators and committees. An administrator is not a good administrator who takes everything to committees with no recommendation. All that is, is a clerk.

What do I mean? Take the case I've just illustrated. Suppose that all that is done is that a committee is called together, and without any study of the matter, someone reports to the committee, "Here is John Jones. He has come in a week late, later than the deadline, and he wants to be admitted. What shall we do about it?"

And there, a group of three or five or seven or nine or eleven people, none of whom apparently have been giving any previous thought to it, sits there and either make a quick decision without proper study or take a long time getting informed on it and arriving at a conclusion. One of the greatest ways that we can expedite institutional work is to bring things to committees studied beforehand and with recommendations.

Now, I'm coming to a few exceptions on this, but they're exceptions. In general, when committees get together, they need recommendations and plans, and the purpose of the committee is to approve those plans before they're carried out.

Come back to the building. Suppose now, we're going to build a lifestyle center, and suppose that a group of half a dozen people get together and sit there and try to draw the plans for the lifestyle center. Wouldn't it take quite a while? Yes.

Take farm work. Suppose that a group of people (I care not how many or how few) get together with nobody having thought anything about it and simply sit down and begin to plan what we're going to grow this year and where we're going to grow it.

Again, either plans will be made quickly without proper thought, or else a lot of time will be wasted in arriving at an answer. You can all see that, can't you? So, if you are a member of a committee or, rather, if you are an officer and you get your directions from some committee, remember, part of your responsibility, in most cases, is to have something ready to present and to recommend.

Take a Sabbath school council. Here is a Sabbath school superintendent. Suppose that he comes to the Sabbath school council and says, "Tonight we have this and this and this that we need to study," but he has no recommendations of any kind. He is afraid that someone will think he is a dictator if he suggests what ought to be done. So, to be very democratic, he just throws in the questions and sits there while the Sabbath school council studies that whole matter with no recommendation from him.

Is he a leader? Not a bit of it. He doesn't understand leadership. Leadership calls for making some recommendations. Now, if the leader does everything without ever counseling with a committee, he probably doesn't need a committee, and we all need committees for some things.

But, if the committee can do it without the leader, then they don't need a leader. You can see that. So, the committee and the leader each need to be aware of their responsibilities and, in most cases, the leader in a particular line is responsible for making some recommendations, laying some plans, and bringing them to the committee. The committee studies them and either approve them or turns them down or amends them, and then the leader can go ahead and carry them out.

Now, I mentioned that there are some exceptions. There may come matters to the leader that, after he is studied and prayed all he can, he still doesn't know what to do. He doesn't even have any recommendations. And a committee is a great help to a leader in a time like that if he can come and frankly say, "Brethren, I've studied and prayed over this. This problem is too big for me to even have a suggestion, but it's a real problem. It's something we've all got to face, and I bring it to you with no recommendation. I want your study and prayer and counsel."

Now, one out of fifty times or one out of twenty times or even one out of ten times that can work, but if it's every time or fifty percent of the time, we need a new leader. We need a new leader because leadership means making recommendations and having a committee to help counsel whether it should be done or not.

Volume three of the *Testimonies*, page 500—here is a picture of a strong executive, James White. Notice, it's right on the point that I've just been studying with you: "In the commencement of this work a man was needed to propose, to execute with determination, and to lead out…" (*Testimonies for the Church, vol. 3*, p. 500).

Those were the three things that James White did as the acknowledged leader of this denomination. What is the first one? Propose. What is another word for that? Plan or recommend. "…a man was needed to propose…" (*ibid.*).

What is the second word here? Execute. What does that mean? Implement or carry out. Who does he propose to? To the group, the committee. But after he is done it, he doesn't just go off and leave it with them. Whatever plans are approved and voted on, then he goes ahead and does what? Executes and leads out in both cases. This is a wonderful statement.

Now I want to add to that the duties of the chairman of the committee. The duties of the chairman of the committee are in addition to his duties as a member of the committee. I'm going to give you seven duties of the committee chairman. But remember, he has all the duties of a committee member plus these seven I'm going to give you now. Is the chairman of the committee a member of the committee? Almost always.

Number one. In some cases, the chairman is responsible for preparing and submitting an agenda. An agenda means a list of the things to be taken up. Sometimes, the chairman may ask the secretary to prepare that. Sometimes the chairman and secretary do it together. Sometimes the work of the committee may be so simple that it isn't necessary to make up an agenda beforehand. It's just one or two things, and those can be mentioned without having an agenda written out.

But where there are a large number of items to be taken up in a committee, it's a very helpful thing to have a list written out. When I go to the board meetings of various institutions, nearly always, I find that the chairman or the secretary has prepared an agenda.

Now sometimes, if it hasn't been done beforehand, the chairman will guide the committee in making up the agenda quickly at the beginning of the committee session. Perhaps he will write it on a blackboard so that the whole committee knows the items that need to be gone over so that they won't spend an hour on some little item and have only five minutes for the big ones.

Number two. The chairman needs to see that the matter before the committee is clear. If he is presenting an item, he will, of course, want to present it clearly. If someone else is presenting an item, he will need to satisfy himself that the committee understands what is being presented. If the committee does not understand what is being presented, the chairman should ask questions or draw out further information to see that the matter becomes clear to everyone.

Number three. He should keep the discussion focused on the point. We have a good statement on this:

> Let them not waste a moment in unimportant conversation; for the Lord's business should be conducted in a businesslike, perfect way. If some member of a committee is careless and irreverent, let him be reminded that he is in the presence of a Witness by whom all actions are weighed. (*Testimonies for the Church, vol. 7*, p. 256)

Now, whose business is it to remind him? Obviously, it is the chairman's business. Then, the chairman calls my attention to the fact that I've rambled off into some unnecessary or irrelevant presentation. If the chairman calls my attention to that, what do you think I ought to say? Do you think I ought to say, "Thank you"? I do. Remember, a chairman who would dare to do this would need some thanks.

Number four. Seek to keep the discussion on a high spiritual plane, avoiding any personal thrusts. The more people's hearts are in a work, the more they put themselves into the discussion of it, and the more they feel bad sometimes if someone differs with them.

And sometimes the chairman has to just kindly say, "Well, brother, sister, let's not say that in a way that makes this brother or sister over here look bad." Again, this brother or sister ought to say what? "Thank you."

Now, it's better to adjourn a committee than it is to carry it on in an atmosphere of strife. This following statement is a beautiful description of group study and group planning. Sister White is talking especially of the early days of the message when they were studying the doctrines of the Seventh-day Adventist Church:

> We tried to make our differences as slight as possible by not dwelling on points that were of minor importance, upon which there were varying opinions. But the burden of every soul was to bring about a condition among the brethren which would answer the prayer of Christ that His disciples might be one as He and the Father are one. (*Christian Experience and Teachings of Ellen G. White*, p. 193)

They wanted to come to what? Unity.

Sometimes one or two of the brethren would stubbornly set themselves against the view presented, and would act out the natural feelings of the heart; but when this disposition appeared, we suspended our investigations and adjourned our meeting, that each one might have an opportunity to go to God in prayer, and without conversation with others, study the point of difference... With expressions of friendliness we parted, to meet again as soon as possible for further investigation... We loved Jesus; we loved one another. (*Christian Experience and Teachings of Ellen G. White*, p. 193)

They loved Jesus, they loved one another, but still, they were strong feeling enough and strong-minded enough that sometimes they had to adjourn the meeting to go home and pray awhile before they could make progress. The chairman shouldn't hesitate to suggest adjournment under those conditions.

Number five, six, and seven are to avoid extremes of three different things. Number five is to avoid the extremes of talking too much or not talking enough.

Now, if you're a perfect chairman, someone will think you talk too much, and someone else will think you don't talk enough. But if everyone thinks you don't talk enough, better talk a little more, and if everyone thinks you're talking too much, better pipe down a bit, as we say.

Number six. Avoid the extremes of running the committee, on the one hand, or a non-committal attitude on the other. One extreme is a one-person rule—one person makes all the decisions. But the other extreme is for the chairman to take this attitude, "Well, I'm just a member of the committee, and I would rather not say what I think about this. Let the committee decide it." That is going too far in the other direction.

Number seven. Avoid extremes of too rapid decisions and too slow decisions. One of the important jobs of a chairman is to sense when the committee is ready to vote and, again, if you're a perfect chairman, someone will think perhaps you call for the vote too fast, and someone else may think, "I wonder when he is ever going to call for the vote." But, if everyone thinks that you wait too long to call for the vote, you had better speed up a bit.

Now, it's a good thing for a chairman to ask different members of the committee sometimes how you are doing. Especially if you're a new chairman and you're inexperienced, just ask someone. If you find that all they do is pat you on the back, go ask someone else.

In closing, I want to read from *Testimonies to Ministers*. This applies to everyone who sits on committees and especially to those who have management responsibilities:

> …the indulgence of a quick temper, a harsh, overbearing spirit, reveals that its possessor should not be placed where he will be called to decide weighty questions that affect God's heritage. A passionate man should have no part to act in dealing with human minds. He cannot be trusted to shape matters which have a relation to those whom Christ has purchased at an infinite price. If he undertakes to manage men, he will hurt and bruise their souls… Those who are thus misrepresenting Christ are placing a wrong mold upon the work, for they encourage all who are connected with them to do as they do. For their soul's sake, for the sake of those who are in danger from their influence, they should resign their positions; for the record will appear in heaven that the wrongdoer has the blood of many souls upon his garments… Brethren, treat men as men, not as servants to be ordered about at your pleasure. He who indulges a harsh, overbearing spirit might better become a tender of sheep as did Moses, and thus learn what it means to be a true shepherd. Moses gained in Egypt an experience as a mighty statesman and as a leader of the armies, but he did not there learn the lessons essential for true greatness. He needed an experience in more humble duties, that he might become a caretaker, tender toward every living thing. In keeping the flocks of Jethro his sympathies were called out to the sheep and lambs, and he learned to guard these creatures of God with the gentlest care… In working for God in this lowly station, Moses learned to be a tender shepherd for Israel. (*Testimonies to Ministers*, pp. 261, 262)

I want to learn to sing the song of Moses, don't you?

Dear Lord, we thank Thee that we can learn to take part in the counsels of committees and that we can learn how to make decisions and carry them out. Help us to be willing to do our best wherever in the army Thou hast placed us at the moment, recognizing that serving with the sheep and lambs out in the desert may prepare us for great leadership in the future.

Help us to be willing, like Joseph, to be a servant, even a slave, if necessary. Help us to be willing even to be unjustly treated, if Thou shouldst allow it, in order that we may learn faithfulness in how to be gentle and fair with others.

Make everyone here wise and strong in the wisdom and strength of God, for Jesus' sake, amen.

CHAPTER 15
Counsel and Committee Work, Part 2

Without counsel purposes are disappointed: but in the multitude of counselors they are established. (Prov. 15:22)

Where no counsel is, the people fall: but in the multitude of counselors there is safety. (Prov. 11:14)

For by wise counsel thou shalt make thy war: and in multitude of counselors there is safety. (Prov. 24:6)

Each of these verses stresses the importance of wise counsel. Could it be possible to get some counsel that isn't wise? Yes. And for this reason, these verses stress the importance of a multitude of counselors.

Someone has wisely noted that if there is wisdom in a multitude of counselors, it's not necessarily found in all of them. If it were found in all of them, we might not need all of them.

I want to study with you about counsel and committee work. Committees, of course, are groups of people drawn together to accomplish a certain purpose.

Now, in worldly organizations, the purpose of a committee is to find a basis for group action, and many people suppose that that is the purpose in the organizations that you and I are interested in, but that is not the primary purpose in anything that can be called a Christian organization.

The great purpose of any Christian organization is not to find out what the people want, it's to find out what God wants. That is the difference between democracy and theocracy.

Americans seem to think that patriotism and Christian principles are the same. It is a Christian principle to be patriotic, but that is not necessarily to believe that the form of government that we live under is the best in the world. There have been various kinds of government down through the history of the world. Daniel lived under a dictatorship. Paul lived under a tyrannical, cruel despotism, and yet those men found it possible to live under governments that weren't ideal and carry on the Lord's work.

Now, we do not need to suppose for a minute that the republican or democratic form of government is the ideal form of government. It may have certain great advantages as far as nations here in this world are concerned, and it has some very great disadvantages, too. As we see what is called democracy being tried by various nations on the earth today, some of the attempts, if they weren't so tragic, would be plain laughable.

God's government is not a democracy, and if anyone thinks it is, I invite you to give it a second look. I'm not in any way suggesting that this nation ought to change its form of government. That is not my thought. I am suggesting that we ought not to think that the church or the school or the institution that we are connected with is primarily and basically a democracy. It is not. It is a theocracy, and democracy means being governed by the people.

Lincoln, in the immortal words of the Gettysburg Address, speaks of this nation as a government of the people, by the people, and for the people. We'll go along with that. But that isn't the way heaven is run, and that isn't the way Israel was run back in the days of Moses, and that is not the way the Christian home is run. Does the father have to run for reelection every four years? No.

"Well," you may say, "yes, but in church organization, don't we have elections, and don't we have committees to nominate?" Yes. But just because we have elections and just because we have committees does not prove that the purpose of those elections and the purpose of those committees is the same as it is in the governments and institutions and organizations of this world. That is the thing I want you to see.

The great purpose of an election in the nation is to find out what the people want or who they want. That is what the voting is for. But in a theocracy, the purpose is to find out who God wants.

Go to the first chapter of Acts, and you will see that that is the great desire of counsel and committee work in the church. You remember that the twelve apostles (the eleven now, with Judas gone) were in the upper room, and a number of other disciples and Mary and the women were there. In verse 15, Peter stood up and talked to them, and he related what had happened to Judas and suggested that they needed to fill the vacancy. Peter outlined what the necessary specifications were, and then, in verse 23, they appointed two that seemed to meet those specifications, and then verse 24 verse says they… "…prayed, and said, Thou, Lord, which knowest the hearts of all men, show whether of these two Thou hast chosen…" (Acts 1:24).

Didn't they know who they wanted? That wasn't what they were anxious to find out. What did they want to know? They wanted to know who the Lord wanted, and that is what they were anxious to discover.

Do you think God is interested in that today?

> From these scriptures we learn that the Lord has certain men to fill certain positions. God will teach His people to move carefully and to make a wise choice of men who will not betray sacred trusts. If in Christ's day the believers needed to be guarded in their choice of men for positions of responsibility, we who are living in this time certainly need to move with great discretion. We are to present every case before God and in earnest prayer ask Him to choose for us. (Testimonies for the Church, vol. 9, p. 264)

"Well," you say, "what in the world is the need of having a committee, then, if God is to do the choosing?" Our text in Proverbs says that there is more safety where there is a number of people counseling together. But it points out the need for wise counsel.

One man that knows the Lord may know a lot more about the mind of the Lord than fifty who just give their own ideas. So, it isn't mere numbers that give us wisdom. But it is more likely that a number of people meeting in a committee (where each member of the committee knows the Lord and can pray and get guidance) can get a view of God's mind than if one person alone were making the decisions.

One would set it in this way, one in another, one in another, and yet God wants to use all of them if they will listen. And so, the word of one will balance the word of another.

Now, we're told plainly that in God's work, one person's word is not to settle things: "In counseling for the advancement of the work, no one man is to be a controlling power, a voice for the whole. Proposed methods and plans are to be carefully considered so that all the brethren may weigh their relative merits and decide which should be followed" (*Testimonies for the Church*, vol. 7, p. 259).

It's a wonderful principle of organization. Every committee, every board, in any institution that is being managed by the Lord needs to follow this principle.

We've just read that no one person is to be a controlling power, a voice for the whole. This is repeated again and again in the Spirit of Prophecy. Take this statement in *Medical Ministry*: "No one in an institution, not even the superintendent, should take the position that he is free to follow his own judgment in all things" (*Medical Ministry*, p. 166).

This is a great help to workers when they know that in the organization they're connected with, every person is under direction. Take even the United States Army. The private, of course, has to listen to the corporal and the sergeant, but the sergeant and the corporal have to listen to the lieutenant and the captain. The captain has to listen to the major and the major to the colonel, and so on to the general, and he has to listen to the chief of staff and the president of the United States.

"Well," someone says, "the president has the final word," but are there a good many things that the president would like to have Congress pass that doesn't always get passed? There are many things that he has to send his representatives to a committee and ask the committee to consider. So, even in the form of government that we have, this principle is recognized to some extent.

In the church, we need to recognize it fully because we're dealing with divine instruction, and no president, no manager, no superintendent should think that his election to the office gives him authority to make the policies and decide, "Well, all right, now, I'm president, so that means I'm a king." Oh, no. Jesus said that those who are great among you would be your servant.

I remember a number of years ago, hearing an administrator tell of an experience that came to him when he was a younger man and a member of a faculty. The principal of the academy that this man was connected with was having some difficulty in the institution, and the chairman of the board came to visit and counsel with him, and in the course of the conversation, again and again, the principal of the school said about the faculty, "They just won't carry out my plans."

And finally, the chairman of the board said, "Brother, it's your business to carry out the plans of the faculty. That is what your position is for." So, leadership is not for the purpose of telling everyone else what to do. Leadership is for the purpose of coordinating group action—carrying out the group policy.

Now, we've already stressed that what the group is trying to find out is what God wishes, but if the group is in touch with God, "…in the multitude of counselors there is safety" (Prov. 11:14).

The leader is the coordinator who takes the policies of the group and gives the signals that make it possible to carry out the group's plan. Someone has to give the signals. The whole group can't decide the exact minute that everyone is to lift the wall when the building is to be erected. Some leader has to say, "All right, John, take hold here, and Harry here, and George here," and so forth. And then say, "Now, let's all get in position. We'll give the signal, and then up we go." Now, that isn't because he is boss. Someone has to give the signals.

When the traffic light may not be working or when it's better to have a human being to direct traffic, the police officer on the corner will stand there and motion, and the president of the railroad or the mayor of the city may be waiting in line on another road, but the officer handles them all in that particular situation. He is acting for the group, the government. That is what presidents and managers and superintendents and supervisors are for.

When we think of these two reins through which God guides the individual—direct guidance and through the group—we must remember that many of the signals of the group are transmitted through an individual. They have to be. But that individual, if he is carrying on his work right, is simply the agent for the group, and the group is behind him, and they ought to be. But he must remember that he is the servant of the group, not the master, and yet—watch the difference in a theocracy, this is vital—no leader must ever forget the fact that behind and above him is the group, and in an infinitely most important way, behind the group is God.

He must remember that there is a line going directly from him to God and from God to him. So, in his sense of responsibility as the servant of the group, he must never forget that he is primarily a servant of the real leader of the group, and that is God.

That is where Aaron missed it. At Mount Sinai, Moses went up to the mount, Aaron was left in charge, and the people all came around. I don't know whether they had a formal committee appointed or not or whether it was just a consensus as it's called today. But at least the leaders of the people agreed, and they to Aaron and said, "Make us gods." Aaron apparently believed in democracy, and the people got what they wanted. They got a calf. And they were well pleased with Aaron.

If you had had an election that day, Moses on the one ticket and Aaron on the other, who do you suppose would have gotten the votes? Aaron, by a landslide. Did that mean he was right? Not in any sense. He was wrong. He was only looking so far. He needed television in the true sense of that word. He needed to be able to see far off. He needed an opportunity and the ability to get orders from heaven.

But when the organization is working as it should with those who sit on committees and boards who are in touch with heaven, then leaders can feel, not that those committees are infallible, but that there is, as we read here in Proverbs, safety. That is the thing. There is safety. There is more likely to be wisdom in a group of God-fearing people thinking and planning together than there is in one person's judgment. "No one man's voice and influence should ever be allowed to become a controlling power… The power to use and disburse the Lord's money is not to be left to the judgment of any one man" (*Medical Ministry,* p. 165).

So, in all these matters, we need committees of counsel. Since we are trying to find out God's will rather than primarily the people's will, prayer should be an important part of committee work.

> Let those who attend committee meetings remember that they are meeting with God, who has given them their work. Let them come together with reverence and consecration of heart. They meet to consider important matters connected with the Lord's cause. In every particular, their actions are to show that they are desirous of understanding His will in regard to the plans to be laid for the advancement of His work. (*Testimonies for the Church*, vol. 7, p. 256)

If we really feel this, I wonder, what will our posture be as we open a committee meeting with prayer? Did you ever attend a committee meeting in which someone looked at the watch and said, "It's time to have our committee, and so let's bow our heads and have a word of prayer and go right into our committee work"?

I wonder if that is a way to show deference to the King of the universe. It may be helpful to look up some references on posture and prayer. Let's get down on our knees with a deep sense of need when we come together in committee or board work. I could almost say, if committee work is so unimportant that we can't take time to kneel, perhaps we can just dispense with the formality of prayer altogether. If all we're going to decide is whether to paint the barn red or brown, maybe we could do that with just human wisdom, but if it's anything more important than that, and most committee work is, then we need wisdom from God. God might even be interested in what color we paint the houses and barns.

We are given some cautions in our committee work, such as wasting time in unimportant conversation: "Let them not waste a moment in unimportant conversation; for the Lord's business should be conducted in a businesslike, perfect way" (*Testimonies for the Church*, vol. 7, p. 256).

On the next page, we're cautioned against something worse than wasting time—being cold, critical, and hard. Then on the same page, we are warned against coming into committee meetings either worn out through lack of sleep or sleepy through overeating too many foods at one meal, or wrong food combinations.

Think of it, friend. God thought it important enough to send His angel from heaven to tell us what to do and what not to do on the diet question in connection with committee and board meetings. I'm afraid that if there is any point that is disregarded in our study on this subject, it's this point. Too many sessions of committees and boards are shadowed by luncheons or dinners or banquets that fill the stomach and deplete the brain.

> At bountiful tables men often eat much more than can be easily digested. The overburdened stomach cannot do its work properly. The result is a disagreeable feeling of dullness in the brain, and the mind does not act quickly. Disturbance is created by improper combinations of food; fermentation sets in; the blood is contaminated and the brain confused ...Some may ask, 'What has this to do with board meetings?' Very much. The effects of wrong eating are brought into council and board meetings ...A diseased stomach produces a diseased condition of the brain and often makes one obstinate in

maintaining erroneous opinions. The supposed wisdom of such a one is foolishness with God.... (*ibid.*, p. 257)

What a challenge to us in committee work!

...I present this as the cause of the situation in many council and board meetings, where questions demanding careful study have been given but little consideration and decisions of the greatest importance have been hurriedly made. Often when there should have been unanimity of sentiment in the affirmative, decided negatives have entirely changed the atmosphere pervading a meeting. (*ibid.*, p. 258)

Committees are apparently not infallible. The Latin proverb, *Vox Populi, Vox Dei* "the voice of the people (is) the voice of God," didn't come out of the Bible or the Spirit of Prophecy. The voice of the people wasn't the voice of God when they got Aaron to make that calf.

The indulgence of appetite back there went along with their idolatry. When people are eating the very things that God told them not to eat and eating in a way He told them not to eat, they should never boast that their decisions represent the voice of God.

An idol can be made of committee work. People can be given the idea that anything committees vote must be what God wants to be done. But this says that often, when there should have been a unanimous, affirmative vote, instead, a decided negative changed this, just because of what some people had been eating. Think of it! So, you can see that it makes a difference who serves on committees and what their state of mind is.

I want to give you a list of seven duties of a committee member, but the first one is number zero. You'll see why I number the first one zero.

Your first duty is to consider your fitness for service. Do you know why I number that one zero? You don't even need to notice the rest unless you pass that one. Do you belong on that committee? "Well," you say, "I must. They asked me to."

In our publishing houses, we have book committees. When someone writes a manuscript for a book, before it's printed, it has to go to the book committee. The book committee has to study that manuscript and decide whether or not it should be printed, and if so, in what form.

In *Counsels to Writers and Editors*, we have a chapter about book committees. It says there that some people shouldn't serve on the book committee, and if they were asked to serve, they should decline. That principle applies to any committee.

> Men have sat in judgment upon books and manuscripts, unwisely placed in their hands, when they should have declined to serve in any such capacity. It would have been only honest for them to say, 'I have had no experience in this line of work, and should certainly do injustice to myself and to others in giving my opinion. Excuse me, brethren; instead of instructing others, I need that someone should teach me.' But this was far from their thoughts. They expressed themselves freely in regard to subjects of which they knew nothing. Conclusions have been accepted as the opinions of wise men, when they were simply the opinions of novices. (*Counsels to Writers and Editors*, p. 159)

Someone's ears must have burned when they heard this. So, when we're asked to serve on any committee: nominating committee, labor committee, finance committee, educational committee, etc., our first duty is to go to God and say, "Lord, do I belong on this committee? Do I have what it takes to make some contribution to it? Will you give it to me?"

"Well," you say, "when you put it that way, Brother Frazee, nobody would serve on any committee." Well, if what I've just read will rule out anyone from serving, then we'd better not have any. Let's not throw the yardstick away merely because we can't find something that is three feet long.

If my appendix were hurting, I would hate to have some of you carpenters and plumbers get together as a committee and decide whether to operate or not, even if there was a multitude of you. I would say, "I'm afraid you don't belong on this committee." What would you say if it were your appendix?

In summary, the number zero is to consider your fitness for serving on the committee.

Now, number one. Prepare yourself through prayer and heart-searching, emptying yourself of pride of opinion: "Before our brethren assemble in council or board meetings, each one should present himself before God, carefully searching the heart and critically examining the motives. Pray that the Lord may reveal self to you so that you may not unwisely criticize or condemn propositions" (*Testimonies for the Church*, vol. 7, p. 257).

So, if I accept the responsibility of serving on a committee, before I go there, I ought to go to prayer. "Well," someone says, "won't they have prayer when they get together in committee?" Yes, but I, as an individual, need to go alone with God and examine my motives.

Oh, how different this is from getting together and having a sort of clique meeting where it is all settled before the committee ever meets what is going to be voted. I need to go alone with God and, in secret, open up the chambers of the soul to the searchlight of the Holy Spirit. God may point out some selfishness, some obstinacy, some stubbornness, some partiality, or some prejudice. It would be wonderful if I could get rid of that rubbish before I go to the board meeting.

Now, number two. Listen carefully and sympathetically to the presentations of your brethren.

That doesn't mean to agree with everything the person presents, but it means sympathetically to try to listen with an open mind and to get their viewpoint. Try to get over there where they are and look at it through their eyes. But it's possible for someone to just sit there and be making up their answers before the other members ever get through presenting their propositions. "Let nothing be done through strife or vainglory, but in lowliness of mind let each esteem other better than themselves" (Phil. 2:3).

If I really feel that way, I will want to hear what my brethren on the committee are saying. They will have my attention when they're speaking.

Number three. Express your own viewpoint. That is what you're on the committee for. Express your own viewpoint freely, plainly, and humbly. "… where the Spirit of the Lord is, there is liberty" (2 Cor. 3:17).

It's a wonderful thing when people can get together and do these last two things I've given you: listen carefully and sympathetically, and then feel free to express their own viewpoint, even if it differs from someone else.

I want to read you something interesting here from Elder McElhaney (1880–1959). He was for many years the president of the General Conference. He was a wonderful leader and a great administrator. He wrote a series of articles on principles of administration in the *Ministry Magazine* in 1938. The following is from the July issue of that year. On the point of expressing your opinion freely:

> Should a man's position in the cause of God be jeopardized because he has courage enough to express his convictions or to differ with a leader? I should dislike to think that this principle obtains in connection with our work… I sometimes hear it said that men fear to express themselves. They fear to differ with the leader because of the possible consequences it might have upon their future standing in the work. But I am more afraid of that feeling in the minds of men than I am of what men will say when they differ with me in expressing their convictions. I am afraid of any leader who will not fully grant his fellow workers the fullest freedom of expression. (*Ministry Magazine*, July 1938)

I've heard Elder Straw, who had done a great deal of administrative work both in conference and self-supporting work, say this more than once, "You know, the only reason for my being on a committee is that sometimes I have to say something that is different from all the others. Otherwise, of what use am I on the committee?"

So, when your time comes, speak freely and plainly. By speaking plainly, I mean, make yourself understood. And speak humbly because you might be wrong. If you carry out that other principle we read in Philippians, you're esteeming others better than yourself.

When a man knows he is right, it's sometimes hard to defer to others. If any of us have that weakness, it would be a good thing to keep a little notebook (you might want to lock it up somewhere) and write down the times you were mistaken. If, after six months, there are no entries in the book, someone might say, "See a psychiatrist."

I would say, "Have a secret session with the Lord and find out what is the matter if you haven't been able to discover any mistakes in your judgment in six months. You might call a committee of your brethren to counsel over your case. Ask them to be really frank with you."

Honestly, some of my most precious memories are connected with times when it was evident that other men had more wisdom than I did. That is one of the great joys of teamwork. That is one of the great blessings of having boards and committees. "...in the multitude of counselors there is safety" (Prov. 11:14).

I would hate to try to run an automobile on one tire and without any spare. Wouldn't you?

Number four. Vote your convictions.

When the time comes for the vote to be taken, you've listened to the others, and they've listened to you. You've expressed yourself freely, and they've done the same. Now, it's time to take the vote. Vote your own convictions.

Too much time is wasted in committees, and even one minute may be too much. It is wasted in looking around to see what someone else is going to vote.

Now, it's right that we should have a humble and unifying spirit, but when I vote, I ought to vote for what I feel is the best. It may be a compromise. I'm coming to that in the next point. I may feel that under the circumstances, we ought to vote this because of what this one feels or that one, but that should be my own conviction that that is what we ought to do. I'm not there as a "yes man" for someone else if I understand God's will.

"At this time God's cause is in need of men and women… who are sanctified by the Spirit of God and can fearlessly say, No, or Yea and Amen, to propositions…" (*Testimonies for the Church*, vol. 7, p. 249). I wonder why she puts in the word "fearlessly." It takes that sometimes to vote convictions.

Number five. Be willing to compromise on policies but never on principles. Compromise is not necessarily a bad word, but it's also not necessarily a good word. Compromise has to be done. Did you know that God even uses compromise? Oh yes, we see that in the Bible again and again. The people came to Samuel and said, "…make us a king…" (1 Sam. 8:5).

Samuel was downhearted, and he went to the Lord and cried about it, and the Lord said to make them a king. You might say, "That is a violation of principle." God let them have the king, and He told the prophet to go ahead and work with them on it.

Now, some people can't do that. Their conscience wouldn't let them do it, but God told Samuel to do it. Study the Bible with those thoughts in mind. There are times that we must compromise, not principle, but policies, plans, and methods. Unless we learn that, we can never do very much group work.

In heaven, everyone will be right on the line, but here in this world of weakness, sin, poor judgment, and dull brains, we have to do quite a bit of compromising in order to have success in group work. Remember, that doesn't mean to do something wicked, but it means that sometimes we have to do second best or third best when we'd like to do what we think is first best. Don't forget that God has been in that position for 6,000 years.

Someone can take what I've just said and run clear off in left field, but don't do that. Let's just stay right in the middle of the road, and that is where we are on this point. "…what power for good a little condescension has" (*Medical Ministry*, p. 172).

It's talking here about business transactions, but the principle applies in committee work.

Number six. Avoid the feeling of winning or losing when the vote is announced. Suppose we're going to have a committee to decide where to go for an excursion, and I want to go to the mountains, and someone else wants to go to the lake. Incidentally, if we carry out the principles we're studying, I will be more interested in finding what God wants for that particular day than what I want. But, as we pray together, I really feel that it would be better if we go to the mountains, yet someone else really feels that we should go to the lake. The pros and cons of it are discussed, and each person expresses his convictions and his reasons, and the vote is taken. It's four to go to the mountains and three to go to the lake. Should I be elated? "We won!" No, no. That may be a democracy, but it's not a theocracy.

On the other hand, suppose it's four to go to the lake and three to the mountains. Where do we go? To the lake. Four voted to go to the lake and three to the mountains. But I wanted to go to the mountains. Should I be dejected? The spirit of contest is not the Spirit of Christ. With Jesus, there is no such thing as failure or loss. So, in committee work, nobody has to lose. "Well," you say, "that is a mystery, Brother Frazee. What are you talking about? Didn't you just say it was four to three?" Yes, nobody lost. We all won.

Number seven, and this is closely linked with number six. Believe that God is ruling and overruling. Sister White was writing to a brother who was all upset because the publishing house hadn't gotten his book printed, and she says: "You speak of humbling yourself by having to wait for the sanction of the board upon your book" (*Counsels to Writers and Editors*, p. 157).

She is explaining to him why the book committee has to be careful, and she says this: "They have many difficulties to meet, and if they err in their action, the Lord knows it all, and can overrule all for the good of those who trust in Him" (*ibid.*).

I would never want to submit anything to a committee, and I would never want to be a member of a committee unless I believed this last principle because we're all just poor fallible human beings. And after we've done the best we can in prayer and study, committees are still limited.

So, after I've done the best that I can on the committee, I can accept the result, not with elation, if it is voted what I've recommended. I simply trust that God is ruling. And not with dejection, if it's something different from what I thought because I believe God is overruling.

Either way, our eyes are on the Lord. He is the One that is guiding His people. He uses the slow, sometimes awkward, and even bungling efforts of human boards and committees, but He is never made Himself entirely dependent on them. One of the reins through which He is guiding goes through these groups, but there is always a rein direct from Him to each individual. Never forget that He is ruling and overruling. "Above the distractions of the earth He sits enthroned; all things are open to His divine survey; and from His great and calm eternity, He orders that which His providence sees best" (*Testimonies for the Church*, vol. 8, p. 272).

CHAPTER 16

How to Start a Leadership

Unto thee lift I up mine eyes, O thou that dwellest in the heavens. Behold, as the eyes of servants look unto the hand of their masters, and as the eyes of a maiden unto the hand of her mistress; so our eyes wait upon the Lord our God, until that he have mercy upon us. (Ps. 123:1, 2)

The psalm compares our looking to God to servants looking to their masters. Servants look to their masters for directions. Is that what we look to God for? Yes.

Remember the illustration of the two reins. You and I, as servants of God and of our fellow men, are to be looking to God directly to know our duty, and we are also to be looking to those who, in God's providence, are placed over us. It shows us that we learn from this experience of looking to human leaders how we're to look to God. "…as the eyes of servants look unto the hand of their masters… so our eyes wait upon the Lord our God…" (Ps. 123:2).

The first human experience of looking to another human is that of a child looking to his or her parents. God intends in the ideal home situation that children shall have a very happy time in looking to their parents for direction. That should be a bond that unites them rather than a gulf that separates them. Isn't it too bad in an institution, church, or home when this experience that ought to draw us together tends to pull people apart—this matter of giving directions and looking for directions?

Let's review. Why are directions necessary? To accomplish what God has placed before us, does it take more than one person? Yes, it takes teamwork. But teamwork means that a group of people are working together.

And while God could have accomplished that by simply inspiring everyone to think the same thought at the same time, He chose to do it instead by having leaders in heaven and on earth to whom we look for directions. That is to give us experiences in love.

The leader gives directions because of love. He gives them in love. And the helper obeys and cooperates because of love. That is the program.

That is the way God's government is run in heaven. He intends that here on earth, in every institution, in every church, in every family, those same principles should be carried out.

Which do we learn first, to obey or to command? Obey. And until we have learned to obey, we're not fitted to command. One of the great things involved in this is mastering the science of love as it applies to this relationship. It's one thing to love people when we come to church, and they don't tell us what to do, and we don't have to tell them what to do. We just sit side by side in the pew and shake hands before or after the meeting. But it's another thing to be linked up in a program where seven days a week, you not only have to rub elbows with people but you have to either take directions or give them.

Dr. Sutherland used to say that a self-supporting unit is a Seventh-day Adventist church that operates seven days a week. I think there is something true about it, and it is a great test of our practical belief in this science of love to live with people. Not merely to live with them in the sense that we eat at the table together or worship together or study together but that we work together where we either take orders or give orders or both. That is really the test of love.

The world has an expression, "Can you take it?" The answer is that we can if we have enough love, and if we don't have enough, the place to get it is from Jesus.

So, day by day, we're looking to God and leaders for direction. Now, I want to ask you something. If, as a follower, I'm looking to someone for directions, what should that someone be doing? They should be getting the directions to pass on to me.

It would be too bad if I'm the foreman on the job, and here come a dozen or two or three helpers, and I have to stand there and say, "Well, I wonder what we're going to do today. Do any of you have any ideas?" The business of a leader is to lead.

To master the science of getting directions and then giving them in such a way that they are clearly understood and that our helpers want to cooperate with us in getting the task accomplished, that is Christian leadership.

If the eyes of the servant look unto the master, oh, how much more important it is that the eyes of that master look to God. The concept of the two reins only works as there is an actual spirit-filled experience in the heart of every follower and every leader having their eyes on Jesus, the great Leader.

Now, how do we learn to do this? The same way people learn to swim—by swimming. Is it a good thing to just throw someone in the water and go off and leave them? Is it a good thing to just jump in the water without anybody around and see what you can do? Some people have tried that and survived, but it doesn't prove that it is wise.

The best way to learn is with someone who knows what to do, who can show us how, let us do it under observation and with their help, and be there to correct us and to save us if we get in a bad position. That is the best way to learn leadership, dear friend. That is the way Paul taught it to Timothy. That is the way Elisha learned it from Elijah. That is the way Peter, John, James, and so on learned it with Jesus. Happy is the individual that can learn it with someone who knows more than they do today.

One problem can be that occasionally we seem to be linked up with someone that doesn't know half as much as we do. That can be imaginary, of course, on our part, but even if it's real, we can accept the providence of God and recognize that our heavenly Father is the manager of our situation.

When Joseph had been in Potiphar's house as a faithful servant for ten years, he doubtless had learned a number of things in such a way that he knew more than Potiphar. In fact, Potiphar seemed to recognize that. He left everything in his hands, and Potiphar went on with his government business. But being falsely accused, Joseph was thrown into prison. Nevertheless, Joseph was eventually placed in charge even there. Don't forget that Joseph was at the bottom when he got there. "His feet they hurt with fetters: he was laid in iron: Until the time that his word came: the word of the Lord tried him" (Ps. 105:18, 19).

Joseph was faithful, not merely as a servant but as a slave and a prisoner right down at the bottom. Did the cream rise to the top? Yes. In God's own time and way, Joseph was in full charge.

God is looking for all the leaders He can get. This denomination is looking for all the leaders it can find—lay leaders and conference workers. This institution is looking for all the leaders it can find. Almost every place is. "Ah, well," someone says, "if that is so, why do I have to spend so long just as a helper, as an apprentice?"

Now, that is a very practical problem, and I want to study it with you. I want to challenge you with something. Let me say first of all, election or appointment to a position doesn't give anyone ability.

Suppose that you were asked to be the governor of Georgia. "Well," you say, "don't worry. I won't." No, that is right, but just suppose. Would such an invitation give you any quality, attribute, or ability that you don't already have? Not a bit.

But my friend, that is just as true of some other situation or position. There is no election or appointment that can give you a single qualification. All it can do is represent someone's confidence that perhaps, with the blessing of God, you can do this or that.

Getting a position is like getting a hunting license. They don't furnish the deer with the hunting license, do they? No. You have to have the license to hunt the deer, but after you get the license, you still have to hunt the deer. You have to find them, and you have to take aim, and the results show whether you're a hunter or not.

And all election or appointment to any office is just a license. It's an opportunity for you to try your skills. Never, then, sigh and think, "Oh, what I could do if…." Remember, God is anxious to get leaders, but people are anxious to find leaders. If God is getting you ready for an important leadership, He will probably give you an important training, but "important" measured by Him.

He kept Jesus, His own dear Son, in the carpenter shop at Nazareth for at least twenty years. I don't think it was because Jesus hadn't learned to plane, saw, or nail. But He was learning obedience in the daily round of common toil. He was fixing in His character that wonderful trait of cooperation with those over Him.

He went down to Nazareth and was " …subject unto them…" (Luke 2:51). He was in that condition of being subject until He was thirty years old. Moses got started in that program when he was forty. He'd been used to commanding the armies of Egypt. People jumped around when he spoke, but God undertook his training and made him an assistant shepherd. Did the sheep jump when he barked? No. He had to learn to nurse and be gentle to them. God kept him in that for forty years until Moses despaired of ever doing anything except that, but that was all right.

No angel came around and gave him a pep talk every few weeks and said, "Well, don't worry, Moses. Someday you're going to be great." No. We're told that after he had followed those sheep around for a while, no longer did he plan to do a great work. He just thought to do faithfully the work that God had assigned him to do. That is all.

One of the greatest lessons you and I have to learn, whether we're thirteen, thirty, or eighty, is to be happy in doing our best in what looks to us like a little job. That is it. Oh, I want to learn that! Don't you? But that is God's training for leadership.

"And if ye have not been faithful in that which is another man's, who shall give you that which is your own?" (Luke 16:12). Was that Jesus' carpenter shop in Nazareth? It was Joseph's, and Jesus was faithful. By learning to be faithful in that carpenter shop that belonged to Joseph, Jesus became the Builder of the church of God, who assembled the parts of this wonderful earthly building in which the heavenly glory is to be revealed.

You and I are to be faithful first in someone else's shop, someone else's lifestyle center, someone else's farm, someone else's home, someone else's schoolroom, someone else's something. We are to learn to be faithful as assistants before we become leaders.

I feel so sorry for the young person that is so restless in his father's house that he has to get out and get married so he can have a home of his own and do as he pleases. That is behind a large share of the marriages that are taking place today, and that restless discontent is a poor foundation on which to build a home.

Oh, how sweet it is when a young man or a young woman is happy to make the home in which they are children and youth a successful one. "Ah but," someone says, "you don't know my father and mother." No, but probably, you don't, either. But God knows them, and He knows you. He knows all about it.

And dear one, that wonderful ideal which you have of how everything would be peaches and cream if you could only get out and run it yourself is going to have some of the same problems that you don't know what to do with where you are. You may think that the reason you don't know what to do with those problems is that you don't have hold of the wheel, but my text says: "...if ye have not been faithful in that which is another man's, who shall give you that which is your own?" (Luke 16:12).

When students come to an institution, do they ever think, "I wonder why they do this around here, or I wonder why they don't do this? Oh my, if I can ever get through this thing and get out, there are some things I'm going to do." Right here where you are is a laboratory where you can learn how to get something accomplished and how to solve problems. The institution you're going to establish someday won't have any problems, or will it? "...If ye have not been faithful in that which is another man's, who shall give you that which is your own?" (Luke 16:12).

Dear one, the challenge to me, to you, to all of us, is to be faithful in helping someone else work out his or her problems. "Ah," but someone says, "I would be glad to if they'd let me." The first thing is prayer life. That is what Elijah learned out in the mountains of Gilead, isn't it? That is what Moses learned in the deserts of Midian. That is what Jesus learned on the mountainside at Nazareth. That is what John the Baptist learned in the hills of Judea—prayer, prayer, prayer, as the way to solve problems.

In each of those four examples I have mentioned, it took prayer over a long period to solve the problems with which those men were grappling. So, as an assistant, do not think, "Well, all I can do now is put in my time. Someday, I'll have a chance." This is not a penitentiary. You're not serving a sentence or just putting in time. You're developing an experience. An experience is not a matter of putting in so many months or years. It is a matter of coming to the place where you and God together can solve human problems, for that is what every Seventh-day Adventist institution and home is for.

I have visitors that have a suggestion or two for me. They come and stay for a few hours or days. Sometimes I ask them for suggestions, but occasionally, the setting is such that it is appropriate for me to tell them that besides all the things they see that need correction, I know quite a list more that they didn't notice. And, of course, if they haven't had any experience in administration, what they're thinking is, "Well then, why don't you do something about it?"

We are not computers. It takes more than pushing some buttons to get something done. One of the great reasons why some problems aren't yet solved is that we are working on some others that have to be solved before those others can be solved. And fortunately, that means that there is some laboratory material for you and me with which to work. Do you know what would have to happen if the place you are in should suddenly become perfect overnight? I know at least one man that the Lord would move somewhere else. It's me. I need the discipline of having to deal with problems brought about by the imperfection of other human beings. That is why God put me where I am. I need that experience. You need it. That is why you're where you are.

Do you remember those stones that David selected to use on the giant? What kind of stones were they? Smooth stones. Why smooth? So they could go out of that sling and to the mark without being diverted. He got them out of a brook. Why out of the brook? The water had been just rubbing those rocks together for hundreds of years, rock on rock, pebble on pebble, until now they were smooth. David knew where to get smooth stones. He'd been over those brooks many times.

When God looks for a smooth stone to put in his sling to use on His great enemy in this closing conflict, He is going to go to a brook where human lives and human hearts have been rubbed together for long enough to make them smooth. I want to learn my lesson. Don't you?

I would like to challenge you with the thought of taking hold of problems right where you are. Do you want to be a leader? Why not go ahead and start? How do you begin? There are two things. Begin with prayer, and begin with one. When I say, "Begin with prayer," I'm referring to the method. When I say, "Begin with one," I'm referring to the number. If God has called you to be a leader, He is going to have you begin by learning to lead one person.

There are people who can give orders to a hundred who don't know how to lead one. It's much more embarrassing to try to lead one than it is to command a hundred. Perhaps it is because if you're telling a hundred, you can give your orders and go off somewhere while they try to do it, but if you're leading one, you have to stay there with them and show them how to do it. God wants you to begin with one.

Let me make a very practical application of this. There are many areas in which we may lead. We may lead in practical work like gardening or cooking or something like that. We might lead in teaching something. But I want to touch something that everyone can do right now, and if you do it, it will eventually lead to many other experiences.

"Again I say unto you, That if two of you shall agree on earth as touching any thing that they shall ask, it shall be done for them of my father which is in heaven" (Matt. 18:19). What unit of organization do you see here in this verse? It's a prayer band with two. One gets the burden, and he prays to God and says, "Lord, give me someone to pray with, as well as someone to pray for." Is that right? Well, that one that gets the burden and says to another, "Will you come with me and pray?" Or, "May I come with you and pray?" The one that suggests that is a prayer band leader. He has gotten someone else to agree. "Can two walk together, except they be agreed?" (Amos 3:3).

One of the greatest things in leadership is to just get some folks to agree with you about getting something done. Prayer is the experience in which to learn that. When two have prayed together about something, then they're ready to get up and do something about it together.

Jesus didn't say that if you can get a dozen people to agree, then this and this will happen. He just said, "two." I think there are a number of reasons why He said just two. One is that that puts the responsibility right back on me personally. This is something I can't say, "Let Jordan do it."

There is another reason. I can never get a dozen people to agree with me until I have gotten one to agree. By the laws of numbers, one comes before two and two before three and three before four, and so on. There is no way to get a dozen and bypass that first addition of one. In the business of leadership, if someday you may lead a thousand people, you're going to begin by leading one.

I've had the privilege, and I say this humbly to the glory of God, of speaking to thousands of people in the last forty years for God. But there is a memory I've mentioned earlier that I want to share with you in more detail. As a fourteen-year-old boy at a summer camp meeting, listening to Elder Meade Maguire, I had given my heart to God in a new consecration, and I wanted to do something for Jesus. I had heard Elder Luther Warren talk about this simple prayer band work. One morning when I was praying, I thought about a boy who was in school with me, whose name was Robert.

After breakfast, before school started, I walked down the road in the direction from which Robert would come, and I met him and I talked to him about meeting together with me from day to day and praying for some of the other boys.

If I were to pick out a moment when an experience in Christian leadership began, I would put it right there. As I look back at it now, I can see that that experience was fraught with infinite potential and that if I had missed it, I would never been in this work. I don't know what I would be doing, but I wouldn't be doing this.

That year, I learned some things about getting other people to agree. Robert and I met together in prayer band day by day, and pretty soon, he had a friend named Irvin whom he invited, and the three of us met together. Then, we got another boy. I said, "Let's divide. Let's go back to two and two." So, I kept one of the boys, Irvin took the other boy, and we had two bands. Then, pretty soon, we had another band, and another. Then the Lord helped me to suggest getting the prayer band leaders together once a week and have a meeting. We did that. I had my little army.

No one urged those bands on me but God. He laid it on my heart. I wasn't perfect, of course. I was just an awkward, bungling fellow, but God had helped me to get hold of a few references. Really, I was better off not knowing a lot of things, if you understand what I mean. I just knew a few things, and so I did those few things.

I knew that God wanted me to get hold of one boy and the two of us pray together for someone else. Then, when we got hold of that boy and had him praying with us for some more boys, we just kept multiplying and dividing and dividing and multiplying.

It was a fairly large school, but before the school year was over, we had over half the school in prayer bands. Week by week, I had this little prayer band staff meeting. I was getting an experience in leading leaders.

No one assigned that to me. It just grew, and it all started with that morning walk down the road to see Robert. It started there, but it could have stopped there, too. It took dedication day after day, week after week, week in and week out. "…this one thing I do…" (Phil. 3:13).

As you read this, you may get hold of something. You may have heard some of these things before or are hearing them for the first time, but whether it's the first time or the tenth time, my dear friend, what are you doing about this particular point? Do you have a little prayer band? Are you a helper to someone else who's leading in a prayer band? If you are, the two of you should be reaching out for someone else and someone else. As soon as you have two "someone else's," it's time for you to take one of them and start off yourself. If you don't have anyone, if no one has ever asked you, I'm asking you right now, for Jesus' sake, to ask someone else, and the two of you start praying together. Just do it. What can stop you? You don't have to wait to be elected. You don't have to wait until some board meets and asks you to be a prayer band leader. No.

Jesus has asked you to be a prayer band leader, and He has offered you mighty inducements. He says that if you just do this, up in heaven, the Father will give you that for which you agree to ask.

> *Praying together brings the atmosphere of heaven here on earth.*

Do you see, friend, how in doing that, you develop the skill of leadership? In the very act of asking someone to associate with you in this, you are using these principles of Christian leadership, and in keeping at it, you're developing one of the most important things, and that is loving persistence.

But that isn't all. As you add, God multiplies. God delights to bless this thing. Oh, what a wonderful thing it would be if all administration were done growing out of a prayer experience!

How could two people who pray together get up and start barking at or biting each other? Praying together brings the atmosphere of heaven here on earth. I feel sorry for any administrator who is attempting to administrate without the prayer bond between him and the people with which he is working.

Suppose you happen to be under someone who hasn't established that bond, then by God's grace, you establish it. If the one under whom you're working is not praying with you, then why not you go and say, "You and I are linked closely together in work. You have to give me directions, and I'm glad about it. I wish we could pray together that God will make our teamwork successful."

This is the most wonderful power in the universe. This is proper training in Christian leadership. This is the way to get it, and there is no school of business administration that can teach you this.

Matthew, John, and Peter learned it with Jesus, and they taught it to others and still others until, within a few years, there were five million Christians. That experience went on the wings of prayer. Will you do it, friend? Will you be a leader for God?

There are some things that you have to be humble and careful about lest they go to your head and inflate you, but you need never worry about two people praying. There is not much about that that is going to make you full of pride like Lucifer. There are just two people getting together without the fanfare of blowing trumpets or saying egotistical things. No. You're down on your knees, humbling your hearts before God. Here, you can learn to be a leader without it puffing you up. Instead of going to your head, it will send you to your knees, and that is the place to be. That is where things happen. "Kneeling in faith at the cross, [we have] reached the highest place to which man can attain" (*Acts of the Apostles*, p. 209).

In 2 Timothy, the second chapter, Paul writes to Timothy. Paul is in the dungeon. His last days have come. He knows he is soon to die, and he writes to Timothy, his son in the faith, the man he is trained in the very things we've been studying, and he says: "Thou therefore, my son, be strong in the grace that is in Christ Jesus. And the things that thou hast heard of me among many witnesses, the same commit thou to faithful men, who shall be able to teach others also" (2 Tim. 2:2, 3).

Do you see that what we have just been studying is right here in this verse? Paul says to Timothy, "Timothy, I taught you. Now, you teach other men. And be sure that the men you teach are people that are faithful and able to teach others."

It wasn't enough for Paul to teach Timothy and for Timothy to teach others.

Those whom Timothy were to teach must be taught to teach others also.

That is why the early Christian church succeeded. That is the secret of the success of the remnant. Power from above is coming to little prayer bands all through this movement. That is the way the work is going to be finished.

Volume seven of *Testimonies for the Church*, page 21, sounds like it had been written for this very moment:

> Why do not believers feel a deeper, more earnest concern for those who are out of Christ? Why do not two or three meet together and plead with God for the salvation of some special one, and then for still another? In our churches let companies be formed for service. Let different ones unite in labor as fishers of men. Let them seek to gather souls... The formation of small companies as a basis of Christian effort has been presented to me by One who cannot err. (*Testimonies for the Church*, vol. 7, p. 21)

This is it. This is the foundation. If we do this, it will spread out in whatever community we are. Reaching first those closest to us, it can spread out in a church, over a campus, out into the outside world around us, fishing for souls and gathering them in. " ...ye shall be gathered one by one, O ye children of Israel" (Isa. 27:12).

Shall we kneel as we pray, friend?

We thank Thee with all our hearts for the invitation and the challenge, for the call, and we thank Thee for the response in our hearts. By Thy grace, we shall be leaders, not that we might be applauded or noticed or recognized by this world, but that we might get a job done for Thee.

Oh, help us to see that there is plenty of room, a great vacancy, a great vacuum that needs to be filled. Thou art looking for men and women and youth who will be leaders for Christ, not to get the applause of the world but to get souls into the circle of salvation and to get them busy in pulling others into the circle.

God bless the reader, and may his or her soul thrill with the joy that comes in doing what we've learned. For Christ's sake, amen.

CHAPTER 17

The Most Expensive Wool

There was nothing extraordinary about the sheep that provided the most expensive wool in the history of the world. There have been millions of sheep like them, before and since. It was the shepherd that was outstanding. See him as he leads his flocks over the deserts of Midian, searching for the green valleys, pasture, and the cool water springs.

Who was he? That man, leading those flocks, was many things. He was the heir apparent to the throne of Egypt—the great empire of that time. Now he was just a shepherd. That man was none other than Moses.

Why a shepherd? The Bible tells us something about the experience of Moses in Acts 7. I would like to have you look at this text and then imagine using a man like that to herd sheep. See if you think it is good economics. "And Moses was learned in all the wisdom of the Egyptians and was mighty in words and in deeds" (Acts 7:22).

Egypt was no stone-age kingdom. They were not like the Hottentots or other primitive people. They excelled in arts and sciences, and Moses was learned in everything that they knew. He had native ability. He was a genius. "There arose not a prophet since in Israel like unto Moses, whom the Lord knew face to face." (Deut. 34:10).

He was not only great in the eyes of men, but he was also great in the eyes of God. You might say, "Well, that is talking about him after he did that great work of delivering Israel."

True. That is the point. With such a past and such a future, what was he doing out there in the desert herding sheep? Behind him is the throne of the world's greatest empire, and ahead of him is an experience that marks him for all time. He is without a peer as a historian, a poet, a philosopher, a lawgiver, and a great general and deliverer of a nation.

How much an hour do you suppose he was worth? Do you think he might have been worth as much as a lawyer? And yet, there he was herding sheep. Why? And why for forty years?

Do you agree with me that the wool was expensive which came off the backs of those sheep he was leading? Indeed, it was the most expensive wool.

A number of people likely made comments about it and thought what a shame it was to use such talent for such a common thing.

It may be that someone came along and said to Moses, "Moses, what are you doing here, anyway? A man with your talent and training? Why, anybody can do this. Of course, Moses, you are not just anybody. You are somebody."

"Man would have dispensed with that long period of toil and obscurity, deeming it a great loss of time. But Infinite Wisdom called him who was to become the leader of His people to spend forty years in the humble work of a shepherd" (*Patriarchs and Prophets*, pp. 247, 248). Was forty years too long? No. Was the price too great? No. What happened to the wool is incidental. What happened to the shepherd is of great importance.

Here is a matchless statement speaking of the forty years in the desert: "Infinite Wisdom counted not the period too long or the price too great" (*Education*, p. 64).

One of these days, you and I, if faithful, are going to join in singing a song on the sea of glass. John writes about it in Revelation 15. He heard the 144,000 singing it, and he tells us it is the song of Moses and the song of the Lamb. The ones in this last generation who sing the song of Moses will have learned some things from the experience of Moses. Let us focus on these two questions: Why did he herd sheep? Why for forty years?

To understand it, we shall have to see some things which happened before that period in the desert. To appreciate it, we will need to note some things that occurred afterward.

You remember, of course, his birth and the interesting experiences in connection with it. Stephen says in Acts 7:20, "In which time Moses was born."

Why at that particular time? A deliverer was to be born. Satan, knowing that, set in motion some oppressive laws. He moved upon Pharaoh to command that all the baby boys be thrown in the river or otherwise killed when they were born. He was trying to destroy that deliverer who was to come, just as hundreds of years later, he tried to destroy the Savior when He was born in Bethlehem.

But you remember that God, in His infinite wisdom, allowed the devil to put that machinery into motion and then used that very thing to bring about something wonderful. Instead of being destroyed, Moses was discovered in the bulrushes by the Egyptian princess.

Through that wonderful arrangement of God, moving upon little Miriam and the others, it was finally arranged that Moses was brought up by his own mother, and she was even paid wages for it.

How the devil must have gnashed his teeth and writhed in agony over that turn of events! That is the way God does things. He lets the devil go so far, and then He lets him hang himself with his own rope.

For twelve years, Moses was trained by his mother, Jochebed. She was a slave, but she was being paid by the Egyptian princess to train her own boy. Jochebed did her job well. She poured into that young heart the truths of God. She taught him the foolishness of idol worship. She taught him obedience, faithfulness, and loyalty. She told him the stories of creation, of Noah, of Abraham, Isaac, Jacob, and Joseph—those very stories that years later, out there with those sheep, he was to write down in the wonderful book of Genesis.

When Moses was finally taken at the age of twelve to the court of Pharaoh, something had gotten into that young boy's heart that never left him. In all those years with the teachers, priests, and princes of Egypt, not once did Moses compromise his principles of loyalty to the true God; not once did he bow to idols; not once did he waiver in his allegiance to the Creator of the universe.

That is a marvelous record! Ponder it. Think of the influence of early training and the importance of true education in the early years. Think of what an influence it must have had all through the court of Egypt. There was a man who was the crowned prince, the heir apparent, and yet he was true to the worship of the God of the Hebrews, those despised slaves down in the land of Goshen.

We are told that the priests of Egypt were given the job of converting Moses to the religion of Egypt. He was told that it was impossible for him to be king and cling to the worship of Jehovah, for part of the responsibilities of the king of Egypt was in connection with its religion.

Note this wonderful description of Moses' attitude written in *Patriarchs and Prophets*, page 245:

> Moses, as the heir apparent, was to be initiated into the mysteries of the national religion. This duty was committed to the priests. But while he was an ardent and untiring student, he could not be induced to participate in the worship of the gods. He was threatened with the loss of the crown, and warned that he would be disowned by the princess should he persist in his adherence to the Hebrew faith. But he was unshaken in his determination to render homage to none save the one God, the Maker of heaven and earth. He reasoned with priests and worshippers, showing the folly of their superstitious veneration of senseless objects. None could refute his arguments or change his purpose. (*Patriarchs and Prophets*, p. 245)

Isn't that a record, friend? We don't need to worry about a young man like that, do we? No. He can go to the University of Egypt. He can go through all the courses in philosophy and theology and psychology and all the rest and come forth still a champion of Jehovah.

So, time goes on. Moses' education is carried to the very pinnacle. He is trained not only in logic, religion, arts, and sciences; he is trained in military tactics. He becomes a general. He became so successful that on one occasion, through his genius, he was able to win a most striking victory over the enemies of Egypt. And as he returned from that expedition, all the armies of Egypt sang his praises.

And yet, he did not give the glory to the gods of Egypt. He did not bow down to those senseless idols. He kept his faith in God as the Creator, and through it all, he cherished the thought which had been taught him by his mother and which had been revealed to him personally by angels—that he was to be the deliverer of Israel. He made the choice not merely once but again and again that he would accept that call and that he would answer that challenge that instead of accepting the throne of Egypt, he would cast his lot with the despised Hebrews and lead them to escape from slavery.

Here was a man that had the highest training, and with it, he had not lost his vision. He'd had all the education that could be given, and still, he had not denied his God. He had genius, talent, training, experience, position, and influence and was ready to throw it all into the work of God to help God do His work and deliver His people.

In Hebrews 11:24–26, we read about how Paul speaks of this decision that Moses made. It is a wonderful description:

> By faith, Moses, when he was come to years, refused to be called the son of Pharaoh's daughter; Choosing rather to suffer affliction with the people of God, than to enjoy the pleasures of sin for a season; esteeming the reproach of Christ greater riches than the treasures in Egypt: for he had respect unto the recompense of the reward. (Heb. 11:24–26)

He turned his back on the gods of Egypt, and he kept his face on the one true God. He forsook the throne of Egypt and cast in his lot with a race of slaves.

I ask very simply, what more could you ask of Moses? There are plenty of people today who have far less than he had when he was forty years of age, who think they are all ready to help finish the work. They have less education, both human and divine, and less loyalty; yet they think they are ready, that all they need is an "opportunity."

Moses not only had all this training, talent, genius, devotion, dedication, and loyalty, but the "opportunity" also presented itself, or so he thought. While visiting his brethren, he saw an Egyptian whipping one of them, and the heart of Moses was moved to do something about the cruelty that he saw. So, he killed the Egyptian and hid his body in the sand.

Do you know what Moses thought? He thought that by the Israelites seeing what he was doing and other Israelites hearing of it, they would understand that Moses was ready to forsake the throne of Egypt and lead his people to victory "He supposed his brethren would have understood how that God by his hand would deliver them: but they understood not" (Acts 7:25).

Apparently, the only reaction he got was that the next day, when he tried to reprove one Israelite who was oppressing another, was that the man turned in an impudent way, defied him, and said, "Are you going to kill me like you did that Egyptian yesterday?"

Moses learned two things from this experience. He saw that his own people were not ready to respond. He would also soon learn that Pharaoh had heard about this and was ready to kill him.

So, what did Moses do? He fled to Midian. That is where he was doing shepherd's work, taking care of the flocks for forty years.

As Moses made his way to Midian, he was accounted a complete failure. He was considered a "has-been." Formerly a general of all the armies of Egypt, he was "reduced" to just looking after some sheep. He was the heir apparent to the throne of the great empire but was later "just" working for his father-in-law. What an apparent come-down!

Moses felt thoroughly defeated. He lost all ideas that anything was going to happen down in Egypt with his involvement. For forty years, he stayed in the desert. Then God called him. What happened during the forty years, and why did it have to happen? You may think of a number of reasons. I would like us to ponder two great reasons why Moses had to be in the desert with sheep for so long.

The first is that, while Moses had maintained his allegiance to God down in Egypt, he had so come to be influenced by the processes of education to which he was exposed that he became a great "reasoner." To some extent, he was substituting reason for faith, and God cannot use a man in that state of mind for a great work. "In slaying the Egyptian, Moses had fallen into the same error so often committed by his fathers, of taking into their own hands the work that God had promised to do" (*Patriarchs and Prophets*, p. 247).

Notice that Moses' mistake was not in apostasy. Moses never gave up the truth. He was not one who went out to shine in the world. No. So, what did he do? He tried to apply worldly wisdom to the doing of God's work. He tried to take that logic and that reason and that type of thinking that he had learned in the halls of the great universities of Egypt and apply that to delivering the people of God.

Well, of course, why wouldn't he? He was putting all he had into it. And that is just the point. All he had was going into it, and he had too much of certain things: "It was not God's will to deliver His people by warfare, as Moses thought, but by His own mighty power, that the glory might be ascribed to Him alone… Moses was not prepared for his great work" (*ibid.*).

There you have it, friends. Moses thought he had figured out how it was going to be. To him, it was very clear. He might have thought, "See, God gave me an early training with my mother to keep me loyal. Then he brought me up here with Pharaoh to get all this wonderful training in military science, organization, administration, and leadership. We are ready. And Lord, you can have all the glory. I am willing to use it all for You. Israel, come. Let's go. I will lead you to victory the way I led those Egyptian armies to victory."

But Moses was not fully prepared. He was substituting reason for faith and was substituting human works for the divinely-revealed blueprint.

There is a second great reason. And if there is any way of measuring it, I would say that this is even greater and more important than the first reason. The two, of course, are connected. But this one sentence from *Education*, page 65, is the key to the whole thing: "In the military schools of Egypt, Moses was taught the law of force, and so strong a hold did this teaching have upon his character that it required forty years of quiet and communion with God and nature to fit him for the leadership of Israel by the law of love" (*Education*, p. 65).

That is it. So, he had to go to Midian. He had to become a shepherd. He had to unlearn the law of force that he had learned in the military schools of Egypt, and he had to learn the law of love. In the counsels of heaven, it was decided that the best way to do that, and the fastest way (for God never wastes any time), was to have Moses herding sheep for forty years.

Oh, friend, can it be that the law of force is so terrible that it needs to be gotten rid of in such a radical way? And can it be so subtle as to take forty years to overcome it? So it seems.

It is interesting how the Lord worked to teach Moses those lessons. In the providence of God, he was led to Midian and found Jethro. Moses became a shepherd. He was used to getting things done. He likely didn't have any lieutenants or sergeants as he had in Egypt to see that his commands were carried out; he just had sheep. So, I can imagine him ordering those sheep around, and they were not used to that.

I suppose many a time Moses thought, "These animals don't know how to obey." The real trouble was that he didn't know how to command. That is the trouble with a lot of parents, teachers, and administrators. They think that the "sheep" don't know how to obey when it's themselves who don't know how to command with love instead of with force. May God be as long-suffering with us as He was with Moses. "Before he could govern wisely, he must be trained to obey" (*Patriarchs and Prophets*, p. 247).

Couldn't Moses already govern wisely? Down in Egypt, he thought he could, and the nation thought he could, and the king thought he could. But out there with the sheep, none of it worked at all. He had to learn an entirely new system of how to govern, direct, and get obedience.

Remember why it took forty years? Because he had been so long down in Egypt in those schools where force was the rule. "The habits of caretaking, of self-forgetfulness and tender solicitude for his flock, thus developed, would prepare him to become the compassionate, longsuffering shepherd of Israel" (*ibid.*).

Are you more like Moses was at age forty or more like Moses at eighty? Can you sing the song of Moses? It is a song of love, my friend, a wonderful song of love.

I want to share a few comments from the book *Fundamentals of Christian Education*. These are in the chapter titled "Speedy Preparation." It's a warning against taking long courses of study. And in page after page of earnest warning, we find comments on how long it took God to train Moses out in the desert. I wonder why. There is a connection. It is neither accidental nor incidental.

"Moses supposed that his education in the wisdom of Egypt had fully qualified him to lead Israel from bondage" (*Fundamentals of Christian Education*, p. 342). He assumed that he was sufficiently trained by his worldly education. Continuing on in *Fundamentals of Christian Education*:

> He first set about his work by trying to gain the favor of his own people by redressing their wrongs. He killed an Egyptian who was imposing upon one of his brethren. In this he manifested the spirit of him who was a murderer from the beginning, and proved himself unfit to represent the God of mercy, love, and tenderness. He made a miserable failure of his first attempt. Like many another, he immediately lost his confidence in God and turned his back upon his appointed work; he fled from the wrath of Pharaoh. He concluded that because of his mistake, his great sin in taking the life of the cruel Egyptian, God would not permit him to have any part in the work of delivering His people from their cruel bondage. But the Lord permitted these things that He might be able to teach him the gentleness, goodness, longsuffering, which it is necessary for every laborer for the Master to possess. (*ibid.*)

Have you ever made any failures in trying to work for God? Because of some failure, have you become discouraged and concluded that you could not do anything, or at least cannot do much? Take courage! Moses made a miserable failure of his first attempt. After forty years of preparation, when he started out to do a great work, it was a flat failure. He was so discouraged that he quit. He thought he was through.

But oh, friend, God was using that very disappointment, that apparent defeat, to take the self-inflation, the self-exaltation, out of Moses; it was to lead him to put aside the sword, the brute force, bigoted authority, and the like, and to learn the burden-bearing, solicitude, and sweet, loving care of a shepherd.

If there is one lesson I long for you to learn, that is it. Call it unselfishness or self-denial, but it boils down to striving to help others instead of advantaging yourself. As many today, what had Moses been taught to expect down in Egypt? "Moses had been taught to expect flattery and praise because of his superior abilities; but now he was to learn a different lesson" (*ibid.*, p. 343).

Moses took a medical missionary course with sheep as patients: "Moses was taught to care for the afflicted, to nurse the sick, to seek patiently after the straying, to bear long with the unruly, to supply with loving solicitude the wants of the young lambs and the necessities of the old and feeble" (*ibid.*).

Surely, with all his talent, if they were going to ask Moses to be a shepherd, they didn't need to add insult to injury by insisting that he look after old and feeble sheep, did they? Why, the very idea! Shouldn't they have hired someone else for that job? Or, if they had to use Moses for a shepherd, they should have at least seen that all the sheep he took care of were in good shape, so he wouldn't have so much trouble, right? No. God was arranging this.

Oh, God help us to learn this lesson—to care for others, to be interested in them, to want to serve them, to go after the straying, to help the sick, to comfort the sad and discouraged, and to bear long with the unruly.

What were the two things that Moses learned in Egypt that he unlearned out in Midian? In Egypt, he learned the world's philosophy, to reason things out, and to only do what was reasonable. But out in Midian, Moses learned something entirely different—a lesson of faith. He came to the place where he did whatever God said, regardless of whether or not it made sense to him.

That is why he could lead His people to the Red Sea. That is why he could lead them through the Red Sea. That is why he could lead them out into the desert, though he knew there wasn't anything out there for a million and a half people to eat. That is why he could lead them by the flinty rocks, where he knew there was not enough water to keep them and their cattle from starving. Step by step, all through the forty years with Israel, he was following God instead of human reason.

Unfortunately, we often don't think that we need faith these days because we have so much light, knowledge, and inventions. There are so many scientific discoveries that some believe that all we have to do, whether in nutrition, medicine, education, and the like, is just to learn of the discoveries made and apply them.

If that is our thinking, we are somewhere along where Moses was in Egypt. It took him forty years to unlearn it, friend. We had better start unlearning fast.

Don't misunderstand. I would not for a minute suggest that nothing in modern science and education is worthy, that there isn't some truth in all those things. The problem is to know which is truth and which is error and to be able to distinguish between them.

A good doctor friend once told me a story that, if it were not so serious, would be laughable. He told me that one of the teachers at a medical college said to his students at the close of the year, "I am sorry. I have to make a confession to you. Half of the things that I have taught you this year are not so. But I have another confession to make which is worse than that. I don't know which half it is."

There is no question that there is a great deal of truth in all the different fields of science and research. There was a great deal of truth in what Moses learned in Egypt. Moses' problem was that he had the truth and the error mixed up. And that is the problem today.

Do you know how Moses sorted it out? He went out to the wilderness with the word and the works of God. He wrote the book of Genesis under the inspiration of the Holy Spirit. He was surrounded by mountain peaks like Horeb and others of the Sinai Peninsula. He led his flocks to the green valleys and the springs. There, in those mountain solitudes, the grandeur of Egypt faded out as the grandeur of God became more and more real.

If we are to be delivered from the peril of rationalism, of exalting reason above faith, we too, must have our minds saturated with the inspired revelations of the Bible and the Spirit of Prophecy. We, too, must bring our souls in contact, not occasionally and spasmodically, but constantly, as Moses did, with the works of God's creation.

On page 360 of *Fundamentals of Christian Education*, note these convicting statements which have impressed my heart very much:

> If many who are connected with the work of the Lord could be isolated as was Moses, and could be compelled by circumstances to follow some humble vocation until their hearts became tender, they would make much more faithful shepherds than they now do in dealing with God's heritage. They would not be so prone to magnify their own abilities, or seek to demonstrate that the wisdom of an advanced education could take the place of a sound knowledge of God. (*Fundamentals of Christian Education, p. 360*)

I submit to you that we need to be saved from the world's wisdom, which is foolishness, and from that selfish use of force, which is the devil's substitute for heaven's power of love.

May we, like Moses, be so saturated with God's word and His works that the influence of Egypt shall be blotted out of our lives, and we finally love as Jesus loved.

CHAPTER 18

Content Without Promotion
[Mark Finley]

Have you ever heard of it? It seems to be a principle in the business world, in the economic world: "There is always room at the top." So here is a man working in a machine shop looking after some machines. Day after day, he comes to that shop. As he is working on his machine, that principle runs over and over in his mind: "There is always room at the top." And so, looking at the foreman's job, he begins thinking, "I would like to be the foreman of this company someday. I would like to have an opportunity of superintending this section of the plant." So, he pushes himself and drives himself until the time comes when he can take over the foreman's job.

Then after he has worked several months at the foreman's job, this thought rings through his mind again: "There is always room at the top." So, he wonders how he can become a plant supervisor. So, through manipulation, hard work, diligence, and pushing himself some more, he becomes the supervisor of that section of the plant.

But after several months, discontented with that position, looking for a still higher-paying job with more prestige, the thought re-echoes in his ears again: "There is always room at the top." So, he sets his sights on a managerial position in the corporation. Through either manipulation or some diligence method, he pushes himself until he becomes a manager in that large corporation.

This seems to be the philosophy of the world. One must set his sights on a higher goal—a higher-paying job with more excellent financial remuneration, a position with more prestige, honor, flattery, and praise.

I would like us to study the contrast of a Man who had prestige and honor, who had all the riches of the universe at His command.

> Let this mind be in you, which was also in Christ Jesus: Who, being in the form of God, thought it not robbery to be equal with God:

> But made Himself of no reputation, and took upon Him the form of a servant, and was made in the likeness of men: And being found in fashion as a man, He humbled Himself, and became obedient unto death, even the death of the cross. Wherefore God also hath highly exalted Him, and given Him a name which is above every name: That at the name of Jesus every knee should bow, of things in heaven, and things in earth, and things under the earth. (Phil. 2:5–10)

This is quite a different picture from the man trying to press his way to the top. Instead, here is a picture of Jesus. I sometimes call Philippians 2:5–10 a description of the cascade of God's love, for it pictures, step by step, Jesus leaving heaven and coming to this earth.

There in verse 6, it speaks about Christ being in the form of God, or Christ being God. Then the next verse tells us about the next step, that Jesus, who was God, became man. Notice what kind of a man He became. He became a servant. Notice what kind of a servant He became—a humble, obedient servant. Notice, as we go on in Philippians 2, not only did He become a humble, obedient servant, but this unassuming, obedient Servant suffered a death. And notice what kind of death He suffered—the death of the cross.

Who was this Christ that became a man? Before we can ever appreciate the incarnation, before we can appreciate the glory and splendor of Christ becoming a man, it is necessary to understand who He was before He became a man. Therefore, let us focus our attention on this Christ.

In Hebrews 1, Paul sets forth for us in clear, explicit language the glory of Jesus before the incarnation:

> For unto which of the angels said He at any time, Thou art my Son, this day have I begotten thee? And again, I will be to Him a Father, and He shall be to me a Son? And again, when He bringeth in the firstbegotten into the world, He saith, And let all the angels of God worship Him. And of the angels He saith, Who maketh His angels spirits, and His ministers a flame of fire. (Heb. 1:5–7)

Now notice in verse 8, this is the Father speaking, and He is speaking to the Son—Jesus: "But unto the Son He saith, Thy throne, O God, is for ever and ever: a sceptre of righteousness is the sceptre of thy kingdom" (Heb. 1:8).

Who was this Christ who became man? According to the clear words of the Bible, He was God. His throne was established as far back in the ages of eternity as our minds can comprehend and an infinite amount beyond. "Thy throne, O God, is for ever and ever..." (Heb. 1:8).

Picture this Jesus in the ages of eternity. Myriads of angels worshiping Him who is the express image of the brightness of the Father's glory. At a word from His mouth, thousands of angels were dispatched to various parts of the creation. At a word from Him, these angels carried out His plans. They worshiped Him. Thousands of angels sang His praise, gave Him adoration and homage, and brought honor to His name.

Who was this Christ who entered into this humiliation; this Christ who became a man; this Christ who became a servant; this Christ who became a humble, obedient servant who died the death of the cross? Who was He? He was God, worshiped by all the angels, the express image of the Father's glory.

But Paul sets Him forth in the book of Hebrews in another function. Besides being God, notice this other interesting aspect that Paul gives us about Jesus the Christ, the One who humbled Himself:

> God, who at sundry times and in divers manners spake in time past unto the fathers by the prophets, Hath in these last days spoken unto us by His Son, whom He hath appointed heir of all things, by whom also He made the worlds; Who being the brightness of His glory, and the express image of His person, and upholding all things by the word of His power, when He had by Himself purged our sins, sat down on the right hand of the Majesty on high. (Heb. 1:1–3)

We have already noted that Christ was God, worshiped by all the angels. Now here in verses 2–3, Paul sets forth these two additional functions of Christ. First, according to Hebrews 1:2, Christ is the Creator. He is the One who made all the worlds, the One who brought the planets into existence, the One who created our world in beauty and splendor.

Let your mind dwell upon Eden and think of the trees—beautiful, without a blight. Think of the trees, heavy laden with fruit. Think of the beautiful lakes and the green foliage of the valleys. It was Jesus Christ who was the Creator of all this. He created the planets that revolve around the sun.

Notice something else that Paul says here about Jesus. Not only was He the Creator, but in verse 3: "Who being the brightness of His glory and the express image of His person, and upholding all things by the word of His power..." (Heb. 1:3).

Not only is Jesus God, worshiped by all the angels, not only was He the Creator, the One that brought all the worlds into existence, but He is the Sustainer of the universe.

It is not by accident that our earth stays on its course around the sun and does not collide with other planets. It's not by accident that, in the springtime, the flowers burst forth in their beauty. It's not by accident that the tulips stick their heads through the damp earth in the spring. It's not by accident that the crocuses bloom. Oh, no. God—Jesus Christ, the Creator of the universe, sustains the universe and causes every flower to burst forth in its beauty. Our heavenly Father, through Jesus, sustains the universe.

And why is this significant in our study? Back to Philippians 2. Notice how this fact that Jesus Christ is God makes more glorious His humiliation and His sacrifice: "Let this mind be in you, which was also in Christ Jesus: Who, being in the form of God, thought it not robbery to be equal with God" (Phil. 2:5, 6).

Was Christ equal with God? Yes. "Who, being in the form of God, thought it not robbery to be equal with God: But made Himself of no reputation, and took upon Him the form of a servant..." (Phil. 2:6, 7).

He "made Himself of no reputation." You think of the great principle of this world—striving to be at the top, pushing men aside, elbowing one's room in, seeking position and flattery and praise and honor, little people aspiring to be first. Then you think of Jesus, the God of the universe, the Creator and Sustainer of the universe, who made Himself of no reputation. He was not interested in that praise and flattery and honor for Himself alone but took upon Himself the form of a servant. "Let this mind be in you, which was also in Christ Jesus" (Phil. 2:5).

Which of the attitudes is yours? Are you interested in employment where you set your goal to reach the top and be independent of other people? And if it means someone else has to be pushed aside, your goal is on the top. Is that your goal? Or are you looking at things the way Jesus looked at them? "Let this mind be in you, which was also in Christ Jesus: Who, being in the form of God, thought it not robbery to be equal with God: But made Himself of no reputation" (Phil. 2:5–7).

We see multitudes dying of coronary heart disease as we look about us today. One of the leading contributors to coronary heart disease in the United States is emotional stress. Could it be possible that one of the great reasons for emotional stress is this dog-eat-dog philosophy, this concept of elbowing one's way in, this concept of striving for the top?

Are there some people in our society today afflicted with stomach ulcers? Could it be possible that one of the great reasons for this is the stress, tension, push, and drive to get ahead? Is our society afflicted with nervous breakdowns? Is it indeed true that many doctors in the United States are treating more people for nervous conditions than primarily physical ailments? Could we have failed to understand the true principle of life and the fundamental law of life?

I would like to share a remarkable statement that sets forth the true principle of life. It's from this beautiful book, *The Desire of Ages*:

> Both the redeemed and the unfallen beings will find in the cross of Christ their science and their song. It will be seen that the glory shining in the face of Jesus is the glory of self-sacrificing love. In the light from Calvary, it will be seen that the law of self-renouncing love is the law of life for earth and heaven.... (*The Desire of Ages*, p. 19)

In Calvary, we see demonstrated before our eyes the law of life. And so, as multitudes press for honor and prestige and think that in attaining that goal, they will have life, we see broken health, nervous breakdowns, and heart attacks. But Jesus invites us into a way of life that is totally different. The law of self-renouncing love is the law of life for the universe.

[W. D. Frazee]

When I was eight years old, I attended a picnic. At that picnic, the one thing I remember was a race for eight-year-old boys. And the prize was a dish of ice cream. For a barefooted boy on a hot summer day, the fourth of July, can you imagine? And I can still see that man standing there with his cap and saying, "Now, boys, all of you put your foot right on this line. When I drop my cap, as soon as my cap hits the dirt, you're off. So go down there to that mark and turn around and come back. The first boy who gets back gets a dish of ice cream."

What do you suppose I did? What do you think all the other little boys did? Why we all ran. But oh, I wanted to win, and I did! And I got that dish of ice cream.

But what about all the other little boys? They didn't get any. Someone says, "That is life."

That is life the way it's lived in this world, isn't it, friends?

I'm so glad that when I got into my teens, I found something better than that. I found a way of life in which I didn't have to beat someone else to win. I found out that there was something that God had for me that didn't have to be grabbed from someone else, that God wasn't in the business of robbing Peter to pay Paul.

There are only two philosophies of life on this planet. Brother Finley has just talked to us about them. One is this idea: "There is room at the top." The other is expressed in these words: "God's plan of life has a place for every human being" (*Education*, p. 225).

And I have come to know that the General Manager of the universe is my best friend, and He runs the whole thing for my benefit. And that doesn't mean, friend, that He will make me president of the United States. No. And I'm not sorry about that. He is not even going to make me a state governor. So that is all right, too.

Sometimes I see young people striving, striving, striving to get hold of something. I think in my heart, "Well, that is something I've already had, and I don't it have anymore." I'm so glad, friends, that I have learned that there is nothing I have to grab from someone else or hold onto if someone else wants to grab it from me. God is in the business of abundantly satisfying every desire of the soul if we will learn from Him how to be content.

The Great Physician says, "Come unto Me, all ye that labour and are heavy laden…" (Matt. 11:28).

You folks who have high blood pressure, nervous tension, ulcers, coronaries: "…And I will give you rest. Take My yoke upon you, and learn of Me; for I am meek and lowly in heart: and ye shall find rest unto your souls. For My yoke is easy, and My burden is light" (Matt. 11:28-30).

In these words, we have a divine prescription for the healing of all physical, mental, and spiritual ills. Of all the causes of disease, the greatest is the one that Brother Finley and I are presenting—this tension that comes to outstrip others, take something that someone else has, climb up on the shoulders or the backs or the faces of other people.

Room at the top? My dear friend, if you follow Jesus Christ, you may not be at what the world calls "the top." As humanity measures position, sharing a cross on Golgotha is not exactly the top. Washing feet in the upper room is not exactly a high position. We are to learn of Jesus the way of meekness and lowliness.

In that beautiful book *Desire of Ages*, which Brother Finley was quoting from, on page 88 is this sentence concerning Christ when He was just a young Man in His teens and twenties: "...He did not strive for worldly greatness, and in even the lowliest position He was content" (*The Desire of Ages*, p. 88).

Someone may say, "Well, Brother Frazee, aren't you afraid that if you give the young people this philosophy, they won't have any incentive to do anything?"

Well, I'll risk it. I want to tell you something, friends: there is something greater than the incentive of force and pressure and trying to rule others.

When Napoleon was banished to the Island of St. Helena and spent his last days there, he had much time for reflection. As he looked back over his life and recognized that at the end, he had made a failure, as he thought of the difference in the life and work of Jesus Christ, he conversed with one of his generals who had chosen to share his exile with him. He spent a great deal of time talking with him. And in one of those dialogues, he expressed these words. I want to read them to you:

> Alexander, Caesar, Charlemagne, and I founded empires, but on what did the creations of our genius rest? On force. Jesus Christ alone founded His empire on love. And at this hour, millions would die for Him.
>
> If we are Christians, we expect one day to live with Him always. Let us accept now the motive which alone causes the angels and the inhabitants of the other worlds to serve Him—the motive of love—with no thought of displacing others, with no thought of bettering ourselves at the expense of others. Napoleon Bonaparte.

Napoleon mentioned Alexander the Great as one of those who had founded an empire on force. You remember how this young man, with his great driving genius, took his soldiers across into Asia Minor and defeated Darius in those battles. And finally, he had the whole known world of that time at his feet. Then he had a grand victory celebration in old Babylon. On that night of revelry and debauchery, he drank and drank and drank until finally, he died as a result. He was just thirty-three years old.

Some 300 years later, there was another young Man who died at the age of thirty-three. That was Jesus; He died on a cross. Alexander died on the throne of the world; Jesus died on the cross. Many years ago, Charles Ross Weede put it in verse. May I share it with you?

> Jesus and Alexander
> Died at thirty-three;
> One lived and died for self,
> One died for you and me.
> The Greek died on a throne;
> The Jew died on a cross;
> One's life a triumph seemed;
> The other but a loss.
> One led vast armies forth;
> The Other walked alone;
> One shed a whole world's blood,
> The Other gave His own.
> One won the world in life,
> And lost it all in death;
> The other lost His life,
> To win the whole world's faith.
> Jesus and Alexander
> Died at thirty-three.
> The Greek made all men slaves;
> The Jew made all men free.
> One built a throne on blood;
> The Other built on love.
> The one was born of earth;
> The Other from above.
> The one won all this earth,
> To lose all earth and heaven;
> The Other gave up all,

That all to Him be given.
The Greek forever died,
The Jew forever lives;
He loses all who gets,
He wins all things who gives.

The devil's most subtle lie is that you can have some of both. But in the end, these things are mutually exclusive. When the Shepherd divides the sheep from the goats, there will be no middle class. Instead, those who have given all for Jesus and those who have lived for self will be clearly distinguished.

Brother Finley has pointed out that this is a very practical thing regarding our daily work. So many people are toiling along in some department, factory, or office, longing for the time when they can have a better job or a higher position.

"Well," someone says, "Sure. Why shouldn't everyone try to advance?" Let me read an interesting statement from what I believe is an inspired source. It is in this old book, *Gospel* Workers: "...Many suffer grief, pain, and disappointment, because they are unwilling to fill the humble place which God's providence assigns them, where they will remain unnoticed and unknown" (*Gospel Workers*, p. 459).

But it is that verb I want you to notice: remain. Many are unhappy and disappointed. Why? "...Because they are unwilling to fill the humble place which God's providence assigns them where they will remain unnoticed and unknown."

Suppose I am a deacon at church. But I've already been a deacon for five years. So I think it's about time they made me an elder.

Suppose that I become an elder and after I've been an elder for several years, where do I go from here?

No matter where we aim at the ladder, there is something we think of as "higher up." Several years ago, I went back to a place where I had been early in my ministry, and I met a man whom I had the joy of seeing baptized in my work. It had been several years since I saw him, and he said to me, "Brother Frazee, what are you doing now?"

"Well," I said, "I'm the pastor of a church in Oklahoma."

"Oh," he said, "I would have thought you'd be conference president by this time." And I saw that I had a little work yet to do with that convert. I explained to him that the Lord didn't call everyone to be a conference president and that no matter how long a man was a pastor, that didn't mean that he was someday to become a conference president.

Did I tell him the truth? Oh, yes.

Let me use a political illustration, for I would rather use that than the religion of Christ for this particular illustration. How many states are there in the United States? Fifty. That is right. Do you suppose that governors who aspire to be president of the United States are among them? It seems to come out every now and then. But do you know how many presidents there are in the White House? There is one. What are the other forty-nine governors going to do?

Do you see what I'm getting at, dear friends? And whether you are thinking of it in government, business, work, or in the church, remember, "God's plan of life has a place for every human being" (*Education*, p. 225).

And the highest place in the universe that you can be in is the place for which God has made you. So that is where you can find real contentment if you accept it.

We drove the highway and smiled as we saw a cow or a horse in a pasture reaching over the fence or through the fence for some grass on the other side. One farmer tried an experiment. He had two fields. He had his cattle in one, and they were reaching through, so he opened the gate and let them in to where they had been reaching. Do you know what some of them did? You guessed it. They started reaching out for that which doesn't seem quite so available.

You and I are not cattle. God has given us brains, and He wants us to use these brain cells to learn from Him the way of life. It is not seeking recognition or position. It is not seeking notice. It is not aiming for promotion. It is seeking to do our best in the place God has put us to reveal the love of Jesus and to live the life of Jesus.

And if God ever wants us to do something else, He can arrange it in His time and way. So it won't be necessary for us to elbow someone else. And as far as recognition is concerned, the Christian can think of no greater honor than to hear Jesus say, "Well done, thou good and faithful servant: ... enter thou into the joy of thy lord" (Matt. 25:21).

"Father, where shall I work today?"
And my love flowed warm and free.

Then he pointed out a tiny spot,
And said, "Tend that for me."
I answered quickly, "Oh, no, not that!
Why, no one would ever see,
No matter how well my work was done;
Not that little place for me."
And the word He spoke, it was not stern;
He answered me tenderly:
"Ah, little one, search that heart of thine.
Art thou working for them or for me?
Nazareth was just a little place,
And so was Galilee."
(Meade McGuire)

But I want to tell you something, friends: everyone in Nazareth wasn't satisfied. It takes more than being in a little, humble place to be satisfied. It takes the light of love that filled the heart of Jesus. It takes the Spirit of the One who once was on the throne of the universe and who humbled Himself, step by step, left heaven, took the form of a man, became a servant, became obedient unto death, even the death of the cross.

The world is thinking of how to climb the ladder. Jesus went down, down, down. For what? That He might reach you and me. That is where we were—down at the bottom. If we let Him fill our hearts with that kind of love, then, like Him, we shall be happy in any position! We shall not seek methods by which we can get above someone else or take someone else's place. We shall gladly accept the position His providence assigns.

"Ah," someone says, "Brother Frazee, I would be glad to if I thought God was doing it. But you don't know how I got where I am. People have just done all kinds of things to me. They have been mean to me. They had lied about me. So that is why I'm not promoted."

The interesting thing about our Lord is that if we are willing to let Him arrange our lives, He sometimes uses the strangest things to accomplish it. Do you know how God got Joseph to Egypt? He used the evil deeds of his brothers. Not that He caused them to do those evil deeds, but when they did them, God said, "Very well, we will use that." So God got Joseph to Egypt as an enslaved person.

For ten years, he worked faithfully in Potiphar's house. Then he was promoted. Where to? The dungeon. His feet were hurt with fetters. Oh, where was God? God was right there with Joseph. There wasn't a day lost. There wasn't a minute wasted. It was all necessary to develop in Joseph this deep, tender love in a practical application to the needs of others.

So now, dear reader, I invite you to think of your own inner heart. Ask the Holy Spirit to illuminate the chambers of the soul and see. Is there any thought, "Oh, if I will do my job well, maybe I can get a different job, a better job"? Listen, friends, if you do your job well, you may have the joy of continuing in it for quite a while.

"Oh, then I think I'll do a bad job."

That is one way to lose the job you have.

It's lovely to be so conscious of God's leading in our lives that we can leave with Him all questions of assignment to other positions.

This is practical; this is real. There are those all over this world who are demonstrating this. And they know that this is something better than all the thievery, rat race, and mad rushing that is filling the world with tension and stress and its results today. Jesus says: "Come unto Me, all ye that labour and are heavy laden, and I will give you rest. Take My yoke upon you, and learn of Me; for I am meek and lowly in heart: and ye shall find rest unto your souls. For My yoke is easy, and My burden is light" (Matt. 11:28–30).

CHAPTER 19

The Three Arks That Didn't Float

Thus he shewed me: and, behold, the Lord stood upon a wall made by a plumbline, with a plumbline in His hand. And the LORD said unto me, Amos, what seest thou? And I said, A plumbline. Then said the LORD, Behold, I will set a plumbline in the midst of My people Israel: I will not again pass by them anymore. (Amos 7:7, 8)

God uses many figures in seeking to convey to us the truth He has to present. Here He is using here an illustration from building—a plumbline.

I heard about some people who were building a church. They had contracted to put up blocks. Some expert masons were going to that job. But the man who was overseeing the whole business came one morning and looked at the wall that they had put up and said to himself, "That wall isn't straight." So pretty soon, the man who was in charge of those brick masons came along and said, "Look here, friend, what about this?" and they put a plumbline on it, and lo and behold, friends, it was out of plumb. It wasn't straight up and down. There was only one thing to do, and that was to knock down the whole thing and start over again, and this time use the plumbline more often as they came up.

It is amazing how simple it is for people to see that with actual bricks and mortar and how hard it is for people to see it when it comes to the work of God. It seems to influence hundreds and thousands of people who seem to be in this state of mind, "Well, I don't know if that wall is so far out of plumb. It probably is a little. But then, after all, there has been a lot of time and money put into it, and it is too late to change it now. So we just have to go on from here."

"No!" God says, "I am not going to accept that work."

"And the LORD said unto me, Amos, what seest thou? And I said, A plumbline. Then said the Lord, Behold, I will set a plumbline in the midst of my people Israel: I will not again pass by them any more" (Amos 7:8). God is the inspector on this job, my friends. And no matter how many piles of brick and mortar we put together, unless God will accept it, what profit or use is it? Let me read this out of Moffatt's: "The Lord eternal showed me this, showed me Himself standing beside a wall, a plumbline in His hand. The Eternal said to me, Amos, what do you see? A plumbline, I replied. The Eternal said, with a plumbline I will test my people" (Amos 7:7, 8, *James Moffatt's Translation*).

Let me tell you, friend, there is something about a plumbline that always says the same thing. There are certain instruments that can get out of true. A square can get twisted and out of shape. But a plumbline always hangs straight up and down. That is why it is used.

God has a plumbline in His hand, and He is testing His people. And nothing but 100 percent straight up and down is going to be accepted.

Do you think it might be a good thing for us to let the plumbline be used on us before the final inspection? It seems to me that instead of arguing that so much of the wall has gone up that after all, we better not worry about it now. It seems to me that the more wall we have up that is not plumb, the more anxious we should be to get it down and start right. What do you say?

> I trust God will help us to make a practical application of that because that is the issue before God's people today; this very thing that I'm discussing with you this morning. It is a hard lesson for men to learn that God means what He says. It is ever proved a dangerous thing for men to carry out their own will in opposition to the requirements of God. (*Sons and Daughters of God*, p. 165)

We are in a time of great backsliding. One of the saddest signs of this backsliding is the disposition to be indifferent and lackadaisical about things being out of plumb; the disposition to accept, as more or less to be expected, a certain amount of deviation from the ideal set before us.

Not long ago, I was in a certain meeting where certain plans were being discussed. One person saw fit to quote some things from the Spirit of Prophecy, indicating that certain procedures being discussed were not in harmony with the blueprint. They were out of plumb in other words. Another person made this comment. He said, "I think it is a good thing for us to have things like this brought to our attention. Even if we feel compelled to do certain things, it is a good thing for us to know that they are not according to what is written."

"It is a hard lesson for men to learn that God means what He says" (*ibid.*).

I want to read an example of a man who used a plumbline. He did exactly what God said. He didn't do less, and he didn't try to do more. He just did what God said. "By faith Noah, being warned of God of things not seen as yet, moved with fear, prepared an ark to the saving of his house; by the which he condemned the world, and became heir of the righteousness which is by faith" (Heb. 11:7).

Noah was the builder. He prepared an ark. Do you suppose he used a plumbline? Notice the comment here:

> 'By faith Noah, being warned of God of things not seen as yet, moved with fear, prepared an ark to the saving of his house; by the which he condemned the world, and became heir of the righteousness which is by faith.' Hebrews 11:7. While Noah was giving his warning message to the world, his works testified of his sincerity. It was thus that his faith was perfected and made evident. He gave the world an example of believing just what God says. All that he possessed, he invested in the ark. (*Patriarchs and Prophets*, p. 95)

Notice that what Noah did was an example of believing just what God says. That is what Paul says. It was an example of faith. And that is just what faith is—believing just what God says. Faith isn't saying, "Well, I have prayed that it will rain tomorrow, so I believe that it will." Or, "I prayed that it will not rain tomorrow, so I don't think it will." Faith is not believing just something. It is believing the thing that God says—nothing less and nothing more. Noah believed a flood was coming, and he believed in the directions God had given.

By the way, who made the blueprint for that ark? God did. God told Noah how large to make it. He tells him about the entrance and the window and so forth. It was arranged according to a divine blueprint, just like the ark, tabernacle, and furniture that Moses made hundreds of years later. It was all made according to the pattern delivered to men by God. And in each case, it was important to build according to the pattern as God told: "Who serve unto the example and shadow of heavenly things, as Moses was admonished of God when he was about to make the tabernacle: for, See, saith He, that thou make all things according to the pattern shewed to thee in the mount" (Heb. 8:5).

So it was in the case of Noah—there was a pattern (a blueprint), and Noah went by it.

Now, did you know that at first, there were quite a number who accepted Noah's preaching and joined with him in building the ark? "Many at first appeared to receive the warning" (*Patriarchs and Prophets*, p. 95). "As Noah proclaimed his warning message, some listened and worked with him in building the ark, but they did not endure.... Thus it will be in the last days of this earth's history" (*Notebook Leaflets from the Elmshaven Library*, vol. 1, p. 48).

As I have been meditating on this, I have in my imagination seen three groups of people back there who joined with Noah in building the ark and were finally drowned in the flood. You can visualize them with me this morning. And remember as we think about it, as it was in the days of Noah, so shall it be in the day when the Son of man is revealed.

I am not dealing with the great godless multitude back then or now. There were thousands upon thousands back then who scoffed and ridiculed from the beginning. They never accepted the message. They went on with their heathenism and all that. I won't study those. We have their counterpart down here today by the millions.

I'm studying these people who accepted Noah's message and joined him in building the ark. But they weren't there when the flood came.

Time went on for 120 years before the flood came. That is a long time, friend. It gives time for character to be developed. It gives time for restlessness to be displayed. It gives time for human ideas to assert themselves. It gives time for human ingenuity to suggest improvements in the plans of the blueprint. So, I imagine that it was back there.

In my imagination this morning, I see a group back there who had been working on the ark. Every now and then, one of them comes to Noah and says, "Noah, I have an idea."

"What is your idea?"

"My idea is this. I think that if we would build this ark a bit more beautiful, and overlay it with gold, and put some overstuffed furniture in some of these rooms and plush carpets, I think, Noah, we could get more people, not only to listen to the message but to accept the message. Wouldn't that be wonderful?"

Noah listens and shakes his head. He says to that young man with bright ideas, "Son, that may sound all right, but it just happens that if God wanted us to do that, He forgot to tell us. So, son, as long as I'm here working on this ark, we are not going to overlay it with gold. We are not going to put in plush carpets."

So, this boy turns and continues to hammer nails in those timbers, and by the way, those were hardwoods back there. It took some strength to get the nails through. It was a good time to dream about things more luxurious, you know. But this young man is not satisfied with Noah's answer. After all, Noah is pretty old. Perhaps he is getting to be an old fogy.

So pretty soon, the young man turns to another one of the workmen and begins to ventilate his ideas. The workman says, "I think that is a good idea. I think that is exactly what we need. I think we need a little more streamlining with this thing. I think we need to bring it up to date. After all, Noah grew up in a former generation. He has his ideas. They may have worked all right back there. And if the flood had come years ago, people would probably have accepted this boat."

And they would have, by the way. There would have been hundreds in that ark if the flood had come within a few years from the time Noah began to preach.

So, these young men, the more they talked and the more they studied, the more they began to feel that there was a way to improve this thing in order to win and hold the people. And finally, it comes to the place where they quietly, or perhaps not quietly, leave Noah.

I can imagine the wonderful suppers that were conducted to raise the money for that other ark. I can imagine the streamlining of fundraising. I can imagine the drive that went one. I can imagine the thermometers that were posted to show the different contesting bands.

It's true that I'm dreaming for the moment, but my dear friend, the lesson is no dream.

Can you see that other boat? Can you see the people… not the godless world, my friends, but the people who have listened to Noah's preaching, say, "Well now, this is more like it. If we can have a gold-plated ark, it will not be bad."

Gold was plentiful in those days. Many people lived where there was plenty of gold. "If we can live in a gold-plated ark, and if we can have these beautiful carpets and elegant furniture and all sorts of luxuries, it will not be so bad to go along with the idea that there is a flood coming."

Do you know what happened to that gold-plated ark? It sank in the waves. "Ah," you say, "but, Brother Frazee, there was no such ark." No. I know it. But I'm carrying you through a parable. Gold may be beautiful, but it is heavy. And that golden ark never floated on those angry waves. It sank, and all who were in it. They had the satisfaction of having a most expensive coffin. So shall it be at the end of this world.

But there is another group I see there, friend. They are building the ark, too. They got ideas. I hear one of them coming around there to Noah one day and say, "Noah, it doesn't seem to me we are getting along very fast with this thing."

"No, it doesn't."

"It looks like to me that we will never get through. It looks like to me that we will never get it done."

Noah shakes his head and says, "Well, brother, the reason I believe we will get it done is that God said to do it, and I know that the biddings of God are enablings and that nothing is impossible to those who have faith. I have faith that God will enable us to finish this ark."

But this man argues with Noah. He says, "Now look, Noah, we have been working all these years, and we've only got so much done."

"Yes."

"Look at all that remains to be done."

"That is true."

"Noah, I have an idea. I think it's a wonderful idea."

"Well, what is it, brother?"

"It's this. Instead of working on this long, expensive, hard work program of building this ark, why don't we just construct some little rafts? Everyone can have a raft. When the waters begin to rise, the raft will rise. Each person can have one and ride safely through the flood. When the waters subside, they come down again and start over again. It is just as simple as that."

Noah says, "Brother, there is just one problem with that. If that is what God meant, He forgot to tell us. Why would He say what He doesn't mean?

"No," Noah says, "I am not going to abandon building this ark. God gave me the blueprint for this ark, and I am not going to abandon for your scheme of rafts."

Do you know what happened to those rafts back then? When the rains came, the rafts rose all right. The people who were on them were in safety for a few hours. But oh, they had not thought of the terrific winds and the awful tempests and terrible storms and those great billows that would sweep over the ocean as they deluged the earth. One by one, every one of those rafts went under, and all the people who were on them perished.

You say, "But, Brother Frazee, people didn't build those rafts." Probably not. But they are building them today, my friend. You notice that it is quite different from the gold-plated idea. There is more than one way to turn from the blueprint of God today. Some people think that what God told us to do is too expensive and takes too much time and work. They don't think it will ever get done.

Friends, I believe the "ark" is going to be built. I believe it is being built. I think that the God who inspects the work is bringing His plumbline from time to time.

There is another group that I want to tell you about. The Bible says that Noah, by faith, built the ark. But these people whom I'm thinking about now thought they were full of faith. In fact, they had so much faith that in my imagination, I hear them going to Noah and saying, "Noah, listen, do you not see that time is passing?"

"Yes."

"Do you not know that there are many yet to be warned about the flood?"

"Yes."

"Listen Noah, we will never get time to tell all the people if you keep on hammering away on this old ark. Come Noah, let's quit this ark building. It would have been fine if it could have been built long ago. But time is going on."

Noah says, "What about the flood?"

"Listen," they say, "Doesn't God love people well enough to protect them if they just believe in Him? And if we will go out and warn everyone, tell them that the flood is coming and they must quit their idols and quit their heathenism and adultery and fornication and their eating of the forbidden foods and all the rest, and get them to accept God and His plan of life, God will somehow protect them when trouble comes. He wouldn't let them be lost in the waters. God will have some way."

"Ah," you say, "But that never happened."

It's happening today, my friend. There are thousands of people that, in one minute, will get up and tell people that certain things are coming and, in another one, indicate that all we have to do about it is just go along and be faithful, and God will somehow take us through. When the God of heaven gave us the warning, He told us exactly what to do in the times ahead. But as I read here, it is a hard lesson for people to learn that God means what He says.

Suppose there were such people back there who thought that faith meant that you could just preach and get people to believe and yet not work on the ark. If there were such people, you know what happened to them, friends. They drowned outside the ark. But Noah, by faith, worked and built an ark to the saving of his house, whereby he condemned the world and became heir of the righteousness which is by faith.

Oh friend, I warn you against those three classic examples of unbelief: the gold-plated ark, the rafts, and simply believing without doing anything. As it was in the days of Noah, so shall it be in the days of the coming of the Son of man.

> Here we see that the church—the Lord's sanctuary—was the first to feel the stroke of the wrath of God. The ancient men, those to whom God had given great light and who had stood as guardians of the spiritual interests of the people, had betrayed their trust. They had taken the position that we need not look for miracles and the marked manifestation of God's power as in former days. Times have changed... (*Testimonies for the Church*, vol. 5, p. 211)

That is the three-word sentence that I want you to get—"Times have changed." Did you ever hear that expression? It is taken from the lips of those who lead God's people away from the blueprint to plans of human devising.

> They had taken the position that we need not look for miracles and the marked manifestation of God's power as in former days. Times have changed. These words strengthen their unbelief, and they say: The Lord will not do good, neither will He do evil. He is too merciful to visit His people in judgment. Thus 'Peace and safety' is the cry from men who will never again lift up their voice like a trumpet to show God's people their transgressions and the house of Jacob their sins. These dumb dogs that would not bark are the ones who feel the just vengeance of an offended God. Men, maidens, and little children all perish together. (*ibid.*)

In the flood, children and their parents likewise perished together. I shall never forget the impression made upon me as a child by a certain picture. It was of animals and people fighting for standing ground on the last bit of land standing above the water as people on that height look out on a shoreless sea. There is a mother tiger pushing her cub up, trying to hold it above the water. There is a human mother pushing her little child up there, hoping the waters will subside before the angry waves wash them into oblivion.

Oh, my friend, this world is soon to be deluged, not with water, but with something worse. So many people are carrying out their own ideas about what to do. Very few are doing what God said to do about getting ready. They think times have changed. They think there are a lot of things that God has told us that might have been all right in former days, but times have changed.

Yes, times have changed. That is the trouble. But God has not changed. That is the point.

"What seest thou, Amos?"

"A plumbline."

The Eternal said, "With a plumbline will I test My people." I want to read you something from Elder J. L. McElhaney, president of the General Conference from 1936 to 1950. This is a sermon he gave to all our educational leaders gathered together in a convention at Blue Ridge, North Carolina, on October 21, 1937. This was published in the *Review and*

Herald of October 14, 1937. Elder McElhaney was, at this time, the president of the general conference. What do you suppose was the topic that he presented? "The Perils of Worldly Trends." Perhaps I shall quote a few sentences here:

> My friends, really, I am concerned about the trends and the tendencies. I confess a great anxiety about them. I tell you solemnly that there are forces and influences at work which, if unchecked, will render us just as unprepared for the second coming of Christ as was Israel for His first coming. Make no mistake about that. I see those influences at work. The spirit of Saduceeism is working like leaven.
>
> This is no ordinary time. The times demand something unusual. I want to stand here before you today as one who believes and believes deeply, seriously, and earnestly that the whole purpose and objective of this movement today is in the balance. I believe these certain principles from the Scriptures ought to be applied today in all our educational centers and in all our institutional centers as well. Too many of our young people today are being led into worldly conformity by some leaders who are themselves adhering to forms of worldly amusement and pleasure.
>
> My friends, I wish our young people could be kept away from all the beach parties and nudity parades and moving picture shows, and other questionable places where they ought not to go, but where they are sometimes led by their leaders. Just how far can we go in this matter of worldly conformity? Let us be done with the spirit of compromise. Let us not be like those people of old who allowed their religious beliefs to be so poisoned by contacts with the world that they were unable to recognize their own Messiah when He appeared.
>
> Would the pioneers know this movement should they awaken? Would they recognize the movement that they started in this world, and handed over to their successors? Would they really recognize it? To me, that is a very appealing and important question.
>
> Oh, some may say, they were a lot of old fogies. They were out of date. They were entirely behind the times. Today's standards have

changed. That is a favorite expression with some, but I do not believe it. I maintain that every right and true and proper standard that has ever prevailed, and that is laid down in God's Word is just as vital today as it ever was. I am not one who is willing to admit that standards have changed. That argument suggests that today we have lower standards, and it is used only by those who want lower standards. The nearer we come to the kingdom of God the higher standards we should have. (*Review and Herald,* October 14, 1937)

What do you say? Oh, God grant it, friend! I care not how many gold-plated arks may be going down the road. I care not how many rafts may be constructed in some hideout. I care not how much preaching of faith and faith only leads people to not even believe anything. Let us be sure that every day our hammer is pounding away on the "ark" according to the blueprint given by God. I return to Elder McElhaney's sermon:

If Jesus were here today would He recognize us? Indeed, may I say, would we recognize Him? Oh, I trust that the inroads of worldly corruption and poisoning have not prevailed to the place where not even Jesus would recognize us. I feel very solemn and very serious when I think about these things.

I may tell you frankly, I have had no desire this morning to preach you a model sermon. I do confess, my friends, to having a heart longing to see something come to us today that will change the whole drift of things, for I believe that the time has come when there ought to be such a change. It is always hard to detect the exact places where we deviate or turn off from some vital path. (*ibid.*)

Oh, friend, I want to be building on that ark. I want to be working with Jesus to help get the ark finished and get people into it. What do you say? And very literally, let us follow the blueprint which God has given from the Bible and Spirit of Prophecy in our homes, in our business activities, and in all aspects of life. In all these things, times have truly changed, but in all these things, I believe, and I must share my profound conviction with you that God has not changed. Bless His holy name. "For I am the LORD, I change not; therefore ye sons of Jacob are not consumed" (Mal. 3:6). "Jesus Christ the same yesterday, and to day, and for ever" (Heb. 13:8).

His changeless love, His changeless wisdom, and His almighty power summon us today from lethargy and unbelief, from every deviation and delusion, to let Him have His way fully, completely, and unreservedly.

CHAPTER 20

Fellow Workers with Him

The purpose of religion is not just to keep us out of jail. It isn't just to make us good citizens and give us happy homes. It will do all those things, but the real objective is something way beyond all of that. And it's because so many people miss the objective that they say it doesn't work for them.

Most recipes have at least one ingredient in the recipe, which, if you leave that ingredient out, the rest doesn't work very well. "Then said Jesus to them again, Peace be unto you: as My Father hath sent Me, even so send I you" (John 20:21).

Jesus invites us to come to Him, but He also says, "Go." His purpose in calling us to Him is that we may come and be filled and then go and share. "As My Father hath sent Me, even so send I you" (John 20:21).

Has He sent you? Well, if you've come to Him and listened and accepted the commission, then you're sent.

Now notice the wording of this, "As My Father hath sent Me, even so send I you" (John 20:21).

Why did He come here? His Father sent Him. What did the Father send Him for? We want to find out because He says He's sent us on the same mission that He sent Jesus on.

Let's look at Matthew 20:28: "Even as the Son of man came not to be ministered unto, but to minister, and to give His life a ransom for many."

The Father sent Jesus for two purposes—to minister and to give His life. He wants you to do the same.

To minister means to serve, to live for others, to spend your life doing things to make other people happy and holy.

That's the way Jesus did. He did it in Nazareth when He was a boy. He did it as a young man in the carpenter shop and in the community. He did it down at Jordan as He drew the disciples to share with Him in His early ministry. He did it at the wedding feast at Capernaum, at the temple at Jerusalem, and everywhere the providence of God sent Him during those three and a half years. But He did more than minister. It says He gave His life. We think, of course, of the cross where His soul was poured out unto death. In some lands, to accept Jesus means to run the risk of being a martyr. It will be here soon. "As my Father hath sent Me, even so send I you…" (John 20:21) …to minister, not to be ministered unto, and to give your life.

The United States' government has a Peace Corp plan in which they invite people to put in a year or two in some foreign land in the service of the federal government, spreading goodwill. It's a wonderful plan. Jesus wants you for His Peace Corp, but not just for a year or two. He wants you to enlist for the duration of the war. That means, until Jesus comes. This is what it means to be a Christian.

Many think that in the church, there are two classes of people: a few who do what I'm reading about, and the rest who fill the pews and give some offerings to help pay the expenses.

But when we look at the early church, we see that the whole group was carrying out this commission. They took the words of Jesus literally: "As My Father hat sent Me, even so send I you" (John 20:21).

And from the apostles right down to the youngest member of the church, they were all witnessing, serving others, and giving their light. That is why within one generation, every creature under heaven had heard the Gospel.

It's also why there were a great many martyrs. The devil gets angry when the church gets on fire, when the church accepts the commission of Jesus, each member giving his or her life in service and sacrifice. When once this commission is accepted, the question of whether we die a martyr's death or live a servant's life is for Jesus to decide. We don't elect that. We enlist. Jesus assigns the particular place we're to fill and the particular work we're to do.

You remember that when Jesus left this world, the last thing He told His disciples was, "I'm going to the Father, and I'm going to pray, and He will give you the Spirit, then I want you to go everywhere."

Read the commission in Matthew, Mark, Luke, John, and Acts. Every one of the Gospel writers echoes and re-echoes this commission of Jesus: "Go ye therefore and teach all nations."

"Go ye into all the world and preach the Gospel to every creature." He sent them to teach and to preach and to heal and to publish glad tidings to the ends of the earth. Thank God they did it.

In this last generation, all that was done back there is to be repeated on a wider stage and on a grander scale. Oh, I hope you will share a part in it! It's your privilege. Yes, it's your duty. God has arranged it so that you could be born at this particular time to fill your place.

I would like to study with you some very practical things about filling your place. In the Lord's plan, He doesn't arrange that we should all do the same work in the same way. He has many different ways of working. One reason for that is because He has many different people to reach. You're different because the people that God has planned for you to reach are different. I can reach some people and help some people that you can never reach. Equally true, you can help some people and reach some people that are not for me.

Isn't it a wonderful thing, friend, to arrive at the conclusion and accept it as a fact that there is a definite, special work for you to do? One of the saddest things I know is to go through life looking around, seeing what other people are doing and thinking, "Oh, I wish I could do this. I wish I could do that. I wish I could do the other thing."

May I say honestly that I do not feel that way? I rejoice in what other people are doing, and so many of them are doing things far more wonderful than anything I can do. But God made me to do a certain work. When He puts me at a certain place at a certain time to meet the need of a certain soul, that thrills my heart. When that happens, I would rather be there than up in heaven with the angels.

There is a place in the ranks for you. And using the language of the army, what difference does it make whether it's the infantry, or the artillery, the quartermaster corps, the medical corps, or what: just so you're helping to win the war? But it isn't just a matter of saying, "It doesn't make any difference where, so I'll just drop into anything that I happen to fall into." No. You had better report to the commanding officer and get your assignment because God has planned for you a certain place, a certain work, and for that work, you were born.

There are three great lines of service. As far as I know, all the different details fit into one of these three plans. Into one of these three phases of activity, your life is to be cast. I can't decide which one of the three it is, but Jesus has it already decided for you, and He will lead you by His Spirit and by His providence, provided you are willing to do anything, go anywhere, at whatever cost to yourself.

Before I give you these three, I suggest you see how different this is from the idea of a church being an organization where you come and listen to a sermon and put some money in an offering plate and go home and say, "Well, we had a good sermon (or a bad one)." I suggest you see how different it is from the idea of just coming to a building and going through a certain ritual or liturgy or some worship of some kind.

The church is organized for service. That is what inspiration says. And that is why the book that gives the history of the early church is called Acts. What does "acts" mean? Actions. Doing things. And every one of those twenty-eight chapters of the book of Acts just teems with experiences of action, action, action.

Now these three phases. I'm not giving these in any particular order, and I'm not trying to emphasize one more than another. We need all three phases or three divisions of this great service program.

Number one in the sequence in which we'll study includes all church members who are laboring day by day in their vocations as carpenters or bricklayers or bookkeepers or cooks or whatever, making a living but doing something more than the workers out in the world who are in those same lines. The church member who has the vision about which we're studying, as he labors with his hands, is watching for opportunities to witness on the job. He is also dedicating time apart from his job to witnessing in his home and in the community. And with part of the money he's earning, he's supporting the missionary program of the church at home and in fields afar with his tithes and offerings.

This is the type of service to which hundreds of thousands of the church are called. Many have responded to that. This is the minimum of service that God expects from everyone. He doesn't expect anyone to just warm a pew. No. He wants our witness on the job. He wants our witness in the home and in the community apart from our job. He wants our tithes and offerings.

Number two. God has also called for certain workers to devote their time and their lives entirely to the service of the Gospel, the ordained ministry particularly, and those associated with them as Bible instructors and helpers in various lines. These are called by God and by the church; they are supported by the church and directed by the church. These are the servants of the church, leading the entire membership of the church in its program of witnessing and ministry to those about. This ministry finds expression in four great lines of activity—preaching, teaching, healing, and publishing. This is the fourfold job that God has given His church. And may I say, there are a lot of things that He hasn't given the church either as a body or the church members as individuals.

May I warn you that there are a great many activities today that are looked upon as perfectly legitimate? In other words, you won't be arrested by the police or the FBI if you engage in them, but God never called a member of the remnant church to perform them.

Now to Ephesians 4:28, "Let him the stole steal no more." Do you know what a thief is? He is one that earns his living by his wits. He is a parasite; he preys on other people. There are hundreds of ways that you can do it today and still not go to the penitentiary. "But rather let him labour, working with his hands the thing which is good, that he may have to give to him that needeth" (Eph. 4:28).

Now, number three:

> For the kingdom of heaven is like unto a man that is an householder, which went out early in the morning to hire labourers into his vineyard. And when he had agreed with the labourers for a penny a day, he sent them into his vineyard. He went out about the third hour, and saw others standing idle in the marketplace. And said unto them; Go ye also into the vineyard, and whatsoever is right I will give you. And they went their way. Again he went out about the sixth and ninth hour, and did likewise. And about the eleventh hour he went out, and found others standing idle, and saith unto them, Why stand ye here all the day idle? They say unto him, because no man hath hired us. He saith unto them, Go ye also into the vineyard; and whatsoever is right, that shall ye receive. (Matt. 20:1–7)

Read the rest of the parable, and you will see how it turned out. But what I want you to notice is this: those who were hired at one point in that day knew they were going to get a certain wage at the end of the day. You noticed that, didn't you? Did they know how much it would be? Yes. It was all agreed on at the beginning of their service. They were hired for a definite time, with a definite wage.

Later in the day, he went out and found some others idle, and what arrangement did he have with them? "Go into the vineyard, and whatsoever is right I will give you." So, you see that there was a difference in those groups.

God has, down through the ages, sometimes called men and women to devote their lives to the work of the church, the work of the Gospel, as fully as though they were hired, and yet without any agreed-on support and without any guaranteed income. This is the third group that I'm presenting to you. And interestingly enough, Jesus and His first disciples are some of the best examples of this.

When Jesus found Peter and John up there at the Sea of Galilee, they were fishing. They were working with their hands. He said, "Come ye after me, and I will make you fishers of men" (Matt. 4:19, ASV).

He called them from the program of making a living to devoting their lives to the work of the Gospel.

Did He guarantee them a certain wage? No, He didn't. They went with Him. They shared with Him. Sometimes they were hungry. Sometimes the only place they had to sleep was under the trees. But all of them, except Judas, stayed with Him to the end. All but John were martyrs for Him after He went back to heaven. They got hold of something, and something got hold of them that sent them to the ends of the earth.

They began on a program in which they had no promise of support except, "Whatsoever is right, I will give you." Later, when the church was better organized, shall we say, more established, money flowed in. And the New Testament teaches that those who preach the Gospel should live of the Gospel.

Consider the early days of the Advent movement. What kind of workers were Joseph Bates and James and Ellen White at the beginning of this movement? Was there a treasury that paid them? Now, this type of worker is called a self-supporting worker in the Spirit of Prophecy. The phrase, self-supporting worker, as used in the Spirit of Prophecy, does not mean the great rank and file of our membership who earn a good living, pay their tithe and offerings, and give some Bible studies on the side. In that sense, everyone should be a self-supporting missionary unless he or she is paid by the church. They're in that first class that I mentioned.

As there are thousands whom God calls to earn their living through the ordinary vocations of life and support the church with their witness and their offerings, and as there are those who God calls to be employed by the church fully, so He calls some to devote their lives as fully as though they were paid, and yet looking to Jesus for the fulfillment of His promise, "Go into the vineyard, and whatsoever is right I will give you."

Now, what is the difference between being self-supporting and the ordinary layman who is engaged in his daily work? One difference is in the size of their bank accounts. It doesn't always work this way. God has given some people the ability to carry on business in order to make money: "Thou shalt remember the Lord thy God: for it is He that giveth thee power to get wealth" (Deut. 8:18).

Abraham was a rich man and got it all honestly. There are men today who have been successful in business. Another reference here to see the point that I am making is in *volume seven of Testimonies*, page 23:

> Self-supporting missionaries are often very successful. Beginning in a small, humble way, their work enlarges as… they move forward under the guidance of the Spirit of God. Let two or more start out together in evangelistic work. They may not receive any particular encouragement from those at… the head of the work that they will be given financial support; nevertheless, let them go forward, praying, singing, teaching, living the truth. They may take up the work of canvassing, and in this way introduce the truth into many families. As they move forward in their work they gain a blessed experience. They are humbled by a sense of their helplessness, but the Lord goes before them, and among the wealthy and the poor they find favor and help. Even the poverty of these devoted missionaries is a means of finding access to the people. (*Testimonies for the Church*, vol. 7, p. 23)

Now, this is a very interesting statement. "Even the poverty of these devoted missionaries is a means of finding access to the people." A self-supporting missionary must be prepared to accept the terms that Jesus offered His disciples, which were nothing. When Jesus called Matthew, who had been making a living and doubtless had a good bank account as a tax collector, Jesus did not say to him, "Matthew, come and I'll match what you've been making" or "Matthew, would you be willing to take 50 percent of what you're making?" He simply called him to leave all that and throw himself entirely with Jesus into soul-winning work. Did it work? Matthew thought it did. And when, at the end of three years, Jesus said to Matthew and the other apostles: "When I sent you without purse, and scrip, and shoes, lacked ye any thing?" (Luke 22:35). What did Matthew and the other apostles say?

"…Nothing."

They hadn't lacked anything. Yet, if you read *Acts of the Apostles*, page 18, you will find that they shared the frugal fare of Jesus. And that doesn't mean ice cream and cake; it doesn't even mean bread and butter at every meal. Do you know what "frugal" means? A lot of people don't know a thing about what it means. Look it up in the dictionary, and if you continue in this work long enough, you'll find what it means by experience. "They shared His frugal fare, and like Him were sometimes hungry and often weary" (*Acts of the Apostles*, p. 18).

Yet, they received something in fellowship with Jesus that was worth more to them than the bank accounts and successful business enterprises that they had left behind. "They are humbled by a sense of their helplessness" (*Testimonies for the Church*, vol. 7, p. 23).

Friend, every person ought to pray about what he or she is engaged in. The man who's running a barbershop ought to pray that God will help him to conduct his business in a way that will bring glory to God. But listen, a barber doesn't have to kneel down every morning and wrestle with God to learn how to cut hair, does he? If he does, he'd better not run a barbershop. A man can be a successful barber even if he doesn't know anything about prayer. Thousands are doing it—making a living, giving good haircuts, and providing for their family. But a self-supporting missionary is dealing with problems, financial and spiritual, that he has got to pray or else quit being a self-supporting missionary. It says, "They are humbled by a sense of their helplessness" (*Testimonies for the Church*, vol. 7, p. 23).

Now, this is what bothers some people about self-supporting work—they can't understand it. They look and see barbers, lumbermen, plumbers, bankers, and others making a good living and making a success of life, and they say, "What is the matter with self-supporting work in that it seems so insecure?" Read this page and ask God why He arranged it this way. I'll tell you a little secret, friend, why God has arranged it this way for some people. It's the only way some people can learn faith. Now, some people can learn it in other ways, but this is the way God has chosen for some people to learn faith. If God calls you into self-supporting work, remember, in a special way, you're going to have to live by faith.

And this brings me to a very important point—just being in a self-supporting institution doesn't give you as an individual this self-supporting experience. You can be in a self-supporting institution and fill your place as a nurse, a bookkeeper, a farmer, a cook, or whatever, and you can be just as dependent on a paycheck or whatever is the equivalent of that as the person down the street who works for a secular business. Don't forget that.

If you really want an experience in self-supporting work and will tell the Lord so, He may answer your prayer, but it may be in unexpected ways. May I suggest one thing that could happen to you? Some sudden financial need may strike you. Or maybe sickness in the family, some accident, or something else may test your faith. If you have not been trained in this philosophy of true self-supporting work, and if you don't understand these principles, do you know what you'll think of? You'll think of the institution as the place that ought to solve and will solve your problems. If that's the way your mind runs, then you're not a self-supporting worker—you're merely an employee.

"Well," you say, "What would a person do?" Let's go back to the parable in Matthew 20. The kingdom of heaven, Jesus says, is like a man who went out in the morning and hired some workers, and he agreed with them for a certain wage. They were to work all day long for a penny. The Roman penny is more than our penny today—it was a day's wage. Those men knew what to expect—work all day and get their day's wage. Did they get it? Yes, read the story. How much did they get? They got just what they had agreed on. But later in the day, the owner of the vineyard went out into the marketplace and found some other people idle, and he said, "Come into the vineyard and whatever is right, I will give you." Did they go? Did they know what they were going to get? But they knew that if the man kept his word, they'd get whatever was right.

By the way, who paid them? The man who called them. And if Brother Frazee calls you, Brother Frazee ought to pay you. But Brother Frazee long ago quit calling people. I don't have that kind of a bank account. My good friend, Brother Neal, said this: "I work for the Lord and I wouldn't work for anybody else." And I advise you, friend, if you really want to have an experience with God, find out what God wants you to do and then do that, and then look to the One that called you to pay you. And remember, He promised to pay you what? Whatever is right. By the way, who decided what was right? The people who picked the grapes? No. The owner of the vineyard. And if Jesus has called you, He is the one to decide what is right.

Dear friends, for years and decades, I've been proving these promises personally and with dozens and scores, yes hundreds of others, and I have seen God keep His word many years. I've never seen God let anyone down. Of course, if you want the security of a permanent job and the settled income and the assured security of social security and all the different arrangements today, then self-supporting work, as we're describing it, is not for you. No. And God doesn't call everyone into this work any more than He calls everyone into the church-supported, conference-paid ministry. Remember, we need all three types of work.

And let me say, friend, nobody should waste one minute comparing these different lines of work and exalting any one of them at the expense of the others. Let me illustrate what I mean. Suppose someone comes up to you and says, "Which do you think is most important—your heart, your lungs, or your brain?" If you had to give up two and keep one, which one would you keep? Well, suppose you only had to give up one and keep the other two? Which one would you let go of? You see, the question is silly, but the application I'm making is not silly.

Let nobody then, for Jesus' sake, waste one minute criticizing any of these three lines of work. It was the Lord Jesus Christ who called for all three lines of work. All three lines were in the early church; all three lines were in the remnant church, placed here by the gift of prophecy. We need all three. Let us uphold one another's hands.

Here is another statement on this from *volume seven* of *Testimonies*. The name of this chapter is "Workers from the Ranks." Listen carefully: "In the future, men in the common walks of life will be impressed by the Spirit of the Lord to leave their ordinary employment and go forth to proclaim the last message of mercy" (*Testimonies for the Church*, vol. 7, p. 27).

You see, they were in class one, and the Spirit of God impresses them to go into class three. These numbers don't mean anything; they're just different ways of describing the three classes. Here are people who have been in ordinary employment, but they're impressed by the Spirit of the Lord to leave their ordinary employment and go forth to proclaim the last message of mercy. "As rapidly as possible they are to be prepared for labor, that success may crown their efforts" (*ibid.*).

Do people need a preparation when they leave their ordinary means of employment and get into self-supporting work? That is what this says. One of the most important things that they need to learn is how to be self-supporting.

In a tract, "An Appeal for the Madison School," Sister White writes, concerning the students at Madison, "They have been learning to become self-supporting and a training more important than this, they could not receive." Let me tell you, it means something to learn the philosophy of self-supporting work and the practical application of the principles in self-supporting work. It isn't something that is learned by breezing into an institution and looking over the grounds and saying, "I've seen that. I guess I could go out and do that."

> In the future, men in the common walks of life will be impressed by the Spirit of the Lord to leave their ordinary employment and go forth to proclaim the last message of mercy. As rapidly as possible they are to be prepared for labor, that success may crown their efforts… Does this indicate that there might be people to try to hinder them? Yes. No one is authorized to hinder these workers. They are to be bidden Godspeed as they go forth to fulfill the great commission. No taunting word is to be spoken of them… Their persevering prayers will bring souls to the cross. (*ibid.*)

If you have given your heart to Jesus (and if you haven't, I hope you'll give your heart to Jesus right now), then He is definitely using you or wants to use you in one of these three lines. And the highest place in all the world, friend, is the place you belong.

If God has called you to be busy making a living for yourself and your family in one of the common vocations of life, ask God to help you to be just as faithful in that as Jesus was when He was a carpenter for many years in Nazareth. Jesus spent more years as a carpenter in Nazareth than He did as a medical missionary in public work. Everyone who is called to the common vocations of life can look to Jesus in the carpenter shop in Nazareth as an example. God may be calling you to give your time to the church-supported, church-directed work. Or, God may be calling you to think seriously about answering the call to self-supporting work. Let the Holy Spirit impress your heart.

Kind Father, we believe that Jesus is interceding at the throne of the universe. We thank Thee that the same Savior who called men from the fisherman's net and the tax-collecting booth is calling men and women today. And we pray that Thou wilt help the reader to know Thy call and give those who already know what it is, the strength to answer it. And as the result, may the reader win souls to Christ. And when Jesus comes, may we see a great harvest of souls as the result of the dedication and devotion. We ask it in Jesus' name, who died for us, amen.

CHAPTER 21

Steps to Miracles

Here is a compelling testimony that came from a friend of mine:

> We came up to yesterday still lacking a few hundred dollars of having enough to pay our bills. There was nothing for the faculty allowance for February. They usually get thirty dollars a month each. This morning, a brother attended our church service and gave us a check for $2,200 marked: 'For Teacher's Salaries.' Oh, for more faith!

Would you like to have an experience like that? These things don't just happen; they're planned. First, they have to be planned in heaven. If I had my life to live over again, I would not choose to miss seeing miracles of this kind. I have seen at least one thousand miracles in my life. I'm not talking about the ordinary working of divine providence. I mean the unusual interpositions of God working. I rejoice that many other people are learning how to work with God to see Him perform miracles. Would you like to see Him work miracles?

I'm going to study with you the road to miracles. There is a road to take to miracles, just as there is a road to get to a major city. There is a road to take to get there. Someone might think it's a rocky road, and it is. Some might think it's a narrow road, and it is. Some might think it's a steep road, and it is. It's all of those.

I read God's invitation to us to enter into partnership with Him: "For My thoughts are not your thoughts, neither are your ways My ways, saith the LORD. For as the heavens are higher than the earth, so are My ways higher than your ways, and My thoughts than your thoughts" (Isa. 55:8, 9).

God's ways are not our ways; our ways are not God's ways. If we are going to walk with God, we'll have to walk a different road from the road we are used to. Which would you rather do: take your road or take God's road? You see, our minds will have to be changed so that they learn to work with God.

God had a man once that He wanted to use to lead Israel from Egypt to Canaan. When Moses was forty years old, he accepted God's invitation. He quit government service and started to work for the kingdom of heaven, but he started to use the methods of earth to advance the interests of heaven. He used his human reason—the methods he had learned in the military schools of Egypt. He meant well. He was perfectly sincere, but he made a flop.

> God's ways are not our ways; our ways are not God's ways. If we are going to walk with God, we'll have to walk a different road from the road we are used to. Which would you rather do: take your road or take God's road? You see, our minds will have to be changed so that they learn to work with God.

It was a good thing he did. God took him out into the desert and swept that out of him. And, thank God, there amid the mountains of Midian, Moses learned God's ways. As the result, he spent the closing forty years of his life in the successful leadership of two million people from Egypt to Canaan.

It was a wonderful trip, but all the way along, God had to work miracles. When they got to the Red Sea, the waters were rolling. How were they going to get through? There were no boats. There was a menacing enemy army behind. There were mountains on either side. What could they do? God said to Moses, "Tell the children of Israel to go forward." What an impossible command! But did it work? Yes. Do you know why it worked? Because they were doing what God told them to do.

Some other people tried it just a few minutes later, and they got drowned. So, just because you see someone experiencing miracles, don't conclude that you can do what they're doing and get the same results. God works miracles for those whom He chooses when they are doing what He has asked them to do. God told Israel to go through the Red Sea, but He never inspired the Egyptians to go in after them. That was a foolish mistake on their part.

Israel went out into the desert. Imagine trying to take two million people through a desert. Pretty soon, they ran out of food. I suppose there were many wise heads that wagged and thought that Moses should have thought of this before he ever left Egypt. He knew they didn't have enough bread to last across the desert. What were they going to do? Had Moses figured that out before he left? Who did? God. And at the right time, the manna fell, and it kept falling for forty years, six days a week—twice as much on the preparation day and none on Sabbath. Thus, it was evident every week that this was not a happenstance; it was a miracle.

When they didn't have water, God told Moses to strike the most impossible-looking place that you could think of—a hard rock. Out of that rock that he struck came water. And all through their journey, as they went from place to place, from the desert rocks, the waters gushed out. God was working a miracle.

There were other miracles. And all this was to prepare them for the conquest of Canaan. When they arrived at the end of the forty years, the River Jordan was overflowing its banks. God could have led them there at a time when it would have been easier to ford the River Jordan. But He deliberately brought them there at a time when the river was overflowing its banks. Why? That people might learn how God does things. God delights in working miracles for His people.

See the promise God gave to Moses early in the trip from Egypt to Canaan: "And He said, Behold, I make a covenant: before all thy people I will do marvels, such as have not been done in all the earth, nor in any nation: and all the people among which thou art shall see the work of the LORD: for it is a terrible thing that I will do with thee" (Exod. 34:10).

Don't you wish you could have lived back there and seen all that? I don't. I would rather be alive right now. "Blessed are the eyes which see the things that ye see" (Luke 10:23). And all that we have seen is but the prelude. Oh, if we will come into line, there is no limit to what God will do. But we have to learn how He works. If we are going to walk with Him on the road to miracles, we must be prepared to take the steep, rough, and narrow road and not turn back.

There are a few words that helped me to understand the road to miracles. We will start with the word vision.

Jesus told His disciples, "Lift up your eyes, and look on the fields; for they are white already to harvest" (John 4:35).

God is not working miracles just to satisfy our curiosity or to amuse us. He is not doing something on a stage while people sit and clap. No, He wants us to participate; He wants us to see a need and fill up.

That vision is to lead to a burden. A burden is more than a desire. It is a sense of mission and a recognition of a commission from God. Moses was given that burden there at the burning bush. God told him to go deliver Israel.

Jesus called His disciples. You and I, as we see about us the needs of suffering humanity, as we see the sick and those tied up with habits that keep them from health and happiness and hope, God puts a burden on us to do something about it.

That burden is to lead us to prayer. If we rush into the work without prayer, we may make Moses' mistake. We may use our own methods or methods we have seen someone else use. Jesus longs to have us come to Him in prayer.

Christ was our example when He was here. Carrying out His Father's work, He spent much time in prayer. He knew that in our humanity, it would be impossible for Him to carry out His mission unless He sought the Lord earnestly. Shall we do less? Oh, that God may teach us the power that there is in prayer!

I want you to see a wonderful promise on prayer: "And all things, whatsoever ye shall ask in prayer, believing, ye shall receive" (Matt. 21:22). "Prayer is the key in the hand of faith to unlock heaven's storehouse, where are treasured the boundless resources of Omnipotence" (*Steps to Christ*, pp. 94, 95).

This was the key that opened up the storehouse to this wonderful miracle story I quoted to you at the beginning of this chapter. This is the key that Moses used again and again in the exodus. When Israel was thrown into panic at the Red Sea, Moses cried to the Lord. When they murmured when the food ran out, Moses cried to the Lord. When they asked what they should do for water, Moses cried to the Lord. Prayer is one of the essential steps in the road to miracles. Those who skip this step will never reach the top. There is more to miracles than prayer, but there are no miracles without prayer.

The way we learn to do things is by doing them. The way we learn to meet problems is by having them. The way we learn to swim is to be in the water. Some of you are having problems. What are you doing with those problems? Are you merely saying? "What shall I do?" Or are you saying, "I wonder when 'they' will get around to solving my problems," whoever "they" may be? This is what many in Israel did back there in the days of the exodus. They were always wondering when Moses was going to do something. Is there some human being or some committee that you are looking to, to solve your problems? Oh, it's a wonderful thing to learn that you can go to God and lock yourself with Him in the closet of communion, and there in the secret place of prayer, you can win victories with which no human being can interfere. You and God are a majority when you are on your knees and claiming His promises.

I trust that the abundance of opportunities, facilities, and means that God has brought us to and brought to us shall not defeat God's purpose in teaching us to pray. Wouldn't it be too bad if God had to cut off our food supply or our money so we would learn to pray? God may cut down our supply of this or that or the other thing upon which we have tended to rely. But in every difficulty, we are to see a call to prayer. That is what these difficulties are for.

The next step after prayer is effort. There is a shorter way to spell effort—W-O-R-K. The same Jesus who was our example in prayer was our example in effort. Hear Him as He says to His disciples: "I must work the works of Him that sent Me, while it is day: the night cometh, when no man can work" (John 9:4).

Jesus was no hermit cut off from the needs of suffering humanity. His sense of need led Him to prayer. But there in prayer, His soul was urged to go out and go to work. This is the kind of prayer that you and I are to experience with Him. Unless our prayer experience leads to effort, it is sterile. Prayer is designed to prepare us for earnest effort in soul-winning and in practical things in solving the problems of life. The mechanic may meet a problem with an engine. He may pray. But does he stand there wondering when the angels will come and assemble the gears? No. Having prayed in faith, he goes to work. The farmer prays. But as he prays, he goes to work; so with soul-winning and with every other experience.

But now we're headed for a miracle. Do you know why we need a miracle? Because the thing we are trying to do is bigger than any human effort can surround. I feel sorry for the man who has a job as small as he is. Oh, friend, I thank God that He has challenged you and me with a task far beyond our capacity. He is calling us up that road to miracles.

But there is another step before we get to miracles. When God has inspired us with a vision and laid upon us a burden when in earnest prayer we have sought Him about that task and then put all we have into doing the work, then comes the acid test—the call to sacrifice.

Do you mean that after I have worked hard for something, then I must give it away? Do you mean that, after I have toiled and sweat, then I must take the money that I have earned or the food that I have grown, and I must share it with others to the point where I myself am poor? This is what Jesus did. He invited His disciples to share that with Him. They shared His frugal fare, we are told, and like Him, were sometimes hungry and often weary. He said to them all: "If any man will come after Me, let him deny himself, and take up his cross daily, and follow Me" (Luke 9:23).

Oh, friends, we are not yet ready for miracles until, in addition to prayer and effort, we take the step of sacrifice. God is not working miracles for lazy people. Neither is He working miracles for people who are industrious but keep what they earn. God is working miracles for people who will work as though it all depended on them and then make a sacrifice. Then and only then can you expect God to work a miracle.

That is the road to miracles. There is something that underlies the whole thing—love. It is love that leads us to lift up our eyes and look on the field. It is love that lays on our hearts a burden to help others. It is love that summons us to prayer and leads us to claim the promises that God's name may be honored and His work extended. It is love that leads us to effort. It makes the burden light. It makes the yoke easy. Toil becomes a delight to the one whose heart is filled with love. It is love and love alone that can turn sacrifice into joy. This is the love of a mother for her child. Greater than the love of any mother is God's love for you and me.

It is that love that we are to receive from Him and impart to the needy around us. It is love that inspires every upward step. And when God finds human beings who will take these steps with Him, He delights to crown their ministry with miracles, one after the other. This is what He did for

Moses. This is what He did for Elijah and Elisha. This is what He did in the ministry of Christ on earth. This is what He did in the ministry of the apostles. This is what He is waiting to do in an unprecedented manner in the closing hours of human history as the remnant church enters upon the final triumph.

Friend, would you like to see miracles? Financial miracles? Miracles of healing? Miracles of solving human problems? Miracles of saving souls? Oh, there is no limit to the usefulness of the one who, by putting self aside, makes room for the working of the Holy Spirit.

Would you pick out mountains for a highway? Most engineers choose to go around the mountains or through them. Why? It's difficult. Some mountains are impossible from the human standpoint. But listen to the thoughts of God made audible: "And I will make all My mountains a way, and My highways shall be exalted" (Isa. 49:11).

Mountains are difficulties—problems, obstacles, impossibilities. God says, "If you will come with Me and put everything else aside, you and I will scale the mountains and make them the highway of miracles."

CHAPTER 22

Less Attempted, More Achieved

What I have to share with you in this chapter is not for everyone; at least, *everything* in the study is not for everyone. You watch for the part that belongs to *you*. The Holy Spirit will help you to see it.

Ahead of us is a great crisis; we speak of it. Many in the world are recognizing that things can't go on the way they are very much longer. Something's going to give; something's going to snap. But the paradox of it is, dear friend, that in order for you and me to get ready for that, some will need to get more relaxed instead of more wrought up. To state it in another way—to accomplish *more*, some need to attempt less. "Come unto Me, all ye that labour and are heavy laden, and I will give you rest. Take My yoke upon you, and learn of Me; for I am meek and lowly in heart: and ye shall find rest unto your souls. For My yoke is easy, and My burden is light" (Matt. 11:28–30).

Jesus tells me if I'll come to Him, I'll find what? Rest. Now, if I haven't found rest, either I haven't come, or else I came, and He didn't keep His word because He says here in this text, "Come unto me, all ye that labor and are heavy laden, and I will give you rest."

May I ask you, friend, what do you think of when you think of coming to Jesus? Do you think of a spur? Do you think of a laugh? Do you think of something happy and cheerful? Jesus says, "Come and I will give you…" what? Rest. Notice it's to those who are weary and heavy-laden that He gives this invitation. Rest is for those who are weary. And weariness comes from work. There are some people that don't know much about what work is, but I don't think that very many of them would care to read a book like this.

I've said that to say this—this text, then, is for *you*. "Come unto me, all ye that labour and are heavy laden, and I will I will give *you* rest" (Matt. 11:28, emphasis added).

"Take My yoke upon you." Is that a rocking chair? What is a yoke for? Work.

"But Lord, I'm already tired."

Jesus says, "You may be, but if you'll take My yoke upon you and learn of Me, you'll find rest unto your souls. For My yoke is easy and My burden is light."

We learn precious lessons in the study of physiology. We know that all the different organs and tissues of the body have their rhythmic cycles of work and rest, work and rest, work and rest. Take the heart. Here it is, beating sixty, seventy, or eighty times a minute, contracting and relaxing. You might not think that the rest it gets in between those contractions amounts to very much, but it makes all the difference between life and death. That is what the difference is. God longs that you and I, in our spiritual life, shall learn to beat rhythmically just like the physical heart. To work and rest, to work and rest, to find an experience where, like an automobile, we recharge the battery as we go along. And that's why Jesus invites us here, to come and take His yoke. And we'll find rest.

How in the world could I find any rest in a *yoke*? Jesus says you'll find it. Of course, I may say, sometimes people have to hunt to find it. We need it, folks. This is called the jet age, but God hasn't made you a jet engine. He never intended that you should work and operate like a jet engine.

The climax of the third angel's message is: "Here is the patience of the saints: here are they that keep the commandments of God, and the faith of Jesus" (Rev. 14:12).

The people who keep His commandments and His faith will be patient people. They can run and keep on. They don't get excited. It's going to mean something to go into this great crisis ahead, having learned that lesson.

"Let your moderation be known unto all men. The Lord is at hand" (Phil. 4:5). Well, if the Lord is at hand, this is no time to be moderate. Let's put on the gas, give it all we've got, and go! No, inspiration says, "Let your moderation be known unto all men. The Lord is at hand" (*ibid.*). "The power of man cannot hasten the work..." (*Testimonies for the Church*, vol. 7, p. 298).

Oh, surely if we'd all just work night and day, we could hasten it! No, no. Tomorrow morning if it's beginning to get light there in the east, but still, the sun hasn't come up, do you suppose if enough people would get a rope and lasso the sun and pull hard, we could get it here a minute sooner?

"Well," you say, "of course, we couldn't. We couldn't get it around it." Well, suppose we *could* get the rope around the sun. Do you think if a large group of people pulled hard enough that they could cause the sun to rise a minute sooner? Or, to get right down to the practical, it's the earth that is turning. Do you suppose if everyone leans heavily enough in the right direction, we could make the earth turn just a minute faster? It would be something to tell to all the world that we had made the sun get up a minute early, wouldn't it? Wouldn't that be a wonderful demonstration?

Well, we're not going to get that done. But this says, talking about the work of God, "The power of man cannot hasten the work…"

"Let no one overtax his God-given powers in an effort to advance the Lord's work more rapidly" (ibid.). Now I know there is a verse that says that we can hasten the coming of Jesus. We sure have been delaying it for over a hundred years.

You say, "How does that agree with what we're studying?" It agrees perfectly, friends. The thing that is delaying the coming of Jesus is not so much our lack of activity; it's the lack of learning *this lesson*. What the world needs is not so much to see us darting here and there like lightning. The world needs to see that you and I have come to Jesus and found rest—rest that's found not by stretching out on the bed and doing nothing, but rest that is found *in the yoke;* rest that we have found a way of life, which for us has settled the question of how to have peace. Not by being released from labor, but by finding satisfaction *in* labor and rest, *in* study and prayer, that causes other people to say, as the woman at the well said to Jesus, "Sir, give me this water."

Well, the text we've just read says, "Let your moderation be known unto all men. The Lord is at hand." What impression do your friends or visitors get as they come in touch with you? Do they get the impression that you have found a way of life, that things are under control? Or do they get the impression that you were born thirty minutes too late and have been seeking all your life to catch up?

Now, I'm not so concerned with the image we create. I'm concerned, my dear friend, with what happens in our own souls. And the interesting thing is that the more conscientious a person is, the more that person may fail to enter into this rest that Jesus is talking about.

Listen, if you knew that the thing that would please Jesus most would be for you to come to Him and get this rest He is talking about and find out how to work with Him in a way that, at the end of the day, you feel happy instead of "Oh, I wonder when I'll ever catch up…" Which is it, friends, which is it? "Come unto Me and I'll…" do what? Give you rest.

Listen, if you knew that coming to Jesus, getting His rest, and working with Him in a way that at the end of the day you feel happy is what would please Jesus the most, would you accept that over the attitude, "Oh, I wonder when I'll ever catch up!"?

"Oh," you say, "Brother Frazee, what pill do you have that is just going to take all our troubles away?"

Do you know what "moderation" is? Moderation is knowing when to stop. Stop what? Stop *any*thing. Moderation in eating means to be able, at the proper time, when something is passed to you, to say what? "No, thank you." Not to say, "Oh, probably I shouldn't eat it, but it tastes so good, I guess I will." Or maybe to cast the blame on the hostess and to say to yourself, "Well, she wouldn't like it if I turned down the second helping, and so just to please her (and myself too), I'll have some more."

That is not moderation. Moderation is being able to say what? "No." "No, thank you," but "no." That is right. And this applies, dear friend, not merely to eating. It applies to everything. "Let your moderation be known unto all men." You and I should be known as moderate people. Another word for that is "temperate."

"And every man that striveth for the mastery is temperate in all things…" (1 Cor. 9:25). Temperate in *all* things. You mean there is a temperance that applies to *everything*? That is what Paul says. Are you temperate in all things? "Excessive indulgence in eating, drinking, sleeping, or seeing, is sin" (Temperance, p. 138).

Can a man eat too much? Yes, people do it. Can a person drink too much, even if it's something good? Yes. Can he sleep too much? That's what this says. The wise man in Proverbs tells us that he went by the vineyard of the sluggard, and he saw it had all grown up to thorns. He said that he looked it over and I thought: "Yet a little sleep, a little slumber, a little folding of the hands to sleep: So shall thy poverty come…" (Prov. 6:10–11).

Yes, a person can eat too much, drink too much, sleep too much, and see too much. There is was something across the page that I didn't want to miss: "We should practice temperance in our labor. It is not our duty to place ourselves where we shall be overworked..." (*Temperance*, p. 139).

"Oh," someone is saying, "I'm so glad Brother Frazee is reading that. I hope someone will listen to that and not give me so much work to do." I hope they will too. May I say very simply, earnestly, and honestly: if you're where you're actually being overworked and can't get it changed, by all means, make a move. "Some may at times be placed where this is necessary, but it should be the exception, not the rule" (ibid.).

It should be what? The exception, not the rule. What is it that should be the exception? Overwork. If a mother has worked all day and then at midnight the baby gets sick, she doesn't say, "Sorry, darling, I'll see you at 8 o'clock in the morning." She doesn't keep union hours or any other kind of hours, does she? She is up and at it. But that is to be the exception, not the rule. Why? Because, friend, God has made us so that we have to have rest just the same as we have to have food. To acknowledge this and practice this is temperance. That is what we read in 1 Corinthians 9. And over in Philippians 4, it's called moderation.

One reason for being temperate in all things is that the Lord is at hand. When He comes, He is going to find a temperate people who are waiting for Him; not on pins and needles, not pacing up and down. They will have expectation, but they will be resting in Him.

I believe that if some people can learn the lesson to work and rest as the human heart does, it will do more for them than anything else I know. The heart can do that, and it can do a lot more than people think it can, provided that we don't overload it and that we give it the opportunity to grow into the bearing of greater burdens.

I'm going to read a few statements now from the book Evangelism:

> If our active temperament gathers in a large amount of work that we have not strength nor the grace of Christ to do understandingly and with order and exactitude, everything we undertake shows imperfection, and the work is constantly marred. God is not glorified however good the motive... The worker complains of constantly having too heavy burdens to bear... (*Evangelism*, pp. 80, 81)

The picture I see when I read that is of a great cafeteria. I take my tray, and I start out. There are the salads, and I think, "Oh my, those salads look so good that I think I'll have two of them! Salads are good for you." So, I get a couple of salads. Then I go on around to the entrees, and they look good, and the vegetables and the desserts and the beverages and bread, and by the time I get through, I need a tray and a half, you understand.

> My dear friend, life is a cafeteria. And one of the biggest things you can learn in life is this: most of what you come in contact with is not for you to put on your tray.

Now I've gotten it on my tray, and I sit down at the table. What have I got to do? Well, I've got to eat it. Or do I? I don't have to, but it'd be a shame to have it go to waste, wouldn't it? It'd be a shame to go to waste either way on this one.

Where was the problem? I took too much on the tray. That's the basic problem. If I'm going to eat at a cafeteria, I'm going to have to learn to think about that whole array and make up my mind that most of it I'm going to pass by and not touch. Is that right?

My dear friend, life is a cafeteria. And one of the biggest things you can learn in life is this: most of what you come in contact with is not for you to put on your tray.

I remember someone years ago, when we were all eating at one table, told the cook that she had to be gone for a few days. So, she said, "Please don't have anything especially good while I'm gone." She didn't want to miss anything. Why, bless your hearts, friend, there are so many good things happening, and you're missing nine-tenths of it every day you live!

"Oh, that is the trouble. I've got to catch up!"

No, you can't. It's impossible. But you can wear your life out trying. It's like a dog trying to keep up with a Cadillac—he can never catch it, but he can sure work hard and wear himself out trying it, can't he? Yes. "Let your moderation be known unto all men."

Let us come to Jesus and find what? Rest! *In* the yoke, *with* the yoke. Jesus wants us to link up with Him and be happy in what He gives us to do and not attempt more.

I want to read an interesting letter that the Lord's messenger wrote to Dr. John Harvey Kellogg. A failure to learn the lesson we're studying is at the foundation of Kellogg's failure to persevere with this message:

> The Lord gave you your work, not to be done in a rush, but in a calm, considerate manner. The Lord never compels hurried, complicated movements. But you have gathered to yourself responsibilities that the Lord, the merciful Father, does not place upon you. (*Testimonies for the Church,* vol. 8, p. 189)

Did Kellogg have more than he could do? Yes. Where did he get it? He gathered those things for himself. The Lord put *some* things on him, and then he put in some more. Did you ever hear of people complaining that a certain food didn't agree with them, and you asked them what else they had for dinner, and there were 13 other things? If they had 14 things in the stomach, how did they know which one didn't agree with them?

> …You have gathered to yourself responsibilities that the Lord, the merciful Father, does not place upon you. Duties He never ordained that you should perform chase one another wildly. Never are His servants to leave one duty marred or incomplete in order to seize hold of another …Not all the burdens that you have been carrying have been laid upon you by the Lord. (ibid.)

The Lord's messenger suggested that one way he could have avoided some of this was to do some counseling with his brethren. But do you know why he didn't? He was afraid they'd interfere with his plans, and they probably would have.

> By prayer and consecration, by seeking the Lord for wisdom and surrendering yourself to His guidance, you would have been prevented from starting many enterprises that have been born, not of the will of God, but of the will of man. You have neglected things of great importance to take up, with impulsive spirit, unadvised by the Lord or your brethren, things of minor importance. Your brethren could have given you counsel, but you despised any word that interfered with your plans. (*ibid.,* pp. 188, 189)

"Oh my! But I wouldn't want to come and tell my brethren, 'Now here, someone's asked me to do this, and someone asked me to do that, and I've thought of this, that, and the other thing that I want to do. Now, which do you think that I ought to do?' They might cut out the thing I want to do most, so I don't think I'll ask them. I'll just try to wedge it all in somewhere."

Do you see the problem? If you want your brethren to help prune out the things in your fruit tree that are keeping you from fruit-bearing, don't cry too hard when they start pruning. Be willing. "There goes that nice branch. Oh my, I was expecting so many things from that." Never mind: "Every branch in Me that beareth not fruit He taketh away: and every branch that beareth fruit, He purgeth it, that it may bring forth more fruit" (John 15:2).

The Lord has been good to us to even tell us what to say when we're tempted to take on more work than we ought:

> There are those who can successfully carry a certain amount of work, but who become overwearied, fractious, and impatient when there is crowded upon them a larger amount of work than they have physical or mental strength to perform. They lose the love of God out of the heart, and then they lose courage and faith, and the blessing of God is not with them. When men are asked or tempted to take more work than they can do, let them say firmly, I cannot consent to do this. I cannot safely do more than I am doing. (*Medical Ministry*, p. 294)

I can't improve on that, friend, for that is inspired. I ought to tell you that these references were all written when men and women were working ten and twelve and fourteen and sixteen hours a day.

While we have so many time and labor-saving devices, and while the workday, in general, has been shortened, the American people have tried to crowd more and more into the twenty-four hours of the day and the seven days of the week. No matter how you pack the suitcase, there are just so many cubic inches in it.

Let your moderation be known. Be temperate in all things. Don't take more work than you can carry. "Come unto Me and I'll give you rest."

Some of us will need to do some cutting. Where shall we start cutting? If we're not careful, we may not start at the right place.

Suppose I was a man out here working in a factory. I'm working eight hours a day, five or six days a week, and I'm earning enough money to support myself and my family. But I'm also doing a lot of things besides my work: around the house, in the yard, etc. Perhaps I have a lodge or a club, or I just go out and visit, or I have some kind of entertainment. Whatever it is, my time is more than filled up. Suppose I read this study, and I think, "I guess that's true, Brother Frazee. I've been trying to get too much done. I think what I need to do is go to my employer and tell him that forty or forty-eight hours a week is too much for me, and I would like to have him cut it down to about thirty hours so I would have more time to sleep and more time to pray and more time to study."

Before we study what "cutting down" means, I want to study with you what it doesn't mean:

> For even when we were with you, we gave you this command: if anyone will not work, let him not eat. For we hear that some of you are living in idleness, mere busybodies, not doing any work. Now of such persons we command and exhort in the Lord Jesus Christ to do their work in quietness, and to earn their own living. (2 Thess. 3:10–12, RSV)

Now from *Phillips Translation* of the same verses:

> When we were actually with you, we gave you this principle to work on. If a man will not work he shall not eat. Now we hear that you have some among you living quite undisciplined lives, never doing a stroke of work, and busy in only other people's affairs. Our order to such men, indeed our appeal by the Lord Jesus Christ is to settle down to work, and eat the food they have earned themselves. (2 Thess. 3:10–12, *Phillips Translation*)

If I understand this plain statement from the Bible, a man's first responsibility in work is to work enough to feed who? Himself. Now suppose he has dependents. Does he have a responsibility for them? That is just as much a part of it as feeding himself, isn't it? Yes. He settled that when he took on dependents. And of course, as children, we have a responsibility to our parents when they become in need of help. The Bible is clear on that. That is not my subject. I merely call attention to the fact.

So, what we're studying is not intended in any way to lessen the duty and responsibility of every man to work sufficiently to take care of himself and all who are dependent on him, whatever that takes. Do you think we ought to have any surplus to help other people who may be unfortunate? The Lord tells us to do that. But *over*work comes from one of two things: either from attempting to hoard riches or not having good management in the way we work. "When one is forever at work, and the work is never done, it is because mind and heart are not put into the work. It takes some persons ten hours to do that which another accomplishes readily in five. Such workmen do not bring tact and method into their labor" (*Fundamentals of Christian Education*, p. 316).

Now listen to this wonderful, encouraging statement: "There is something to be learned every day as to how to improve in the manner of labor so as to get through the work and have time for something else" (ibid.).

Every day it's my privilege to do what? Learn something about how to get more done in less time, so I'll have time for other things—missionary work, study and prayer, sleep, recreation, visiting, and so forth.

I found another suggestion here that might help some of us to know where to cut a little: "Let the talkative man remember that there are times when he has no right to talk. There are those who take time to stand still... Make not others idle by tempting them to listen to your talk. The time of many is lost when a man uses his tongue instead of his tool." (*Evangelism*, pp. 653, 654).

This can be true not merely in building a house. It can be true in the office, in the hospital, and even in our homes. I give you these suggestions so that you will take them to the Lord in prayer and see if we can't all learn how to help one another to find time enough to do the things we really need to do.

Here is the key to the whole thing: "The Lord GOD hath given me the tongue of the learned, that I should know how to speak a word in season to him that is weary: He wakeneth morning by morning, He wakeneth mine ear to hear as the learned" (Isa. 50:4).

Dear friends, if you and I will give God the first part of our day in the morning, He will help us to know what to do for the rest of the day. If you're in a bind financially, if it's obvious that some things you've been spending money for have got to stop so you can get out of debt, what do you do? Do you start with the tithe and say, "Well, I guess I'll have to cut that until I get out of debt"? No. You'd say, "No, Lord, whatever I cut, I can't do that. That is yours." So, it is with this time we spend with Jesus. The heavier your burden, the more you need Jesus. "Come unto Me, all ye that labour and are heavy laden, and I will give you rest" (Matt. 11:28).

Who will give you rest? Jesus

If you come, where? To Him. Let's come to Him, what do you say? But let us accept as our goal nothing short of finding that rest that Christ has promised. Let us not consider it a halo of martyrdom to go about so burdened that people wonder what our problem is. Let us rather rejoice in being a part of that demonstration of moderation that says, "Thank God, I have come to Jesus, and although He hasn't put me in the rocking chair, He's put me in the yoke with Him, and it feels good. I've got something worthwhile pulling, but oh, He gives me rest while I work!"

This will mean that we will take to God in prayer the requests that come to us to do this and do that and do the other thing. It will mean that we'll take it for granted that we are going to miss many things. But it will mean that we will know that the work we're doing is the work appointed by God and that there is joy and satisfaction in the service of our Lord.

> Come unto Me, all ye that labour and are heavy laden, and I will give you rest. Take My yoke upon you, and learn of Me; for I am meek and lowly in heart: and ye shall find rest unto your souls. For My yoke is easy, and My burden is light. (Matt. 11:28–30)

CHAPTER 23
The Secret Formula of Success

Everyone wants to be a success, and God wants everyone to succeed. So I want to give you the secret formula for success.

A large corporation engaged in the manufacture and service of various machinery has a sign in its repair shop that reads something like this, "When all else fails, read the manufacturer's instructions."

I want to share some of the secrets of success given to us in this beautiful Book, the Bible. Everyone wants to be successful. Everyone could be. Very few are.

> Only be thou strong and very courageous, that thou mayest observe to do according to all the law, which Moses My servant commanded thee: turn not from it to the right hand or to the left, that thou mayest prosper whithersoever thou goest. This book of the law shall not depart out of thy mouth; but thou shalt meditate therein day and night, that thou mayest observe to do according to all that is written therein: for then thou shalt make thy way prosperous, and then thou shalt have good success. (Josh. 1:7, 8)

If we'll listen, learn, and live out of the law of God, we will have good success. That is the recipe. These are the manufacturer's instructions.

You want to be successful, I'm sure. Nobody loves failure, and here is the formula for success. God said that if you just read what He had His prophet write and then do what it says—don't turn from it to the right hand or the left—meditate in it day and night, and then carry it out, and then you'll have good success.

Did it happen? Yes, it did. Joshua stubbed his toe a time or two when he slipped up on what this says, but he learned a lesson. We can learn lessons from all our failures. The great lesson, friend, is that the plan and the power are in this Book.

If you were the devil, what would you do about it? I'll tell you what he *is* doing about it—he is trying to interfere with this communication of the instructions of the Bible to me and you. He is trying to block this excellent channel. He brings in doubt. Some say, "Oh, I don't believe it." But, of course, without faith, it doesn't mean anything. So, doubt devalues and destroys the instructions in this Book.

"Well," someone says, "How can I get faith?"

" ...faith cometh by hearing, and hearing by the Word of God" (Rom. 10:17).

If you want more faith, study this Book. But faith won't come by listening to all the arguments, objections, and doubts of others. Oh, no. Faith comes by listening to God, and God will kindle faith in your heart as you study this Book.

The devil has other snares for those who believe the Book. Millions say, "Sure, I believe this Book." But the devil's game for those people is to get them busy with other things: other books, other magazines, TV programs, radio broadcasts, or just listening to their friends and relatives—*anything* to keep them from studying this Book. Do you know what I'm talking about? Bless the Lord that we don't have to walk into that spider web.

But now, let me tell you one of the most insidious things of all, and that is this—after we have found faith in this Bible, and as we read it and study it, and even learn to love it, there is a danger of getting all the blessing that there is in it through failure to carry out what we read. By looking at what people around us are doing instead of listening to what the Book says. Oh, my dear friends, the burden of my heart is to warn you on this point. The pilgrim's pathway is ever onward, ever upward. This Book is not instruction on reaching a certain plateau and staying there, waiting around until Jesus comes. This Book is a map on which we're to make progress every day. This Book portrays a journey that never stops this side of heaven.

Whatever God teaches you from this Book, why not follow it and follow it at once? This is the way to make rapid progress in the pilgrim journey.

Is God the One that made us body, mind, and spirit? Does He know what will make us successful? You'd think everyone would be anxious to get the instructions and follow them. Instead, listen, learn, and live according to the law of God.

> Therefore shall ye lay up these My words in your heart and in your soul, and bind them for a sign upon your hand, that they may be as frontlets between your eyes. And ye shall teach them your children, speaking of them when thou sittest in thine house, and when thou walkest by the way, when thou liest down, and when thou risest up. And thou shalt write them upon the door posts of thine house, and upon thy gates: That your days may be multiplied, and the days of your children, in the land which the LORD sware unto your fathers to give them, as the days of heaven upon the earth. (Deut. 11:18–21)

Do you want heaven on earth? You can have it. Just listen to what God says, learn His program, and live it. Fill your mind with the words of God. Fill your hands with the works of God. Fill your heart with the love of God.

Notice the three areas that we're told by inspiration that the following verse represents God's desire for every human being: "Beloved, I wish above all things that thou mayest prosper and be in health, even as thy soul prospereth" (3 John 2).

Most people are aware that God is interested in their spiritual life. But isn't it wonderful that God is as interested in our prosperity and physical health as He is the other?

You see, God loves us. If you love someone, you don't love just a part of that person. God is interested in our total health, prosperity, and whole spiritual life and happiness.

As we shall see, the secret recipe in all these is to listen to what He says, learn His principles, and live them in harmony with His law. That is the program. If we do it, we'll have the results.

Now, we're studying the secret formula of success. And remember, when all else fails, read the manufacturer's instructions. That is what we're doing. We're not exhausting the instructions. The whole Bible is a manual on the health of body, mind, and soul. And thank God for the fifty volumes of the inspired counsels in these latter days that magnify these beautiful things in the Bible and bring them down to our needs today.

Now, the secret formula of success for material prosperity. Is God interested in it? Yes. Just as in spiritual success, there are specific laws, rules, and principles that God wants us to follow. He wants us to live in cooperation with Him.

Turn to Malachi 3:10–12. This is God's secret formula for prosperity. Look at the recipe for prosperity. It's talking not just about spiritual things. It's talking about crops, a very material and financial item.

> Bring ye all the tithes into the storehouse, that there may be meat in Mine house, and prove Me now herewith, saith the LORD of hosts, if I will not open you the windows of heaven, and pour you out a blessing, that there shall not be room enough to receive it. And I will rebuke the devourer for your sakes, and he shall not destroy the fruits of your ground; neither shall your vine cast her fruit before the time in the field, saith the LORD of hosts. And all nations shall call you blessed: for ye shall be a delightsome land, saith the LORD of hosts. (Mal. 3:10–12)

The inspiration that has come to this people tells us that if the children of Israel had done what God told them to, they would have been the world's object lesson of health and prosperity. They would have been known all over the world. And that is what this says: "And all nations shall call you blessed: for ye shall be a delightsome land, saith the LORD of hosts" (Mal. 3:12).

And notice that the cornerstone of financial prosperity is to tithe. Now, see in Isaiah 58, another phase of this matter of financial prosperity:

> Is not this the fast that I have chosen? to loose the bands of wickedness, to undo the heavy burdens, and to let the oppressed go free, and that ye break every yoke? Is it not to deal thy bread to the hungry, and that thou bring the poor that are cast out to thy house? when thou seest the naked, that thou cover him; and that thou hide not thyself from thine own flesh? Then shall thy light break forth as the morning, and thine health shall spring forth speedily: and thy righteousness shall go before thee; the glory of the LORD shall be thy rearward.
>
> And if thou draw out thy soul to the hungry, and satisfy the afflicted soul; then shall thy light rise in obscurity, and thy darkness be as the

noon day: And the LORD shall guide thee continually, and satisfy thy soul in drought, and make fat thy bones: and thou shalt be like a watered garden, and like a spring of water, whose waters fail not. (Isa. 58:6–8, 10–11)

Health and prosperity depend upon sharing the good things that God gives us with others in need. That is the program.

Now, please go back to that seventh verse and notice some details. What very practical things are in that first line of the seventh verse? Bread. It's not talking just about spiritual matters. It's talking about actual food for the hungry.

And bring the poor where? To *your* house. There is an interesting statement in *Welfare Ministry*, page 322. This is a statement by one who knew James White very well. Please notice how he carried out this instruction.

> Elder White was himself a very philanthropic man. He always lived in a large house, but there were no vacant rooms in it. Although his immediate family was small, his house was always filled with widows and their children, poor friends, poor brethren in the ministry, and those who need a home. His heart and his pocketbook were always open, and he was ready to help those who needed help. He certainly set a most noble example to our denomination in his large heartedness and liberality of spirit. (*Welfare Ministry*, p. 322)

This was written after his death by a man who knew him well. Sister White herself was a lifetime example of this. I have a fascinating story. You can read more of them there in *Welfare Ministry* about Elder and Sister White. But I have something extraordinary I want to share with you here.

This is *Letter 68*, 1898. This is a simple recital of what I think is a beautiful example of philanthropic interest in humanity, hospitality, and love. And remember, God says if you and I do it, our health will be improved and our prosperity.

> It is selfish actions that keep the soul in feebleness, and deprive it of its power.

> A lady who has just recently embraced the truth, and who conducted a large dressmaking establishment, thought she would be able to take treatment at our sanitarium in Sydney and then come

> to the school and be educated as a missionary. She remained there paying out her little hoard of means until she dared not remain longer. Then she went to the mission home where she was boarded for ten shillings per week. But money was going out and none coming in. It was thought that if she could get into the quiet of the country, into the pure air of Cooranbong, it would be beneficial to her. I invited her to my house and told her to make her home with me, although we had to crowd up our own family to do this. I could not see her pay out her last shilling for board. She is now located in my family, and is having all the opportunities she desires in riding out and sitting at my family board. She is treated as a member of my family without the cost to herself of a penny. I thought that Jesus would do just this. (Ellen G. White *letter 68*, 1898)

Isn't that a sweet statement?

I thought that Jesus would do just this.

> It had been thought that she would remain here only four weeks, and then return to the city. But she shall remain just as long as she pleases. I tell her that this is her home. We must do these works just as Christ would do them if He were in our place. We want to show Christian warmth and hardiness, not as though we were doing some wonderful thing, for this is just what we would expect any real Christian to do in our own case, were we placed in like circumstances. (ibid.)

Isn't that wonderful? Now, notice Deuteronomy 15:7–11. I want you to see that in the plainest language, it links the promise of prosperity with this attitude and state of mind:

> If there be among you a poor man of one of thy brethren within any of thy gates in thy land which the LORD thy God giveth thee, thou shalt not harden thine heart, nor shut thine hand from thy poor brother: But thou shalt open thine hand wide unto him, and shalt surely lend him sufficient for his need, in that which he wanteth. Beware that there be not a thought in thy wicked heart, saying, The seventh year, the year of release, is at hand; and thine eye be evil against thy poor brother, and thou givest him nought... (Deut. 15:7–9)

Do you know what that means? As the cycle went on, the Jews had to forgive their brethren their debts every seventh year.

And God says, "Now, be careful. If there is a poor man who needs help in the sixth year and you say, 'Well, I would better not give him very much because I've got to forgive it all next year,'" God says that is a what kind of a heart? A wicked heart. It says, in essence, "Be careful you don't listen to that sort of business."

"Thou shalt surely give him, and thine heart shall not be grieved when thou givest unto him: because that for this thing the LORD thy God shall bless thee in all thy works, and in all that thou puttest thine hand unto" (Deut. 15:10).

"Don't be grieved," he says. In the New Testament, Paul says God loves a cheerful giver. Wouldn't you hate to have someone give you something and you knew they didn't want to give it to you? God is like that.

I tell my wife I'm so glad I have someone around who loves me, cooks my meals, and washes my dishes. I even help her sometimes. Love is like that. God wants everything we do for our brothers and sisters and others in need to be cheerful and in love.

But now, notice, here is what we might call the bottom line. God says in essence, "Don't be worried and fearful and anxious and grieved when you give because for this thing the Lord will bless you."

For what thing? For being generous with the needy, helping them when they need help or bringing them to your home, or giving them food, clothing, or whatever they need. Sometimes they need counsel and prayer more than they need anything material. But whatever it is, meet that need, "...For this thing the LORD thy God shall bless thee" (Deut. 15:10).

If you want to be prosperous, God knows how to make you successful according to His terms.

"Well," you say, "that means that nobody will ever be poor." Read the next verse, "For the poor shall never cease out of the land..." (Deut. 15:11).

"Well," you say, "I thought you would tell us how to be prosperous according to God's plan."

Do you know why God doesn't let the poor ever cease? "...Therefore I command thee, saying, Thou shalt open thine hand wide unto thy brother, to thy poor, and to thy needy, in thy land" (Deut. 15:11).

Wouldn't it be wonderful if nobody was ever poor? No, it wouldn't be wonderful at all. Do you know what it would be like? It would be as if every part of this world was just as level as any other part. How many rivers would we have? How many waterfalls would we have? None. Ah friend, I'm thankful for God's plan. "It was not the purpose of God that poverty should ever leave the world. The ranks of society were never to be equalized, for the diversity of condition which characterizes our race is one of the means by which God has designed to prove and develop character" (*Testimonies for the Church, vol. 4*, pp. 551, 552).

Character is being demonstrated, and it's being developed. Whenever someone is brought in touch with me and needs something I have, and I'm better off than they are, what is it demonstrating in my life? Character.

But suppose it's the other way around.

Some people say, "Well, I can give, but I hate to have anybody do things for me. I'm too independent."

The Bible says, "...It is more blessed to give than to receive" (Acts 20:35).

"So, I want to do all the giving."

Listen, if everyone did all the giving, who'd do the receiving? Should I be willing whichever way God arranges it?

> Many have urged with great enthusiasm that all men should have an equal share in the temporal blessings of God, but this was not the purpose of the Creator. Christ has said that we shall have the poor always with us... It would be the greatest misfortune that has ever befallen mankind if all were to be placed upon an equality in worldly possessions. (*Testimonies for the Church, vol. 4*, pp. 551, 552)

Does God intend that the stronger shall help the weak? Yes. I have an interesting statement on this in the book *Education*, page 268. Now, listen carefully to this statement. Someone reading this may get a re-emphasis on something you already know, but someone else may get the dawning of a new light on disabled people. "Whether in the home, the neighborhood, or the school, the presence of the poor, the afflicted, the ignorant, or the unfortunate should be regarded, not as a misfortune, but as affording precious opportunity for service" (*Education*, p. 268).

What do you think of that? So, whether it's a physical disability or financial poverty, whether the need is one of health, ministry in sickness, or some other need, we should think of it not as a misfortune but as a what? A blessed, precious opportunity. Oh friend, how different this is from the viewpoint of this world! And for this thing, the Lord will bless you. I know it's true.

My wife and I have been married for over fifty years. But I want to tell you something. We're not in debt, and we've been in missionary work not making much money for almost all our lives. But, yet, we're not in debt. We're not millionaires, but we thank God for everything He has given us through the years. We've held it in trust to go into helping others. It's a happy way to live.

Talk about prosperity. I say this thoughtfully, I wouldn't trade with the most prominent billionaire on Wall Street. But I've got something that many of them would give a lot to have, but they don't know how.

So, look around you and see if there is someone who needs help, so you can give it. And remember, you don't have to be rich to help others. All you have to find is someone who needs something you have.

You can see that this program all the way through is so different from what the world has. It is more blessed, happier, a greater experience in prosperity to give than to what? Receive. So, in heaven's balance sheet, the richest person is the one who gives away the most. Ah, that is what Jesus did. And that will be our experience if we follow Him.

CHAPTER 24

Married to the Work

I trust, as the result of reading this chapter, that you will have a clearer view of your privileges and responsibilities in connection with God's work in this closing hour. It may be possible that some minds will undergo a complete revolution in feeling and attitude. That would not be too much for God to do, and it shouldn't be too much for us to expect.

> For Zion's sake will I not hold my peace, and for Jerusalem's sake I will not rest, until the righteousness thereof go forth as brightness, and the salvation thereof as a lamp that burneth. And the Gentiles shall see thy righteousness, and all kings thy glory: and thou shalt be called by a new name, which the mouth of the Lord shall name. Thou shalt also be a crown of glory in the hand of the Lord, and a royal diadem in the hand of thy God. Thou shalt no more be termed Forsaken; neither shall thy land any more be termed Desolate: but thou shalt be called Hephzibah, and thy land Beulah: for the Lord delighteth in thee, and thy land shall be married. For as a young man marrieth a virgin, so shall thy sons marry thee: and as the bridegroom rejoiceth over the bride, so shall thy God rejoice over thee. I have set watchmen upon thy walls, O Jerusalem, which shall never hold their peace day nor night: ye that make mention of the Lord, keep not silence, And give Him no rest, till He establish, and till He make Jerusalem a praise in the earth. (Isa. 62:1-7)

These prophecies find their fulfillment in the closing work of the church into which we are now entering. God wants His people to share with Him in longing for a finished work, a completed task, a glorious demonstration of the character of God. His longing should be echoed in every heart.

"For Zion's sake will I not hold my peace, and for Jerusalem's sake I will not rest, until the righteousness thereof go forth as brightness, and

> *God wants His people to share with Him in longing for a finished work, a completed task, a glorious demonstration of the character of God. His longing should be echoed in every heart.*

the salvation thereof as a lamp that burneth" (Isa. 62:1). Other translations render that as a blazing torch. So, as a great torch blazing upon a mountain, the church of God today is to shine. And the results will be that "the Gentiles shall see thy righteousness, and all kings thy glory."

God's work is not to close in obscurity. The loud cry will be the greatest burst of glory that this world has ever seen. Upon that loud cry experience, the heart of each one of us should be set to have a part in it. I want a part in the loud cry, don't you? That is what is going to make heaven happy. That is what is going to thrill the heart of each child of God. And it's what is going to gather in the people from every fold into the one true fold and the finishing of this work. You notice that God lays upon us a responsibility to keep this before Him in prayer, in earnest intercession.

I will read part of the sixth and seventh verses as given in other translations. Notice the margin in verse 6: "I have set watchmen on the walls, O Jerusalem, which shall never hold their peace day nor night: ye that are the Lord's remembrancers [marginal reading] take no rest and give Him no rest until He make Jerusalem a praise in the earth" (Isa. 62:6).

In ancient times, if someone came to the king and asked for a favor, sometimes those favors were things that could be done at once, sometimes they involved the future. Once the promise of the king had been given, the good name of royalty and the honor of the throne was at stake. It was very important that whatever the king had promised should be fulfilled.

So, there were "remembrancers"—people to remind the king of what he had promised. In my imagination, I see one of them as, from time to time, he approaches the king and says, "Your Majesty, you remember that some time ago you made a certain promise?"

"Oh, yes," the king says.

"Well, that promise has not yet been fulfilled."

The king replies, "That hasn't been done? We must do that. The honor of the throne must be upheld."

The remembrancer was responsible not for doing the work but for seeing to it that the king didn't forget it, for only the king could do it. The finishing of this work is something that only God can do. The finishing of the work in our own hearts and lives, the finishing of the work in all the world, must be and will be a divine accomplishment. But, thank God, He has permitted you and me to have a part in it. The part He assigns us in these verses is that of remembrancers. We are to remind heaven.

Someone says, "Can He forget?" No, of course, He doesn't forget. Then why does He tell us to remind Him? To give us something to do. A wise parent arranges that the children shall have something to do. Our heavenly Father is a wise Father. He has arranged for you and me to have something to do. But I do not mean to suggest that it makes no difference whether we do it or not; it makes all the difference in the world. If enough remembrancers were reminding the King and then living in harmony with their prayers, we would soon see every promise of God fulfilled, and this work closed in that blaze of glory which we love to contemplate. Let us give ourselves to intercessory prayer that God shall arise and let His glory shine upon Zion and that the church shall appear in all her apostolic purity and simplicity as a living demonstration of the character of God.

That is not all that this chapter brings to view concerning our privileges, opportunities, and responsibilities. God is speaking to Zion—His church on earth. We are familiar with this figure of marriage as used in verses 4 and 5 to represent the relationship of God and His children. Often God speaks of His church as His bride and Himself as the husband.

In this chapter, we are given a most interesting application of this figure to another phase of the relationship. The sons of the church are represented as marrying the church in this closing hour—in this demonstration time, this glory burst which closes the work of God. I would like to study God's invitation to you and me to enter into such a relationship to the work, the church, and the cause of Christ. In studying this, we shall think of the fact that, just as God uses that sweet, sacred, and close tie of marriage to represent His devotion to us, so He desires in this figure to represent our devotion to the work of God.

Marriage has well been called the sacrament of love. We are told that to marry anyone without love is a sin. It is both a travesty and a tragedy. True, pure, sanctified love is the basis of marriage. It is in this marriage that God wants you and me to enter into the work of God. Love is the basis. Do we love God with all our heart, mind, and soul? Do we love His work?

Remember the story of Jesus sitting by the well at Sychar while the disciples had gone into the village to buy food, and the woman from the village came out, and the conversation with her resulted in her *conversion*—how it thrilled the heart of Jesus! The disciples came and marveled that He was talking to the woman. Later, she went her way. They offered Him something to eat, and He said, "I have food to eat ye know not of." Materialistic in their thinking, as they so often were, they questioned among themselves, "Has anybody given Him something to eat?" So slow they were to catch the lesson. He said: "My meat is to do the will of Him that sent Me, and to finish His work" (John 4:34).

Jesus was so devoted to the business of His Father that to Him the great object of life was to get that work done. That showed at the early age of twelve. As Mary and Joseph came to find Him witnessing to those religious leaders in the temple at Jerusalem, His mother reproved him, "Why have you dealt with us this way?" According to inspiration, they were the ones who were under reproof because they had forgotten Him. He didn't argue that with them. Pointing up to heaven, He said, "How is it that ye sought me? Whist ye not that I must be about My Father's business?" That was the keynote of His life. He lived for just one thing—to get the Father's work done. That was His meat and drink. It was more important to Him than meals or sleep or convenience or comfort or anything else. As a result, He could say, "I have finished the work which Thou gavest Me to do" (John 17:4).

Thank God, He finished the work. I pray that you and I shall have a similar devotion to the work of God. What do you say? Love must be the basis. Devotion is the basis for marriage; it's the basis of the connection with the work of God to which heaven is calling us.

Pursuing further the figure of marriage, you know what is involved in marriage in the matter of one's relationship to other things and other people. God laid down the fundamental law of marriage at the beginning: "Therefore shall a man leave his father and his mother, and shall cleave unto his wife: and they shall be one flesh" (Gen. 2:24).

The marriage ceremony takes cognizance of this expression. And so, in the vows that are said, the question is asked something like this: "Will you leave everything and everyone else and take this one?" That is the question. Is the companion that important? And, of course, the ready answer is: "I do." Would that it was always sincere and intelligent, for I should remind you that thousands of people who take those vows have not the slightest conception of what it means to "forsake all others" and keep themselves only to that *one*. They do not know whether they can do it or not, for they've never done it; they have never restricted or denied their inclinations. They do not know what it means to say "No" to any whim or clamor or appetite or passion or affection. That is something to meditate on.

Marriage is based fundamentally upon such channeling of affection toward one as to exclude all others from that intimate close love that marriage embraces. I repeat: there are few who take those vows both intelligently *and* sincerely. In what we are studying in connection with the work of God, He says, "Will you do that? Will you so relate yourself to the work of God that everything is left to one side?" Hear the words of Jesus as He challenges us on this, pausing to speak to the multitudes who followed Him:

> He turned, and said unto them, If any man come to Me, and hate not his father, and mother, and wife, and children, and brethren, and sisters, yea, and his own life also, he cannot be My disciple. And whosoever doth not bear his cross, and come after Me, cannot be My disciple. (Luke 14:25, 26)

Now verse 33: "So likewise, whosoever he be of you that forsaketh not all that he hath, he cannot be My disciple" (Luke 14:33).

That is what Jesus said; that is what He is saying today. There are thousands of people with whom the work of God comes in third. What do I mean by that? I mean myself first, my family second, and the work of God third. There are thousands of decisions being made today that are being made on just that basis. People don't always think it through and recognize the motives that are prompting them. And there is a lot of pious quoting of Scripture and the Spirit of Prophecy to justify and excuse all such attitudes. They say, "Oh, my family must come first." But Jesus does not say so here. He says that if they take that attitude, they cannot be His disciple. Family is not to be first at all; God and His work are to be first. Oh, that we may sense the implications of that great principle!

The work of God will never be finished on the easy-going, lackadaisical, comfort-consuming program that many are on today. It never will. God is looking for some people who will be married to the work of God on the basis of leaving everything and everyone and devoting themselves full-time, all they have, without any diversion or distraction, to the one objective of getting the work finished so Jesus can come. Isn't it worth that? Jesus thought so. He left His Father; He left everyone in heaven who loved Him; He came down here where people did not treat Him very well; He gave His life that this work might be finished, and He's calling someone today to hear and answer and unite with Him. But the lament of God's messenger was "How few are heart to heart with God in His solemn, closing work" (*Testimonies for the Church, vol. 7*, p. 13).

Let the Spirit of God awaken our hearts so that we will be with Him heart to heart. Now I know that people can take what I have said and make an extreme application of it, but most people today are so far on the other end of this thing that we would have to run a long way to get within shouting distance of extremism on this matter of making God first and family second. There is an extreme, of course, but that extreme is from a perversion, a *mis*application, not from a *full* application of it.

Love is the basis. Then we must forsake all else, and then the next thing is cherishing. That is part of the marriage ceremony: "Will you love her, honor her, cherish her in sickness, in health, in prosperity, in adversity, and forsaking all others keep you only unto her as long as you both shall live?"

Will you cherish the work of God? Will you cherish the cause of Christ? What does "cherish" mean? To care for, to support, to take care of in a nice, sweet, tender way. God wants you to do that with His work. Will you do it?

I want to come to grips with one of the greatest problems of this hour. What is the work of God for? To support you or for you to support it? I'm sorry to say that there are too many young people today, and older ones too, to whom the expression "getting into the work" means getting a job and getting a place on the payroll because that means security.

Let me hasten to make very clear because the devil would like to twist and turn the things that are said in this chapter, that we believe in tithing, we believe in the support of the ministry in God's ordained way through the tithe administered by the conference, we believe in the foreign mission program, the Ingathering, and the other mission offerings that make possible sending missionaries to the four corners of the earth. And nothing I have said or will say is in any way to *lessen* that; rather, it's to *exalt* it. But I want to repeat: One of the tragedies of this hour is that thousands of young people are being conditioned, by the very atmosphere of the hour in which we're living, to look upon the work of God as something to support *them* rather than something for them to support. May I tell you, it's just as great a danger in what is called self-supporting work as it is in any other phase of the Master's business today. There are thousands of people who would like to be in what is called self-supporting work if someone would support *them* if someone would give *them* a job and guarantee that they will have a place to live and something to eat and money for clothes. Shouldn't that be done? That is what I want to study with you.

"As a young man marrieth a virgin, so shall thy sons marry thee" (Isa. 62:5). Are you interested in that kind of thing? Suppose that when a minister asks a young man if he is willing to forsake everyone else for a young woman and love her and honor her and cherish her, he would answer, "Frankly, sir, my intention is that this young woman shall support me." Do you think the wedding ceremony would proceed?

As we stand at the altar of God with the thought in our minds that we're going to be devoted to the work, married to the work, are we going to support the work, or is the work going to support us in sickness and in health, in prosperity or in adversity?

When Elijah called Elisha into this program, he put the mantle on him. Elisha came after him saying he had some things to do at home. Elijah said it was all right that he could go home and *stay* there, that he didn't have to go with Elijah. You know what Elisha did; he burned his bridges behind him. He took the implements of agriculture he was using and burned them. He took the oxen he was using to plow and cooked them. Everything was settled. He was going with the prophet. He counted the cost. He was going with the prophet to *give* service, not to be served. He was going with the prophet to give his life, not to be waited upon. We're told that the life he shared with the prophet was an uncertain life.

In the days of Jesus, the story is told of the calling of Peter, John, James, and Andrew. Those men were fishermen—not wealthy, but apparently, they were making "a decent living." Jesus came one morning and used Peter's boat as a platform from which to preach. He worked a miracle to get some fish they had not gotten through the night, and then He invited them to leave all that. Jesus didn't offer to buy out their boats and fishing business. Neither did He, in any way, hire them on a settled salary basis or give them any guarantee that they would have it as good as they had it. On the contrary, He was careful to teach them, and others who came to Him from time to time, that they were getting into a program of uncertainty, as far as this world is concerned—that it would cost them instead of paying them, that *they* would need to support *it* instead of *it* supporting them.

The interesting thing is, they did it: "And when they had brought their ships to land, they forsook all, and followed Him" (Luke 5:11).

What a strange thing to walk off of a good job and go with Jesus in an uncertain life.

A little later, Jesus came to Matthew the tax collector. I don't suppose he was rich, but I don't suppose he was a pauper, either. He had plenty. Jesus said that He wanted Matthew to leave tax collecting and follow Him. Before giving service, Matthew did not see to it that he was going to be supported in the style to which he had become accustomed; not at all. He left a good bed to sleep in the park. He left the certainty of a good job with the government for the uncertainty of traveling around with Jesus.

Those men came into such a relationship with Jesus that they did not regret the decision they had made. And believe me, where love is the basis, fellowship is worth more than all that it costs. The reason some people do not find more joy in the work of God is that they're looking to it to support them. About all they get out of it is the money, and the money goes so fast that they don't get much pleasure out of it. But that is not the basis for pleasure and satisfaction.

The greatest joy in this world is the joy of love, and love will be revealed in sacrifice. If you and I will enter into that relationship with God and His work, it will abundantly satisfy every longing of the soul, even if it means that we are left in poverty and hardship.

When Jesus met the apostle Paul on the road to Damascus, He didn't say, "You have quite a high position down there in the Sanhedrin. Suppose I could arrange to give you a high position in the Christian church. Would you consider making a transfer? What are your wages, Paul? You get a pretty good salary. Well, we might have to arrange a bit of a sacrifice on that. But on a missionary basis, would you be willing to take half what you've been getting down there in Jerusalem?" Can you picture Paul thinking that would be a real sacrifice? Why, there was no such interview as that. Instead, Jesus said He would show Paul what great things he must suffer. But that didn't scare Paul; it didn't daunt Paul; it didn't turn Paul back.

The thing that challenges the loving heart is not ease, convenience, and security; it's filling a need. What our young people today need is not to be shown what comfortable quarters they're going to have and what abundant provision for their security has been made. They need to be shown a needy world and a loving Christ who is calling them to share with Him His longing desire to get the work finished. That is what James and Ellen White saw over 100 years ago. They set out to do that very thing—to finish the work of God in this world. They had no other thought than that.

If you haven't read the book *Life Sketches* lately, pick it up and read these first 200 pages. See how this work got started, and remember, it's going to be finished in greater sacrifice than it began. Sister White is speaking of the time just about a year after their marriage: "Brother and Sister Howland, of Topsham, kindly offered us a part of their dwelling, which we

> *The greatest joy in this world is the joy of love, and love will be revealed in sacrifice. If you and I will enter into that relationship with God and His work, it will abundantly satisfy every longing of the soul, even if it means that we are left in poverty and hardship.*

gladly accepted, and commenced housekeeping with borrowed furniture. We were poor and saw close times" (*Life Sketches,* p. 105).

Someone says, "Why, the very idea of living in a home with other people! I never saw a house yet that was big enough for two families. The very idea that God would require His people to be so poor that they had to borrow furniture in order to set up housekeeping and accept someone's charity to get a roof over their head." Did you ever hear anybody talk like that? Well, I have. The enemy talks to us just that way. But listen to what the messenger of God says.

> We had resolved not to be dependent, but to support ourselves and have something with which to help others. But we were not prosperous. My husband worked very hard hauling stone on the railroad, but could not get what was due him for his labor. Brother and Sister Howland freely divided with us whatever they could… (ibid.*)*

Some may say, "Ah, the very idea of having to accept charity from brothers and sisters. I don't like that. I wouldn't get myself in a place like that." Well, that all depends on how much you love the work of God. Reading on:

> Brother and Sister Howland freely divided with us whatever they could; but they also were in close circumstances. They fully believed the first and second messages, and had generously imparted of their substance to forward the work until they were dependent on their daily labor. (ibid.)

They started in good circumstances. They had taken hold of the first and second messages and poured in their money until they had to work from day to day to get something to eat. Were they happy with it or sorry? Oh, they were happy.

> My husband stopped hauling stone and with his axe went into the woods to chop cord wood. With a continual pain in his side, he worked from early morning till dark to earn about fifty cents a day. We endeavored to keep up good courage and trust in the Lord. I did not murmur. In the morning I felt thankful to God that He had preserved us through another night. (ibid.)

Are we, as their successors, to insist that every one of us shall have at least decent living conditions, which means these days, having a good home with nice furniture and assured income, a good up-to-date car, with enough allowance to be sure that all the expenses of the car are paid, and probably a radio and television thrown in for good measure? And, of course, all the other things like a refrigerator, etc.

I'm reminded of a young woman who, shortly after her marriage, was called to the mission field out in the middle of Africa, hundreds of miles from what is called civilization. She was inquiring about taking her electric refrigerator and electric iron, and a number of other electric appliances. Of course, that part of Africa didn't happen to have any electricity.

There are some young people today who won't venture beyond electricity. There are plenty of needs to be filled where there *is* electricity. Someone says, "That is the point. Let someone go out there who *likes* that pioneer life; I like electricity."

I'm not sure that the caves we go into in the time of trouble are going to be wired for 110 or 220.

> One day when our provisions were gone my husband went to his employer to get money or provisions. It was a stormy day and he walked three miles and back in the rain. He brought home on his back a bag of provisions tied in different compartments, having in this manner passed through the village of Brunswick where he had often lectured. As he entered the house, very weary… (ibid.)

Would God require that of His people? He did. Oh, aren't you glad that *you* don't live back there? Aren't you glad that you live in these wonderful days of the modern world when there is so much money that you don't have to do anything like that?

"In the future our work is to be carried forward in self-denial and sacrifice even beyond that which we have seen in past years" (*Called to Medical Evangelism*, p. 13). Friend, if we'll get *married* to the work of God, we'll want to be in it no matter how poor the wife gets. We'll want to be right there with the wife.

The people who finish this work are going to stick with it to the end. All the way through, they're going to think about how to support *it* instead of how it supports *them*. That is the thing I am seeking to explain in plain English, and God give us the spirit to see it and to love it.

There was a man in China who was a leading minister. When the communists came, they saw to it that before long, this minister was put out of office and more or less under house arrest. What did he do? He set about to do what he could with his hands to make some money. But instead of devoting all his time to making money, even to feed himself, he had been translating *The Desire of Ages* into the language that is read by millions of earth's inhabitants. That wonderful book has now been printed down in Hong Kong. That young man has been translating other books of the Spirit of Prophecy, one book after the other, and he is going ahead with his work as a self-supporting worker. Why? Because he is married to the work of God. He can't even think of giving it up any more than a man could give up his wife just because things got in a hard place. A young man loves his bride, and the worker that God can use in this closing work loves the *church*, and the *work* of the church, for it's the work of God.

This man has devoted his life to it, not on the basis of whether there is money in the treasury to pay him or not; not on the basis of *if* he can get a good home, and *if* he can get living conditions, and *if* he can get security. No. It has nothing to do with that.

Someone says, "Don't we have to have a living?"

The martyrs didn't; they had to have a *dying*. Fifty million of them went to their death because they believed what we're studying. God hasn't called you to make a living, friend; He has called you to put yourself and all you have into His work. And if you do that, God says He will give you everything else you need.

He made that clear in the parable of the laborers in Matthew 20. He said to go into the vineyard, and whatever is right, He'll give you. Of course, that means that whatever He gives you is right.

Paul and Silas got what was right, and one night, they spent the night in the dungeon. And I'm not so sure that the dietician came down and asked them what they'd like for breakfast either. But they sang praises at midnight, rejoicing that they were counted worthy to suffer for Jesus' sake.

"But seek ye first the kingdom of God and His righteousness, and all these things shall be added unto you…" (Matt. 6:33). Food and clothing and all the rest. If we make God and His work first, everything else that we need for this life and the next will be added unto us.

> My brethren and sisters in America, I make my appeal to you… The lives of many are too delicate and dainty. They know nothing of bearing hardship as good soldiers of Christ. They are hindrances to the work of soul-saving. They have many wants; everything must be convenient and easy to suit their taste. They will not do anything themselves, and those who would do something they hinder by their suppositions and imaginary wants, and their love of idols. They think themselves Christians, but they do not know what practical Christian life signifies. What does it mean to be a Christian? It means to be Christlike.

> When the Lord sees His people restricting their imaginary wants and practicing self-denial, not in a mournful, regretful spirit, as Lot's wife left Sodom, but joyfully, for Christ's sake, and because it is the right thing to do, the work will go forward with power. (*Testimonies for the Church, vol. 8*, pp. 52, 53)

Oh, let's say, "Jesus, I am with You. I am going to be married to the work of God, not to *be supported* but to support."

What would you think of a husband who would say to a woman, "Yes, I want to marry you, and we'll arrange to share 50/50 what comes in, but I do have some money laid by in the bank, and I want it clearly understood that you are not to touch any of that or to get the benefit of any of it. If anything should ever happen and we'd get divorced, I want it understood that I am to have all of that because I had it when I got married, and I want to be sure to have it if we get unmarried"?

But there are a number of people who say, "Yes, I'm willing to be in the Lord's work, and I'm willing that everything that I earn shall go right into it, but I do have certain things over here that I've gotten, and I wouldn't want to deplete my capital."

I think of an experience that I had several years ago. I was holding an effort in one of our large American cities. There was a man and his wife with their two children who attended. They gave good attention. We were introducing the work through the agency of the health program. They gave up their beer and tobacco and tea and coffee and Coca-Cola. They accepted the full health program. Of course, it made them feel better, so they began to take hold of the rest of the message. They started to keep the Sabbath. They were getting ready for baptism. We were having our studies and classes.

One night, I noticed that they did not attend the meeting. I asked the Bible worker about it. We went down to see what we could find out. We visited for a little while, but I could tell that things were a little cold. Finally, the man asked me a question. At once, I knew I had the key.

He said, "Brother Frazee, when a person joins the Seventh-day Adventist church, do they have to turn all their property over to the church?"

We'd found the problem. Someone had told him that if he became a Seventh-day Adventist, it would mean giving up everything he had.

> Whether you've got a penny or a million dollars, if you're married to the work of God, every penny you have will be for one thing—to get this work finished. And every hour of your time, every day of the week, you'll be wanting to do just one thing—help to finish the work.

I answered him, "No, brother, you don't need to worry about that. You don't have to turn over your property to the church at all. You understand, of course, about the tithe, but the paying of your tithe is between you and God. The church teaches that. That is part of what the Lord has given the church to teach. But the church is not going to come around and check up to make certain that you've paid every penny of tithe you're supposed to."

He was greatly relieved. But before he could sigh too much relief, I said, "Brother, what I have told you is the truth, but I want to tell you something else. While it's true that the church does not require you to turn over your property, I wouldn't want you to even think of being a Seventh-day Adventist unless you are willing and ready to turn over everything you have because that is what it's going to take before you get through."

That is the program that you enter into when you become a Seventh-day Adventist. That is what it took with the early disciples. I read it to him and let him read it in the Bible. I told him that the *church* doesn't require it, but if he gave his heart to God, *God* would require it of him and that he should settle it in his soul that everything is on the altar.

Do you know what happened? He did not come in. He did just what the rich young ruler did when Jesus told him the same thing. That young man with great possessions went away sorrowful. And that is why he did, it says, "…for he had great possessions" (Matt. 19:22).

Whether you've got a penny or a million dollars, if you're married to the work of God, every penny you have will be for one thing—to get this work finished. And every hour of your time, every day of the week, you'll be wanting to do just one thing—help to finish the work. "We have no time now to give our energies and talents to worldly enterprises… Let every talent be employed in the work of God" (*Testimonies for the Church, vol. 9*, p. 104).

"Not one in a hundred among us is doing anything beyond engaging in common, worldly enterprises" (*Testimonies for the Church, vol. 8*, p. 148). Someone says, "I don't know how to do anything but that." Peter and John had never done a thing but catch fish. Jesus said if they came with Him, He would make them fishers of men. Did it work? Matthew hadn't done anything but collect taxes. That is quite different from evangelism. But Jesus said if Matthew came with Him, He would help him collect souls instead of money. Matthew said he would come. Did it work?

Whatever your experience has been in the past, if you are willing to give God what you have (your time, your money, your service, your life) and if you are willing to be married to the work of God, He will see to it that your talents, your time, your money, and your life are used in the greatest business in this universe—the business of winning souls to Christ in this closing hour of human history.

This is the last hour. This is a very personal invitation from Jesus to you:

From the fields so white with harvest,
We may glean the golden grain;
For the Master seeketh reapers,
Hark, I hear Him call my name.
By Ina Duley Ogdon

Copyright 2024. All rights reserved.

W. D. Frazee Sermons, P.O. Box 102, Wildwood, GA 30757

1-800-WDF-1840 / 706-820-9755

support@WDFsermons.org

www.WDFsermons.org

TEACH Services, Inc.
PUBLISHING

We invite you to view the complete
selection of titles we publish at:
www.TEACHServices.com

We encourage you to write us
with your thoughts about this,
or any other book we publish at:
info@TEACHServices.com

TEACH Services' titles may be purchased in
bulk quantities for educational, fund-raising,
business, or promotional use.
bulksales@TEACHServices.com

Finally, if you are interested in seeing
your own book in print, please contact us at:
publishing@TEACHServices.com
We are happy to review your manuscript at no charge.

www.ingramcontent.com/pod-product-compliance
Lightning Source LLC
Chambersburg PA
CBHW071655160426
43195CB00012B/1480